KT-195-588

OXFORD HISTORICAL SERIES

Editors

G. N. CLARK   F. M. POWICKE

NOTE

This Series comprises carefully selected studies which have been submitted, or are based upon theses submitted, for higher degrees in this University. The general aim of the Editors is to make the Series a collection of works which advance knowledge of the structural development, whether political, ecclesiastical, or economic, of British Society.

RECENT VOLUMES

Public Order and Popular Disturbances, 1660–1714
By M. BELOFF. 1938.

The Corporation of Leicester
By R. W. GREAVES. 1939.

English Diplomatic Administration, 1259–1339
By G. P. CUTTINO. 1940.

The Social Ideas of Religious Leaders, 1660–1688
By R. B. SCHLATTER. 1940.

Northamptonshire County Elections and Electioneering, 1695–1832. By ERIC G. FORRESTER. 1941.

The Wiltshire Woollen Industry in the 16th and 17th Centuries. By G. D. RAMSAY. 1943. *Out of print.*

Elizabeth's Army. By C. G. CRUICKSHANK. 1946.

THE ENGLISH LANDS OF THE ABBEY OF BEC

BY

MARJORIE MORGAN

LECTURER IN MEDIEVAL HISTORY IN
THE UNIVERSITY OF ABERDEEN

OXFORD UNIVERSITY PRESS
LONDON : GEOFFREY CUMBERLEGE
1946

OXFORD UNIVERSITY PRESS
AMEN HOUSE, E.C. 4
London Edinburgh Glasgow New York
Toronto Melbourne Cape Town Bombay
Calcutta Madras
GEOFFREY CUMBERLEGE
PUBLISHER TO THE UNIVERSITY

PRINTED IN GREAT BRITAIN

PREFACE

THIS book is virtually a collection of studies—monastic, administrative, and economic—relating to the English priories and manors of the abbey of Bec-Hellouin. The form was imposed by the nature of the subject; for the alien priories in England were without any vital life of their own to hold and direct the attention of the historian. Nevertheless they are important for their place in monastic and social history, and for this reason a study of them is not without value in the study of medieval institutions.

The work, which touches more sides of history than I myself could know intimately, owes its completion to many. The extent of my debt to the late Professor Eileen Power, who for a time directed my researches, can be fully appreciated only by those who have had the privilege and pleasure of working under her. Professor M. M. Postan, Professor F. M. Powicke, Dr. Helen Cam, Mr. R. V. Lennard, Dom David Knowles, and the late Mr. R. A. L. Smith, read the book at various stages in its composition ranging from the thesis to the final proofs; to them and to the many friends who have discussed special points with me I owe advice, encouragement, and numerous corrections. My thanks are due to the Provost and Fellows of King's College, Cambridge, the Dean and Chapter of St. George's Chapel, Windsor, and the Provost and Fellows of Eton College for permission to work in their private archives; and in particular to those in charge of the records who gave me every facility for carrying on my search in spite of the grave inconvenience caused by the removal of manuscripts during the war: Canon S. L. Ollard of Windsor, Sir Henry Marten, Provost of Eton, and Mr. J. Saltmarsh of King's. Mr. A. J. Taylor, who had unknown to me begun work on the subject, very generously placed his transcripts at my disposal; these included transcripts of documents relating to Cowick Priory which had been made available by the courtesy of His Grace the Duke of Bedford. My debt to Lady Margaret Hall, Oxford, is manifold, extending from undergraduate years to the period of my tenure of a Susette Taylor Research

Fellowship; and to the Council of the College I owe a grant from the Eleanor Lodge Historical Fund in aid of the expenses of publication. The Council of the British Archaeological Association kindly allowed me to reproduce material published by them in their *Journal* for 1940.

War-time paper restrictions prevent a separate dedication, but I am permitted to inscribe here the dedication of this book to my mother and father.

M. M.

KING'S COLLEGE
ABERDEEN

CONTENTS

LIST OF MAPS

ABBREVIATIONS

C.Ch.R. . .	Calendar of Charter Rolls.
C.Cl.R. . .	Calendar of Close Rolls.
C.D.F. . .	Calendar of Documents preserved in France.
C.F.R. . .	Calendar of Fine Rolls.
C.P.L. . .	Calendar of Papal Letters.
C.P.R. . .	Calendar of Patent Rolls.
D.B. . . .	Domesday Book.
E.H.R. . .	English Historical Review.
F.A. . . .	Inquisitions and Assessments relating to Feudal Aids.
H.M.C. . .	Report of the Historical Manuscripts Commission.
J.B.A.A. . .	Journal of the British Archaeological Association.
K.C.C. . .	MSS. of King's College, Cambridge.
L.F. . . .	Liber Feodorum.
P.L. . . .	Patrologia Latina, ed. Migne.
Porée . . .	A. A. Porée: Histoire de l'Abbaye du Bec.
P.Q.W. . .	Placita de Quo Warranto.
R.H. . . .	Rotuli Hundredorum.
R.S. . . .	Rolls Series.
Select Pleas . .	Select Pleas in Manorial and other Seignorial Courts, ed. F. W. Maitland (Selden Society, vol. ii).
T.P.N. . .	Taxatio Ecclesiastica Angliae et Walliae, auctoritate P. Nicholai IV, *circa* A.D. 1291 (Record Commission).
T.R.H.S. . .	Transactions of the Royal Historical Society.
V.C.H. . .	Victoria County History.

INTRODUCTION

(i)

THE history of the alien priories in England has for many years attracted the attention of scholars on both sides of the Channel. Numerous scattered references among the records of French abbeys have invited the compilation of an Anglo-Norman cartulary, and even the writing of a complete history. Yet the subject has never produced a rounded work, and often the once eager antiquaries laid aside their notes before they were complete enough to appear in print. Léchaudé d'Anisy's *Cartulaire de la Basse Normandie* remains an isolated manuscript in the Public Record Office;[1] Delisle's miscellaneous notes on the English possessions of Norman abbeys were preserved only by being pasted into a scrap-book in the Bibliothèque nationale.[2] Some collections of documents planned on a wider basis were completed in both countries: De la Rue's *Cartularium Normannicum ex autographis tam in turri Londinense quam in Musaeo Britannico*, and Round's *Calendar of Documents preserved in France*, though not confined to the alien priories, are potentially useful source-books for later histories. But, on the whole, work on the subject has been confined to the unsystematic collection of data. Nichols, Tanner, and the continuators of Dugdale casually cleared a few paths of established truth in a jungle of unassimilated fact and left them to become the seeding-ground of error.

The first difficulty was one of definition. The term 'alien priory' became current when Edward I seized the possessions of French priories during the wars with France. It was used from that time to describe all dependencies of French monasteries in England and included every type of religious establishment from the prosperous and fully conventual Cluniac priories to tiny cells like Wootton Wawen or Ogbourne which had more in common with an estate office than a Benedictine priory. For administrative convenience the inhabitants of all these places were classed as 'foreign religious subject to the King of France and his allies'.

[1] P.R.O. Trans. 8 140/B.

[2] MS. Nouv. Acq. Fran. 21807.

The order of Cîteaux and the dependencies of monasteries outside enemy territory were unmolested. The fate of the other priories varied a little because the influence of their English patrons varied, and also because the obligation of allowing religious life to continue necessitated some distinction between conventual and non-conventual priories. Yet on the whole the classification was arbitrary and artificial. This 'large but spiritually insignificant class of cells and priories'[1] lacks any true unity and is less encouraging to the historian than any of the great monastic orders.

The scattered sources present another difficulty. Charters preserved by the mother abbeys have found their way into French archives, whilst cartularies and manorial records entrusted to the English priors and proctors are widely distributed in college and private libraries or the British Museum; and the Alien Priories Bundles in the Public Record Office have barely been classified. A complete history of all the alien priories would necessitate years of work, and even then might be unsatisfactory. Only one modern scholar has attempted it, and he, though he attacked the subject with much energy, has left a great deal more to be done.[2]

On the whole, recent research has been directed towards the history of single houses and orders. Dr. Rose Graham's distinguished work on the dependencies of Cluny is outstanding. Thanks to the publications of Dom David Knowles, Dr. Salter, Mr. A. J. Taylor, and others, it is no longer necessary to begin any account of the alien priories with an explanation that many of them never were priories in any sense of the word. But in spite of the general introduction to investigation, a large group of priories, cells, and manors dependent on the great Norman abbeys remains unstudied. Manors, churches, and prebends were showered upon the abbeys, either for the enrichment of the mother house or for the foundation of new priories to be colonized with French monks. Practically all the great monasteries received gifts, although their English possessions ranged from a few acres to manors scattered over the length and breadth of England

[1] Dom David Knowles, *The Religious Houses of Medieval England*, p. 56.

[2] C. H. New, *History of the Alien Priories in England to the Confiscation of Henry V*. This book is uncritical of sources and must be used with great caution.

and conventual priories as well. Their interest in their English estates varied proportionately; the abbess of Montivilliers, for example, disembarrassed herself of her single Dorsetshire manor in the mid-thirteenth century.[1] But for more than three hundred years all the more richly endowed abbeys clung tenaciously to their property and rights across the Channel with a sublime disregard for geographical convenience. They had to face problems of monastic discipline complicated by the jealous encroachment of diocesan bishops, difficulties of estate organization on their widely separated manors, and finally the steady drain upon their resources imposed by the royal confiscations. Manors and priories alike had to fit into their local background without being severed from the Norman abbeys. Some of the obstinacy with which the abbots defended their rights is reflected in a letter written by a fifteenth-century abbot of St. Florent by Saumur, in which—years after the allocation of his property to English colleges—he upheld his predecessor's decision not to part with his English priories even in return for money.[2]

The abbey of Bec-Hellouin is worth studying for the variety and wealth of its possessions. It colonized an abbey and gradually acquired in England four conventual priories, three or four granges, over twenty manors, and innumerable churches, tithes, and pensions. No one group of alien priories can be regarded as a pattern for all the rest. Yet a history of the order of Bec involves some consideration, however cursory, of the English cells and priories and their disciplinary problems from the Conquest to the Suppression; of manorial administration and the economic conditions of the abbot's tenants, and of royal and ecclesiastical policy towards the French dependencies, especially after the end of the thirteenth century. And so it may, within limits, be regarded as a microcosm of the history of the alien priories.

(ii)

Sources, in spite of disappointing gaps, are unusually abundant. The French records have suffered most since

[1] *C.P.R. 1232–47*, p. 333.

[2] P. Marchegay, 'Les prieurés anglais de Saint-Florent près Saumur', in *Bibliothèque de l'École des Chartes*, xl (1879), pp. 161–2.

practically all the original records at Bec were burnt during the revolution of 1789; but two good collections of transcripts were made before this catastrophe by Dom Thibault and Dom Jouvelin, and there are also a few scattered documents in Norman departmental archives. Most of the manors in the bailiwick of Ogbourne were given after the suppression to King's College, Cambridge, St. George's Chapel, Windsor, and Eton College; institutions whose continued existence until the present day has favoured the preservation of their legal records. In addition, a custumal and a formulary have found their way by devious routes into the British Museum, the formulary passing through Corpus Christi library and thence, in the time of Cotton's predatory librarian Richard James, into the Cottonian collection (MS. Cotton Domitian A XI).

The earliest surviving documents are charters. There are still a few originals in the Archives de l'Eure, and a handsome charter roll of the early thirteenth century at Windsor (XI G 11) contains some charters of the early Norman period granting land to the abbey. A note before the last document in the roll: *Scriptum est in libro novo* indicates the existence of a later cartulary of English property, now lost. The transcripts of Dom Thibault (MS. Lat. 12884) and Dom Jouvelin (MS. Lat. 13905) preserve a record of many more of the original donations. Charters describing little transactions in the thirteenth and fourteenth centuries survive for a few manors: Eton has the records of Cottisford, Blakenham, Bledlow, and Weedon; and King's College, Cambridge, possesses a very few charters for Ogbourne, Ruislip, Combe, and Dunton.

Chronologically the next manuscripts are the custumals.[1] Maitland noted in passing the long roll among the muniments of King's College (Dd 33) and dated it from the handwriting as early thirteenth century.[2] Internal evidence confirms this assumption. The beginning is missing, and the roll opens with part of a survey of the manor of Ogbourne St. George, followed by surveys of Ogbourne St. Andrew,

[1] The text of the earliest custumals is to be printed in a collection of economic documents forthcoming in the Camden Series.

[2] *Select Pleas in Manorial and Other Seignorial Courts*, p. 4.

Combe, Monxton, Wantage, Chisenbury, Quarley, Povington, and Deverill, with a note of a few revenues from Hungerford. The survey of all the manors except Ogbourne St. George and Wantage was brought up to date about half a generation after its compilation, for the names of tenants and some customs have been crossed or scratched out, and others written in. Slightly more than half have been changed, and as comparison of the names of tenants with those who took up tenements in the early court rolls gives a date slightly earlier than 1248 for the second survey, the first cannot be much later than 1230. A second roll at King's College contains in the main a fair copy of the second version of Dd 33, written more grammatically. It begins, however, with a fragment of a full survey of Hungerford, and includes Combe, Monxton, Quarley, and Deverill.

These surveys were later digested into a book, together with a slightly later survey of Ogbourne St. George and surveys of all the other manors except Hooe, Tooting, and Dunton. Evidence from the eastern manors confirms *c.* 1245 as a likely date: a note before the record of the customs of Swyncombe mentions William de Guineville, proctor-general from 1239 to 1254,[1] and in 1246 the proctor was engaged in a suit with the tenants of Atherstone about the villein services which he demanded for their tenements—the type of case which might have originated in an inquiry into tenure.[2] It is impossible to know if surveys of Dunton, Hooe, and Tooting were taken at the same time; the only existing details about the customs of Dunton are in two late-fourteenth-century rentals (King's College, M 18 and M 19) and of Tooting in court rolls of the same period.[3] There are in addition two fourteenth-century rentals of Weedon at Eton.

The court rolls begin in 1246. Like the rolls of St. Albans and Ramsey they are composite, at least for the first eighty years: each roll is in a single handwriting, and probably they were written up yearly from rough drafts;

[1] MS. Add. 24316, f. 13: 'Consuetudines manerii de Swincumbe, iuramento legalium hominum presentate et recognite tempore fratris W. de Guineville.'

[2] *Feet of Fines for Warwickshire* (Dugdale Society), nos. 621, 667.

[3] *Court Rolls of Tooting Beck*, pp. 2 seqq.

they cannot have been written day by day after each court since occasionally the courts are slightly out of chronological order. As usual they begin at Michaelmas; the series is not complete, but rolls exist for the years 1246, 1247–8, 1249–50, 1269–70, 1275–6, 1280–1, 1289–91, 1295–6, 1307–8, 1311–12, 1314–15, 1316–17, 1320–1 (King's College, C 1–15). The first and last membranes of most rolls have partially decayed, and one roll (C 5) is so mutilated that it cannot be dated.

Separate rolls were kept for Blakenham from the reign of Edward I, and these are at Eton (D 5). After the end of Edward II's reign separate rolls were kept for most of the manors. There is one composite roll for the five manors of Combe, Monxton, Quarley, Chisenbury, and Deverill of 1334–5 (C 19) and one of 1349–50 (C 21). Separate rolls exist for Ogbourne, 1333–4, 1336–7, 1341–2, 1349–50 (C 16, 17, 20, 22); Dunton, 1349–77 (M 7), 1377–99 (M 8), and 1399–1412 (M 9); Ruislip, 1334–5, 1393–6 (Q 44–9); Lessingham, 1349–51, 1383–94, 1396–1409 (P 4); Atherstone, 1336–7, 1346–51 (H 4); and Brixton-Deverill, 1404–5 (C 24). There are later rolls for Tooting in the possession of the L.C.C., some of which have been printed;[1] and Maitland has printed selections from the earliest composite rolls.[2]

Early account rolls exist for the following manors:

Combe, 1306–18 (King's College).[3]

Ogbourne St. Andrew, 1332–8 (King's College).[3]

Cottisford, 1292, 1316–17, 1318–22, 1340–3, 1360 (Eton, C 14).

Blakenham, 1294–5, 1297–1303, 1331–3, 1334–7, 1347–8; view of account, 1350–1 (Eton, D 5).

East Wretham, 1303–8, 1335, 1336–9, 1341–March 1342; views of account, 1339–40, 1350–1 (Eton, A 20).

Weedon Beck, 1304–5, 1325 (Eton, B 11).

There are no examples of the *status domus* which the prior of Ogbourne was expected to submit to his abbot. It is

[1] *Court Rolls of Tooting Beck*, ed. Gomme.

[2] *Select Pleas in Manorial and Other Seignorial Courts* (Selden Society), vol. ii.

[3] These rolls have no reference mark.

possible that most of the financial records of the bailiwick of Ogbourne were sent to France: Richard de Beausevalle told Edward III that he was unable to give him full particulars of pensions and corrodies held out of the property, since most of the records concerning the bailiwick of Ogbourne were at Bec.[1] And in the seventeenth century the abbey still possessed the following documents:

'Two parchment rolls fastened together containing receipts from the English possessions dependent on Bec.

'A parchment roll recording the customs to which the farmers of manors and lands possessed by Bec in England were subject.

'Another parchment roll, in which are inscribed the revenues of Great Ogbourne.'[2]

Not a trace of them now remains in the French archives, and they must be presumed burnt. There is, however, one central financial document of great interest. Eton College possesses in the drawer of Cottisford documents the first four membranes of a pipe roll of 1288–9. This contains the accounts of sixteen manors enrolled after the audit of October–December 1289. It gives a full statement of receipts and an abbreviated list of expenses, the latter consisting of various forinsec expenses, the total running costs of the manor, and the liveries to the lord. On the dorse is a fairly full corn account, but no mention of stock.[3]

In addition to the records compiled by the monks for their own benefit, certain royal records have preserved valuable details about customs and economic conditions. Customs of Swyncombe and Cottisford, which tally reasonably closely with the custumal of Ogbourne, are in the printed hundred rolls,[4] and the tenants of Ogbourne stated traditionally accepted services and alleged new burdens imposed by the abbot, when they claimed ancient demesne in the king's court.[5] The extents taken each time the estates of alien

1 P.R.O. Ancient Petitions, S.C. 8, E. 1394: 'E treshonurable seignur daltres enpensiouns dount la dite baillie est chargee en nule manere ne vous sai certifier quant a me, gar ioe su noveaux venuz en Engleterre, e toux les lettres e remembraunces tochauntz la dite baillie sont demorretz devers mon mestre labbe du Bekherlewin.'

2 *Inventaire des Titres du Bec* (MS. Cinq Cents Colbert, 190), p. 59.

3 Forthcoming in the Camden Series.

4 *Rotuli Hundredorum*, ii. 757, 761, 837.

5 P.R.O. Plea Rolls, K.B. 27/207, 27/288.

religious houses were confiscated are very numerous for 1294 and 1324,[1] though they become sparser later. If the statements about the status and services of the tenants are normally too generalized for comparison with the earlier surveys, these extents contain useful figures of the number of acres—arable, meadow, and pasture—in the demesne, the amount of stock kept, and the corn grown.

The spiritualities passed in their entirety to St. George's Chapel, Windsor, and all the records concerning them are now in the possession of the dean and chapter. A miscellaneous collection of records of tithe suits, leases of tithes, charters granting and confirming churches, and documents relating to the peculiar jurisdiction of the prebend of Ogbourne is in box XI G. Leases of the manors of Preston, Tooting, and Lessingham have accidentally been included amongst them. Many of the ecclesiastical documents, and others of which the originals have perished, have been copied into the Arundel White Book, ff. 90 seq., and there are copies of papal bulls, mostly those delegating tithe disputes, in the Denton Black Book, ff. 26*v.*–41.

These records are mainly of two types: documents from the central archives describing the relationship of the abbey of Bec to its dependencies, and detailed local records relating to property in the bailiwick of Ogbourne. There are scattered sources for the history of the other priories and cells: cartularies for Stoke-by-Clare and St. Neot's in the British Museum, and a collection of miscellaneous documents relating to Cowick priory in the possession of the duke of Bedford. In the absence of account rolls, court rolls, and custumals no detailed history of conditions on these estates could be written, and I have not attempted it. There are two sides to the following study: first, the general history of the 'order of Bec', beginning with the acquisition of the scattered English property and passing through four hundred years of constitutional development and political and economic adjustment until the last English dependencies were cut off; secondly, the detailed organization of the estates in the bailiwick of Ogbourne, by far the most unusual and interesting of the abbey's dependencies.

[1] Exch. K.R., E. 106, 1–12.

PART I
THE ORDER OF BEC

(i)

THE expansion of monasticism following the Norman Conquest brought remarkable and unforeseen consequences. The revival of religious life in Normandy, with its fervour and dynamic force, was in its prime when the Norman lords—often personal friends of neighbouring abbots—acquired a wealth of lands across the Channel. Their natural impulse was to grant at least a small proportion of their estates to religious houses of deservedly high reputation; either a single manor to swell the resources of a Norman abbey, or land and churches enough to support a colony of monks sent out from the mother house. It was not unusual in the eleventh century for a monastery to possess estates or cells in remote regions, but the Norman plantation produced in a few decades a remarkably large number of minute dependencies scattered over the whole of England. Possibly their numbers in part accounted for their stunted growth; certainly the coming of the Cistercians and the newer orders tended to draw donations away from the older Benedictine houses. There are examples of abbeys colonized by monks from Normandy which were independent from the beginning,[1] but very few, if any, of the subject priories became independent communities until political events in the late fourteenth century forced them to choose between denization and slow ruin. In the larger houses, such as St. Neot's, Spalding, or Stoke-by-Clare, where there was room for a full development of monastic life, the supervision of the abbot may have been a salutary influence on monastic discipline. But the continued existence of tiny cells of four or even fewer monks must have imposed unnecessary hardship and mental difficulty on all monks who had a real vocation for the claustral life and provided unparalleled opportunities of worldly living for those who had not. In spite of this, development of these cells was not arrested;

[1] Dom Knowles, *The Monastic Order in England*, p. 154, cites Battle and Chester.

although they almost never grew to support large communities, they were rarely suppressed. 'When once monasteries have been dedicated with the consent of bishops they must always remain monasteries; and the possessions depending on them must always belong to monasteries; they can never again become secular habitations.'[1] Alienation of monastic lands to seculars was illegal; union of them with the lands of other monasteries was a last desperate resort. Innocent III occasionally sponsored the suppression of a decaying religious community for the benefit of another,[2] yet in spite of this illustrious example the numerous small alien cells continued their separate and often rather material existences. Custom lay upon them like frost.

Amongst the monasteries that acquired property and influence in England none is more famous than the abbey of Bec-Hellouin. In the age of Herluin, Lanfranc, and Anselm it became a spiritual and intellectual centre, constantly called upon to send out monks to other communities. It was in fact a seminary of bishops and abbots, and the mother house of numerous priories in France as well as in England. Lanfranc's policy of bringing monks from Normandy to infuse new life into English monasteries would alone have served to spread its influence, but there were also lay friends of the abbots no less anxious to see monks from Bec settled in Duke William's newly acquired kingdom. Hugh, earl of Chester, was one of them; his gifts made possible the foundation of St. Werburgh's, Chester, which was colonized by monks from Bec. Though Dom Thibault and after him Canon Porée believed St. Werburgh's to be a dependency of Bec during the first years of its existence,[3] there is no evidence to support this view; Anselm himself wrote of it very shortly after its foundation as an independent abbey.[4]

[1] *Decretum*, II. XIX. III. iv (Council of Chalcedon, c. 24). This canon was cited by the monks of Tavistock in the fifteenth century, when they opposed the grant of Cowick priory to Eton (Cowick Priory Documents, D 82/32).

[2] Dom U. Berlière, 'Innocent III et la réorganisation des monastères bénédictines', in *Revue bénédictine*, xxxii (1920), pp. 22–42, 144–59.

[3] MS. Lat. 12884, f. 87; Porée, *Histoire de l'Abbaye du Bec*, i. 451.

[4] Anselm, *Epistolae* (Migne, *P.L.* clix), lib. III, ep. xlix. The evidence produced by Tait in his edition of the Cartulary implies that St. Werburgh's Abbey was independent from the time of its re-foundation by Earl Hugh (*The*

But the most conspicuous lay friends of the abbey were Gilbert of Brionne and his descendants. Gilbert himself had been Herluin's feudal overlord; he had made possible his retreat into a monastery by releasing him from the secular services which he owed, as well as giving land to swell Herluin's modest patrimony.[1] His son Richard, the founder of the house of Clare, brought one of the first colonies of monks to England. A few monks of Ely who still inhabited the decayed priory of St. Neot's were expelled, and monks of Bec established in their place, probably about 1079. The community was endowed by Richard, his wife Rohais, and their dependants, and for several centuries supported from twelve to eighteen monks and a prior.[2] A foundation of a slightly different kind was made in the next generation by Gilbert of Clare, who in 1090 gave Bec the collegiate church of St. John Baptist of Clare, with the stipulation that the monks were to occupy the prebends one by one as they fell vacant. The collegiate church was situated actually within Clare castle and was probably in an unsuitable spot for the erection of a monastery, though its prebends were an important source of revenue; in 1124 the community was definitely established at Stoke.[3] Like St. Neot's, this priory remained conventual and recited full choral offices.[4] The third conventual priory was founded a little later by a member of a different family, Robert of Chandos, who founded Goldcliff in 1113;[5] but it came in time into the patronage of William the Marshal, and after his death into the main stem of the Clare family.

William, son of Baldwin, sheriff of Exeter, was a cousin of the Clares; we do not know if he expressly stated when he gave Cowick manor to the abbey of Bec that a priory was to be established there, but certainly by the middle of the twelfth century a cell was in existence at Cowick.[6] The

Chartulary or Register of the Abbey of St. Werburgh, Chester, ed. J. Tait (Chetham Society, 1920), pp. xxiv–xxv).

[1] Porée, i. 34 seq.

[2] Porée, i. 453 seq.

[3] Porée, i. 444 seq.

[4] Porée, ii. 164.

[5] R. Graham, 'Four Alien Priories in Monmouthshire', in *Journal of the British Archaeological Association*, xxxv. 104 seq.

[6] Cowick Priory Documents, G. 4, no. 26; J. Ramackers, *Papsturkunden in Frankreich*, neue Folge, 2. Bde., Normandie, no. 21.

intention of the donors of other manors is equally obscure. Possibly the earlier gifts were made in the hope that a community might be founded; however, by 1100 the abbot of Bec was lord of the manors of Atherstone, Blakenham, Brixton-Deverill, Lessingham, Povington, Monxton, Quarley, Ruislip, Swyncombe, Tooting, East Wretham, Christow, and possibly Combe; and not one of them ever became the nucleus of a fully conventual priory. One or two may have been cells or granges supporting a prior and his *socius* who administered the estates; Ruislip certainly was a cell of this type, but the early history of the other manors is a blank. Probably early-eleventh-century donations were made solely to swell the revenues of the Norman abbey, or the intentions of the donors were vague. The abbey's wealth in manors and churches grew steadily until the middle of the thirteenth century, when four conventual and three non-conventual priories owed allegiance to Bec.[1]

Anselm was abbot of Bec when the first communities set out for England. He gave the monks the advantage of his counsel and guidance, and recommended them to prelates and others in England. To Gundulf, formerly a monk of Bec, then bishop of Rochester, he wrote: 'I commend to your fatherly love . . . our brothers and yours, whom we are sending into England; so that in all time of need they may be supported by your aid and guided by your counsel; and that their lives may be carefully examined by you and judiciously praised or corrected';[2] and he made the same request to Henry, abbot of Battle, and Baldwin, abbot of Bury.[3] His letter to Richard and Rohais of Clare reminded them of their responsibility towards the monks: 'We are sending our brothers to you, as you commanded. And therefore we commend them to you; because they are going to England at your command and by your wish what they do, and how and by what means they live, ought to be your care and consideration.'[4] Faced with a definite disciplinary problem—the drunkenness of brother Henry, the chamberlain[5]—he

[1] See *infra*, Appendix, for details of the English property of the abbey.

[2] *Epistolae*, lib. II, ep. iii (Migne, *P.L.* clviii).

[3] Ibid., ep. iv, v.

[4] Ibid., ep. vi.

[5] Probably of St. Neot's.

urged that penance should be imposed by Lanfranc or Gundulf of Rochester or brother Richard, the head of the community in England, and added: 'But if he obstinately refuses correction, I prefer that (in spite of the profit we should derive from his presence in England) he should return to us to be ruled by discipline, rather than remain far from discipline to be ruined.'[1] For the general guidance of the monks he promulgated statutes that were to be read annually in the chapter of Stoke-by-Clare, but their substance is no longer known.[2]

For a century afterwards the relations of Bec with its daughter houses in England are very obscure. It seems improbable that Anselm or his immediate successors visualized any kind of constitutional bond to maintain the abbot's authority in the subject priories; Anselm entrusted the temporal welfare of his monks to the patrons—the Clare family—and their spiritual welfare to wise and distinguished friends among the bishops and abbots in England. In fact he relied entirely upon personal relationships and the personal judgement of the abbot of Bec when any particular problem of discipline was brought to his notice. He may have expected that in time, like the abbey of Chester, the priories would become independent. Meanwhile the monks had his statutes, the rule of St. Benedict, and the authority of their abbot to guide them; permanent, stereotyped relationships with the abbot, the patrons, and other ecclesiastical authorities were left to the moulding of time and circumstances.

The example of Cîteaux was not immediately followed by the abbey of Bec. Faced with the problem of uniting in spirit widely separated monasteries, the abbot and senior monks of Cîteaux drew up the *Carta caritatis*, which imposed upon the abbot the duty of visiting once a year the cells subject to him,[3] and on the subordinate priors and abbots the duty of

1 *Epistolae*, lib. II, ep. vii.

2 MS. Lat. 9211, no. 15. Probably these were statutes for the whole order; cf. MS. Dom. A. XI, f. 121*v*., where the monks speak of customs common to the whole order of Bec, approved by Anselm and others.

3 'Semel per annum visitet abbas maioris ecclesie vel per se vel per aliquem de coabbatibus suis omnia cenobia que ipse fundaverit. Et si fratres amplius visitaverit, inde magis gaudeant. . . .' (J. M. Canivez, *Statuta Capitulorum Generalium Ordinis Cisterciensis*, i. p. xxvii.)

attending the annual general chapter.[1] Other religious orders copied this institution.[2] Abbots of Bec certainly visited the English priors whenever they went to England; Anselm visited them, and so did Theobald: the obligations of many tenants in the thirteenth-century custumal to ride with the abbot or fetch food for him when he came suggest that he made periodical progresses round his English possessions.[3] But of any kind of general chapter, apart from the chapter that met to elect each new abbot,[4] there is no trace during the twelfth century. When Abbot William II visited the English priories in 1200 and extracted letters of obedience, the priors recognized his right to appoint and remove them as well as their monks, but confessed to no other obligations towards him.[5]

The change seems to have begun early in the thirteenth century. Innocent III's work for the Benedictine monasteries has already been given its deserved prominence by Dom Berlière;[6] and his pontificate brought the monks of Bec organization, definition, and perhaps some innovation. Whereas the bulls of previous popes had merely confirmed the abbey's possessions, Innocent III's letters dealt with points of discipline. He gave the abbot of Bec power to suppress small cells of two or three monks where regular life was neglected, and recall the monks to the cloister; to punish his monks, notwithstanding any appeal to Rome, and to absolve any who incurred excommunication through assault with violence.[7]

But the decision of Innocent III most influential in the development of all Benedictine monasteries was embodied in the twelfth canon of the Fourth Lateran Council. This decreed that in every ecclesiastical province a chapter of

[1] 'Omnes abbates de ordine nostro singulis annis ad generale capitulum Cisterciense omni postposita occasione convenient' (*Carta caritatis*).

[2] E. Martène, *De antiquis monachorum ritibus*, lib. III, c. xxvii. 3.

[3] MS. Add. 24316, f. 57*v*. [58*v*.] and *passim*.

[4] In the thirteenth century this consisted of the monks of Bec and the French priors only; Porée believes that the English priors also were present in the twelfth century (i. 495).

[5] Porée, i. 446–7; MS. Lat. 9211, no. 15.

[6] Op. cit. (*Revue bénédictine*, xxxii (1920).)

[7] Potthast, no. 4159; *P.L.* ccxvii. 275, no. 236. MS. Lat. 12884, f. 294; MS. Lat. 13905, f. 3*v*. Potthast, 4160.

religious orders who had not previously had regular chapters was to be held; its decisions were to be observed by all, and specially appointed visitors were to enforce them. Moreover, every bishop was to take upon himself the reform of the monasteries of his diocese subject to his jurisdiction, and prevent laymen from infringing the rights of the religious.[1] The importance of this decision has been justly stressed by many modern writers. Its interest for the order of Bec was that, by creating a machinery to enforce monastic discipline, it compelled the monks almost in self-defence to create a similar machinery of their own. Before 1215 we have no evidence for the existence of a general chapter; but on 23 June 1219 the priors of the order met under the presidency of Abbot Richard of Saint-Léger and promulgated statutes for the reform of monastic life.[2] It seems probable that this chapter was designed to preserve the unity of the small group of priories dependent on Bec; if the subject priors, already liable to visitation and correction by their diocesan bishops, had also been drawn into the provincial chapters and forced to adopt varying rites and customs the slender ties that bound them to the mother house would soon have been broken. From the thirteenth century the expression *ordo Beccensis* appears in documents;[3] and the constitution of the priories, united under the abbot, with special statutes, ritual, and even a distinctive white habit justifies the description of Bec and its dependencies as an 'order'.[4]

By the late thirteenth century the abbot's authority had been built upon legislation in the general chapter, with the solid backing of papal privilege. In spiritual matters the abbot was supreme; he sent out monks and recalled them at will, as well as appointing the priors and removing them. The priors themselves were only entrusted for a time with the administration of the estates and the maintenance of discipline. Legally they were only proctors of the abbot and needed his letters of proxy to defend their rights and posses-

[1] Mansi, *Sacrorum Conciliorum Nova et Amplissima Collectio*, xxii. 999–1002.

[2] Porée, i. 547–8.

[3] Cf. *Chronique du Bec*, p. 35.

[4] See R. Molitor, *Aus der Rechtsgeschichte benediktinischer Verbände*, i. 89.

sions in courts of law or to alienate property.[1] Sometimes, however, they received the professions of monks.[2] In England the conventual priors presented to some churches; but, in order to save the French cells the expenses of litigation, the abbot decided to present to all benefices in their gift and bear the expense of any lawsuits that might arise about advowson. In the province of Rouen the abbot himself was to present his nominee to the bishop; in the sees of Paris, Chartres, Beauvais, and Amiens, on account of opposition from the diocesans, he was merely to designate someone and leave the actual presentation to the prior.[3]

Against alienation and the unwarranted granting of benefices the struggle had been long and slow. Papal bulls on the subject were common during the early thirteenth century, and the abbey of Bec received its share. Honorius III first authorized Abbot Richard of Saint-Léger to refuse pensions *gratie expectative* to clerks who declined to accept a proffered benefice,[4] and later forbade the granting of any pensions to the detriment of the monastery.[5] Another of his bulls ratified Abbot Richard's letter prohibiting the division or alienation of conventual property by English priors;[6] these priors, however, were particularly intransigent, and in spite of abbatial and papal letters in 1220 Peter de la Cambe had to renew the prohibition fifty years later.[7] An insidious form of alienation began with letting out property at farm: Alexander IV commanded the abbot and convent of Bec to resume possession of goods which, under cover of a temporary farm, had been annexed by laymen and clerks, and even annulled previous papal bulls authorizing the farming of tithes and other monastic goods.[8] Urban IV was attacking

[1] Jouvelin, cited Porée, i. 441. MS. Dom. A. XI, ff. 124–5, 137–8, contains letters of proxy for the French priors.

[2] MS. Dom. A. XI, f. 129: 'Item supplicant quatinus indulgeatis eisdem ut ipsi vel priores sibi subditi ad recepcionem alicuius in monachum seu conversum . . . de cetero compelli non possint. . . .'

[3] Ibid., f. 126.

[4] Porée, i. 568; MS. Dom. A. XI, f. 127.

[5] Porée, i. 568 (23 May 1223). Gregory IX also dispensed the religious from granting pensions except by formal papal concession (Porée, i. 569; MS. Lat. 12884, f. 329; MS. Lat. 13905, f. 5).

[6] Porée, ii. 211; MS. Lat. 12884, f. 299*v*.

[7] MS. Dom. A. XI, ff. 112–112*v*.

[8] MS. Lat. 12884, f. 363. Honorius III had permitted the farming of tithes.

the same problem when he warned all farmers and usurpers of revenues, lands, tithes, meadows, woods, jurisdictions, privileges, or other goods belonging to the abbey of Bec to restore them forthwith,[1] and renewed Alexander IV's prohibition of the farming of tithes.[2] The period is rich in bulls trying to protect the abbey's estates from loss and molestation.[3] Other papal privileges buttressed the abbot's authority by repeating the provisions of Innocent III.[4]

The abbot himself enforced his authority by visiting the priories personally and issuing monitory letters, and after the early thirteenth century through the general chapter. Dom Thibault asserted that the English priors took an oath of obedience in the general chapter, though he antedated it.[5] It was in the chapter that disciplinary measures were considered and liturgical modifications approved; probably the decision that the abbot should present to all French benefices was reached there. Statutes were promulgated by Abbot Ymerius in 1304 'by his power and authority, and also by the will and assent of the prior and convent of his monastery and all the priors of his order of Bec present in the general chapter', declaring that monks in English priories were to be recalled to Bec or one of the French priories after an absence of six years at the most, and were to bring with them a certificate of good conduct.[6] The chapter was, moreover, concerned with finance as well as discipline, and Ymerius, by asking the priors to bring their priory accounts with them, added auditing to its other functions.[7]

1 Porée, i. 604–5; MS. Lat. 12884, f. 381.

2 Ibid. The abbot of Bec, through his proctor-general in England, made a regular practice of farming tithes throughout the thirteenth and fourteenth centuries.

3 Bulls were issued by Urban IV (Porée, i. 605, 606); Gregory X (ibid., p. 627); Nicholas III (ibid., p. 628). The abbey was in particular need of a steady revenue on account of the disastrous fire of 1265.

4 Thus Innocent IV and Martin IV condemned monks who made frivolous appeals against their abbot (Porée, i. 546, n. 2); and Alexander IV recognized the abbot's power of instituting and revoking priors (Porée, i. 604; MS. Lat. 12884, f. 365*v.*). Alexander IV also 'concessit . . . ut abbas et capitulum Becci possint revocare monachos ex cellis ubi duo vel tres non satis ordinate vivunt, et bona . . . dictarum cellarum applicandi usibus monasterii, vel ex eis unum vel plures conventus noviter ordinandi licentiam dedit' (Porée, i. 604).

5 MS. Lat. 12884, f. 299*v.* He states that the priors began to refuse the obedience they had sworn immediately after the loss of Normandy.

6 Porée, ii. 566–7.

7 *Chronique du Bec*, ed. Porée, p. 131.

To understand this new duty some consideration of temporal administration is necessary. The abbey of Bec, in common with most other Norman abbeys, had no unified central financial system.[1] From an early date some of the donations had been set aside for a special purpose—thus Ogbourne was given *ad vestiendum monachos*—and by the thirteenth century the more important obedientiaries had certain revenues assigned to them. Apart from the abbot and prior, the sacristan, chamberlain, gardener, granetar, almoner, cellarer, treasurer, infirmarian, and precentor had charge of special lands and revenues.[2] The treasurer was mentioned in one act only and may have been no more than a keeper of records and valuables in the treasury. The revenues allocated to each office were fixed and stable, unless the abbot in consultation with the chapter decided to redistribute them to meet new needs more equitably.[3] As far as temporal administration was concerned, the priories were a type of obedience; lands were assigned to them for the purpose of supporting a fixed number of monks. Their obligations to the abbot were as clearly established as their revenues, and debts owed by one priory to another were carefully recorded. Thus in 1286 the prior of St. Neot's owed 186 marks to the prior of Meulan,[4] and the register of Archbishop Rigaud shows that almost every French prior had incurred a debt towards the abbot. During emergencies the abbot raised money by levying a graduated tax on the French priories and obedientiaries.[5]

Departmentalization and the absence of central control,

[1] R. N. Sauvage considers the powers of the treasurer of Troarn unusually extensive (*Histoire de l'Abbaye de St. Martin de Troarn*, p. 117: 'À Troarn, fait vraiment exceptionnel parmi les abbayes bénédictines normandes, il existait un fonctionnaire, un officier spécial chargé de la garde et de la surveillance des fonds de la maison: le *bursarius conventualis*, ou *custos burse conventualis*'). Some abbeys, for example Jumièges, had no treasurer at all. See J. Loth, *Histoire de l'Abbaye royale de Saint Pierre de Jumièges*, ii. 71–7.

[2] Porée, ii. 137–43.

[3] Thus Ymerius ordered the precentor to pay 50 s.t. annually to the succentor 'qui multo ecclesiae labores die noctuque portat' (*Chronique du Bec*, p. 134). This was a course recommended by the English abbots in the general chapter of 1343: 'Statuimus quod si in monasterio quocunque aliquod officium in temporalibus sit habundans, et sit aliud in eodem quod sufficere sibi non valeat, insufficiencia unius per alterius habundanciam relevetur' (W. A. Pantin, *Chapters of the English Black Monks*, ii. 39).

[4] Porée, ii. 111.

[5] Porée, ii. 80; *Chronique du Bec*, p. 132, n. 1.

common to most French Benedictine monasteries at this period, left ample scope for incompetence and dishonesty.[1] Innocent III, however, introduced a far-reaching reform by commanding the abbot and obedientiaries of Monte Cassino and other monasteries to render account annually.[2] From this time the regular auditing of accounts became a general panacea for all financial ills and was proclaimed throughout Europe by provincial chapters and reforming abbots. Even before the time of Gregory IX it had been demanded in the provincial chapters of Tours, Rouen, and York at least,[3] and from 1249 it gradually found its place among the statutes of the province of Canterbury.[4] Gregory IX formally pronounced the duty of abbot and obedientiaries alike to render account;[5] and Odo Rigaud, basing his injunctions on the statutes of Gregory, reminded most of the abbots and priors of Normandy of this duty.[6] So Ymerius, although the chronicler of Bec thought his decision worth recording, was carrying out a long-overdue reform, not innovating, when he commanded the priors of the order to bring their accounts to the general chapter. Not very long afterwards, indeed, Benedict XII assumed that this system was common to all Benedictine monasteries with dependent cells.[7]

(ii)

The relationship between the English priories and the abbey was in process of definition. During the early twelfth

[1] Some English monasteries, notably Christ Church, Canterbury, had a more centralized and unified financial system. See R. A. L. Smith, 'The Central Financial System of Canterbury Cathedral Priory', in *E.H.R.* lv. 353 seq. (1940).

[2] Cf. Dom Berlière, loc. cit.

[3] For Tours see M. Prou, 'Statuts d'un chapitre général bénédictin tenu à Angers en 1220', in *Mélanges d'Archéologie et d'Histoire de l'École Française de Rome*, iv. (1884); for Rouen, D. Bessin, *Concilia Rothom. Provinciae*, i. 114–22, 154; for York, W. A. Pantin, op. cit. i. 238.

[4] W. A. Pantin, op. cit., i. 36, 84; ii. 87.

[5] *Statuta super reformatione monachorum ordinis S. Benedicti*, nos. 26–7 (*Régistres*, ed. L. Auvray, ii. 316–31): 'Et ut domorum status certior habeatur, singulis tribus mensibus, coram abbate, sive priore, si ibi non est abbas, et senioribus, reddant officiales de suis officiis rationem, computationem de omnibus expensis et receptis fideliter facientes. Abbates et priores bis in anno . . . statum domus sue in capitulo vel coram senioribus . . . plenarie manifestent.'

[6] Amongst others, the abbot of Bec. *Reg. Visit.*, p. 427.

[7] *Constitutiones Benedicti XII*, in Wilkins, *Concilia*, ii. 591–3, *De capitulis generalibus cuiuslibet ecclesie*.

century organization must have varied almost from year to year as new donations came in; the conventual priories were fixed and separate entities from the time of their foundation, but any of the scattered manors bestowed on the abbey of Bec may have become the home of a monk or two for a few decades. The experience of at least one French abbot proved that to place a manor in the hands of farmers was to lose the profit from it;[1] the abbot of Bec had no alternative on his distant English estates but to plant a few monks in convenient centres. These tiny cells or granges needed no conventual buildings; the manor-house and a chapel, or the chancel of the parish church, were enough.[2] They multiplied rapidly on the English as well as the French estates of most Norman abbeys. With the advance of the thirteenth century administrative development, as well as papal legislation, cut down their number. Innocent III encouraged the suppression of unnecessary and corrupt cells;[3] Gregory IX tried to regularize life in the smaller cells by decreeing that at least two monks must reside in each one, and more if the revenues were adequate.[4] Archbishop Rigaud found over and over again during his visitations that solitary monks were residing in England and commanded the French abbots to remedy this fault.[5] Gradually the number of Bec's English cells was reduced to the minimum. Manors were allocated to each according to the purpose of the donors, with a limited regard for administrative convenience. By the middle of the thirteenth century there were seven

[1] Suger, *Liber de Rebus in Administracione sua Gestis.* Cf. Marc Bloch's comments on Suger's policy in *Les Caractères originaux de l'histoire rurale française*, pp. 101–3.

[2] I have described the buildings of three of these granges in 'Inventories of Three Small Alien Priories', in *J.B.A.A.*, 3rd Series, iv (1939), pp. 141–9. Chapels might be built on manors that cannot be proved ever to have been priories. Wretham is an example: in 1339 the indenture of property received by a new bailiff included the following: 'In capella, j calicem de argento, ij tuell', j albam cum aurica, j casulam cum stola, manupul' corporal', j superaltar' cum quadam cista pro vestimentis imponendis' (Eton, A. 20, Wretham Account Rolls, 1339).

[3] *Supra*, p. 10.

[4] *Régistres*, ed. Auvray, ii. 321, no. 12.

[5] *Reg. Visit.*, pp. 76, 110, 191, 316, 578. Rigaud found one case of a monk who refused to have a companion sent to him, 'Unus, videlicet dominus Eustachius, erat in Anglia, qui noviter remiserat quendam monachum quem eidem abbas adiunxerat, ita quod solus remanserat; quod quidem displicuit abbati et nobis' (ibid., p. 608).

groups, each with a priory or grange at its centre; some simplification had taken place, but a map shows that the manors of the seven cells still lay intermingled as chance dictated, without much regard to the difficulties of estate management. Each group of estates, however, was assigned for a peculiar purpose, and so remained distinct. There was one small and obvious exception to the complete economic self-containedness of each group; monks of Bec and their servants in their journeyings across England were given hospitality in any of the manors that lay on their route.[1]

First, Bec had four conventual priories. The revenues of St. Neot's, Stoke-by-Clare, and Goldcliff were needed to support the communities of monks, and these priories paid only small apports annually as a token of their submission to Bec.[2] Cowick also had a community of five to support; it was poorly endowed and from the middle of the thirteenth century held the manor of Christow and land in Harwood at perpetual fee-farm from the abbot of Bec.[3] The prior of Cowick owed 18 marks for the farm of Christow, but unless his apport to his abbot was also 18 marks the farm covered all his obligations.[4] The revenues of the other manors were intended to swell the resources of French houses and supported the minimum number of monks necessary for efficient administration. Steventon and Westbury had, however, from the first been assigned to the prior of Notre-Dame du Pré, and their revenues, like the revenues of the tiny Norman cell of Bures,[5] were intended to support the monks of Le Pré.

1 Manorial accounts frequently record expenses on their behalf; for example at Cottisford in 1292 the oats account included two bushels for the horse of the prior of Goldcliff on the vigil of the Ascension, and one bushel for the horse of the sub-prior of Steventon in June (Eton, C. 14); and the manor of Wretham regularly bore the expenses of the carters and horses of the prior of Stoke, travelling to Yarmouth to fetch herrings (Eton, A. 20).

2 Goldcliff and Stoke-by-Clare owed 20*s.* each, and St. Neot's 30*s.* (P.R.O. Exch. K.R., E. 106, 3/19; MS. Add. 24316, f. 31*v*).

3 Oliver, *Monasticon*, pp. 156–7.

4 The custumal of Ogbourne states that the prior of Cowick owed 18 marks for Christow and Harwood (MS. Add. 24316, f. 31). The inquiry of 1295 found that he owed 18 marks to his abbot (Exch. K.R., E. 106, 3/19) and the prior paid £12 to his abbot in 1286 (MS. Cinq Cents Colbert, 190, p. 67, 'Reconaissance d'obéissance faite à l'abbé de Bec par le priour et religieus de Cowyk avec une redevance de douze livres sterling de rente, 1286'). But these two last references may refer to the farm for Christow.

5 The prior of Le Pré once received 600 livres from Bures (*Reg. Visit.*, p. 267);

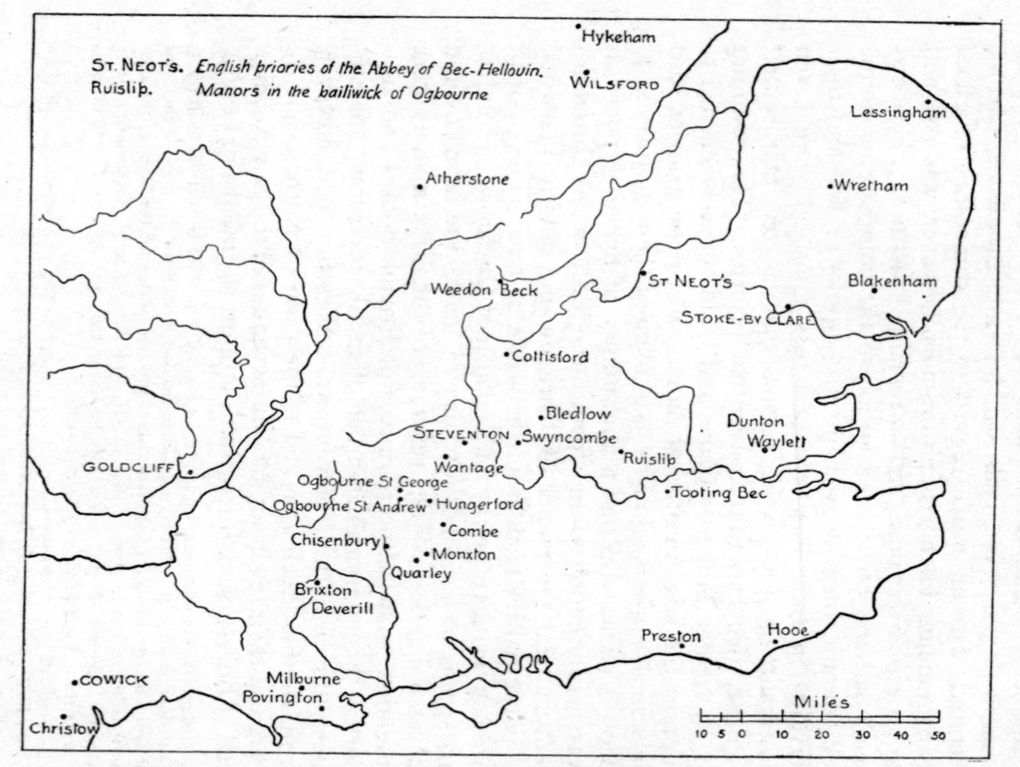

English Priories of the Abbey of Bec-Hellouin; Manors in the Bailiwick of Ogbourne

A prior and his companion lived at Steventon to look after the property and transmitted a small annual sum to the French priory; the inquiry of 1295 found 20 marks to be the customary apport,[1] and in 1258 the abbot of Bec received 60 marks from the English property as part payment of the prior of Le Pré's debt to him.[2] Wilsford was in a similar position; the manor had been assigned to the priory of Envermeu and supported a prior and one monk. By the middle of the thirteenth century the prior held the manor of Hykeham at farm from the proctor of Ogbourne and rendered 14 marks to him,[3] as well as an apport which the royal inquisitors assessed at £10.[4] According to the register of Odo Rigaud the prior of Envermeu had a revenue of 50 marks annually from England, which must have come from Wilsford; but already he had difficulty in collecting it.[5] Thus the temporal economy of these two small priories was subordinated to the economy of Le Pré and Envermeu, but, as in all priories of the order of Bec, the abbot of Bec was supreme in spiritual matters.[6]

The remaining manors came in time to be known as the priory or bailiwick of Ogbourne. During the twelfth century cells may have been established for a time on any of them; but after the turn of the century, when records begin to be more numerous, we hear only of a prior of Ruislip and a proctor of Ogbourne. Between them they managed the estates and presented clerks to churches in the abbot's gift.[7] There had already been some slight readjustment of

the amount as stated seems incredibly large, unless Bures was a centre for the collection of revenues from a wide area. There is certainly one reference to a large household there (ibid., p. 380).

[1] Exch. K.R., E. 106, 3/19.

[2] *Reg. Visit.*, p. 326, 'Debebant circa vii^c libras abbati, verumtamen abbas receperat in Anglia pro eis lx marchas stellingorum.' There is no trace of any apport owed to Bec.

[3] MS. Add. 24316, f. 5*v.*

[4] Exch. K.R., E. 106, 3/19.

[5] *Reg. Visit.*, p. 301: 'In Anglia l marcas, sed sex anni transierunt quod non receperunt aliquid de illis, nisi xviii marcas hoc anno, et quondam alio anno v marcas.'

[6] The prior of Envermeu was, however, occasionally associated with the abbot of Bec in the nomination of a prior of Wilsford (*Rot. Hug. de Welles*, iii. 151; *Rot. Rob. Grosseteste*, p. 46).

[7] The custumal of *c.* 1247 (MS. Add. 24316) shows that some revenues, mostly in the east, were owed to the prior of Ruislip, and others in the west to the prior of Ogbourne. During the collection of the Prelate's Aid of 1235–6 the prior of Ogbourne rendered account for 50 marks 'pro se et priore de Ruslepe' (*Liber

endowment during the twelfth century, for Weedon, originally given to St. Lambert-de-Malassis,[1] and Hooe, at first a manor of St. Martin-au-Bosc,[2] became parcels of Ogbourne. Also the pension from Saltwood church, once due to the prior of St. Philbert, seems later to have been collected for the abbot of Bec.[3] Later, the two most remote manors were leased to priories of the order of Bec.[4] Centralization was, however, to advance still further; the separation of Normandy from the kingdom of England increased difficulties of communication, whilst legal procedure became more lengthy and complex; consequently the monks were often drawn into lawsuits 'in order that, by default, lands and services might more easily be extorted from them'.[5] They sought remedy, like other French abbots, by appointing a proctor-general. By the mid-thirteenth century he was the real link between the abbot of Bec and his English manors; for a time he was known indifferently as prior or proctor of Ogbourne or Ruislip, thus creating the illusion that the estates were still divided into two custodies,[6] but later his title was usually prior of Ogbourne. The administration of this property and the collection of the scattered revenues will be the subject of a later chapter. We do not know to which household department the total profits were paid; since Ogbourne had been given to the wardrobe of the monks the chamberlain seems a likely recipient. Of the woollen cloths and other goods owed to the abbey, however, some were sent for the use of the abbot and prior and others

Feodorum, i. 563). Cf. also *V.C.H. Suffolk*, ii. 152–3, and Newcourt, *Repertorium*, ii. 230, note a.

[1] MS. Cartulaire de St. Lambert, Collection Mancel de Caen, no. 200, pp. 2–12.

[2] *C.D.F.*, ed. Round, nos. 399–401.

[3] A judgement of Stephen Langton (Reg. Pecham, f. 171*v*) stated that the pension was due to St. Philbert; but it is described as a pension of the abbot of Bec in the *Taxation of Pope Nicholas*, p. 2*b*, and in a judgement of Boniface VIII (Canterbury, Dean and Chapter Muniments, S. 334).

[4] *Supra*, pp. 21–3.

[5] *C.P.R. 1232–47*, pp. 272, 291.

[6] William de Guineville, proctor-general from *c.* 1239, is called at various times prior of Ogbourne (*C.P.R. 1232–47*, pp. 272, 291) and proctor of Ruislip (K.C.C., Q 7); and Richard de Flammaville, who received letters of attorney in 1261 (*C.P.R. 1258–66*, p. 135) and seems already to have been proctor-general, was called prior of Ruislip in a judgement of 1259 (K.C.C., Q 4). The name 'prior of Russel' was still attached to the recipient of a pension out of Sampford church in 1291, and caused Newcourt some perplexity (*Repertorium*, ii. 516).

for the use of the convent,[1] and the surplus may have been paid into the abbot's chamber.

(iii)

It remains to consider the relations of the English priories with their diocesan bishops, their patrons, and other Benedictine abbots. The undefined personal bonds that had existed in the time of Anselm had no enduring qualities; they could exist between a prior and a bishop, not between a priory and an episcopate. The twelfth and thirteenth centuries were a period for the precise definition of legal rights, with its inevitable concomitant, disputes about jurisdiction; and from these a formal procedure was gradually evolved.

Unlike the cells of Cluny and Cîteaux, the priories of Bec had no claim to exemption from episcopal control. Bec itself was not exempt, and even if it had been, its dependent cells in other dioceses might have been subject to visitation.[2] Consequently each new prior had to take with him letters of presentation to his diocesan. The precise wording of these letters was a nice point and led to several heated disputes, though never apparently to litigation. The abbots of Bec worded their letters of presentation with as much independence as the suffragans allowed; thus Henry of Leone, the chosen prior of Stoke-by-Clare, was sent to the bishop of Norwich with two letters: the first saying *ad vos mittimus*, the second, which was to be submitted only after the rejection of the first, *vobis presentamus*. Since the bishop made no difficulties about accepting the first formula, the second was sent back to Bec.[3] Osbern, prior of Goldcliff, had two similar latters when he was presented to the bishop of Llandaff, and again there was no difficulty about his admission.[4] But there were several disputes with the bishop of Lincoln. Oliver Sutton refused to accept the form in which Ymerius presented John of Bois Renaud because it contained a clause committing the cure of the monks' souls to the

[1] MS. Add. 24316, f. 31*v*.

[2] Cf. R. Molitor, *Aus der Rechtsgeschichte benediktinischer Verbände*, i. 88. Exempt monasteries, however, sometimes disputed the right of a bishop to visit their dependent priories.

[3] MS. Dom. A XI, f. 113*v*.

[4] Ibid.

prior, and to commit the cure of souls in another diocese was contrary to reason and canonical custom. He enclosed a shorter form of presentation which had been used before: Ymerius, after taking counsel, decided to use it without protest.[1] During the next vacancy at St. Neot's the bishop of Lincoln showed himself a little unwilling to accept even this form of presentation; but there had already been considerable delay because the retiring prior had omitted to send a proper letter of resignation, and the bishop graciously decided not to hold up the appointment any longer, 'although the letter of presentation seemed of doubtful validity, in the words "to whom we have committed the cure and administration of our priory etc.", since the abbot had no right to commit a cure, but only to present.'[2] Oliver Sutton showed the same attitude towards presentations to the priory of Wilsford, and in 1290 he insisted on Walter of Pont Audemer renouncing the offending form and obtaining a new letter of presentation before he would admit him as prior.[3] The priory of Cowick was very closely under diocesan control, and Peter Quivil even claimed that his undisputed right of admitting and instituting the priors of Cowick gave him also the right of removing them. On one occasion the abbot of Bec yielded to the bishop's insistence and forbore to transfer a prior of Cowick to St. Neot's, thus provoking from an anonymous monk of Bec the plaintive cry: 'But God knows that this counsel was against the jurisdiction of the lord abbot of Bec, and against his privileges.'[4] The letter from a newly appointed prior of Cowick to his abbot contains a very full account of the claims of the bishop of Exeter, which included the right of forbidding the prior to cross the sea without special licence, and the guardianship of the property during vacancy.[5]

Of Steventon nothing definite is known; there is no record of a presentation to it in either the Formulary of Bec or the Register of Simon of Ghent. Ogbourne was part of

[1] MS. Dom. A XI, ff. 113*v*–14.

[2] G. C. Gorham, Supplement to *The History and Antiquities of Eynesbury and St. Neot's*, p. cxlii, note *h*.

[3] Reg. Sutton, ff. 212–212*v*.

[4] MS. Dom. A XI, ff. 114*v*–15.

[5] MS. Lat. 13905, f. 12. See Oliver, *Monasticon*, pp. 161–2 for a list of licences.

the abbot of Bec's Salisbury prebend and was exempt from diocesan control.[1]

The priors once instituted, the bishop unquestionably enjoyed the right of canonical visitation. Since Archbishop Rigaud visited both the abbey of Bec and its Norman priories, and the English priors took an oath of obedience to their diocesans, they would have had no good reason for claiming exemption.[2] Cowick was visited several times, by both the bishop of Exeter and the guardian of the spiritualities *sede vacante*.[3] No injunctions have survived, but we know that after the visitation of 1315 the bishop was dissatisfied with the prior's conduct and informed the prior of Ogbourne of his displeasure.[4] Archbishop Pecham included Goldcliff priory in his visitation of the diocese of Llandaff in 1282 and issued stereotyped injunctions; his chief complaint was that the prior did not render account.[5] There appear to have been few cases of open scandal in the priories of Bec; the history of other alien cells shows that as a rule bishops dealt with scandals by writing monitory letters to the French abbots,[6] though occasionally they took the law into their own hands.[7]

At intervals during the thirteenth century the Benedictine abbots of the province of Canterbury, assembled in their general chapter, attempted to extend their jurisdiction over the alien priories. According to the statutes of 1249 any *monachi transmarini* who refused to be visited were to prove their exemption at the next general chapter.[8] More positive claims were raised in 1278, when the priors of Stoke and St. Neot's were cited, as priors having no superior abbot, to

[1] *Infra*, pp. 138–9.

[2] In 1279 the abbot of Bec wrote: 'Cum igitur secundum antiquam monasterii nostri Beccensis consuetudinem approbatam et hactenus observatam, soli abbates dicti monasterii et locorum dyocesani visitacionem habuerint in prioratibus seu cellis predictis ab antiquo. . . .' W. A. Pantin, op. cit. iii. 270.

[3] *Reg. Grandisson*, p. 392; H.M.C., *Various Collections*, i. 274.

[4] MS. Lat. 13905, f. 12.

[5] *Reg. Epist. Joh. Peckham*, iii. 800. The same injunctions were issued on the same day to the priory of Monmouth.

[6] Cf. Grosseteste's complaints about the prior of Minting to the abbot of Fleury. *Epistolae*, nos. liii, liv, cviii; also *Reg. Epist. Joh. Peckham*, ii. 561.

[7] For example, Pecham's excommunication of the monk-bailiff of Fécamp *Reg. Epist.* ii. 604–6), and his removal of the prior of Pembroke (ibid. iii. 786–8).

[8] W. A. Pantin, op. cit. i. 44.

appear in the next chapter. When the visitors appointed in the chapter actually tried to enforce new statutes and collect contributions for the Benedictine house of studies in Oxford, Abbot Peter de la Cambe took up the case and appealed to Rome.[1] The claims he put forward related to abstract rights rather than actual practice, but were logically convincing; namely that the priors had a superior abbot, owed attendance every three years at the general chapter of Bec, and were visited annually by the diocesan bishop, that the abbot's authority in his dependent priories was confirmed by papal bulls, and the monastery had received customs from Lanfranc and Anselm. 'How', he asked, 'can you who are members of the monastery of Bec observe statutes other than those observed by the head without grievous injury to it?'

Although the appeal was abandoned after the death of Nicholas IV, the priors established their claims; Archbishop Pecham supported them, and the Benedictine abbots ceased to treat them as contumacious for not appearing in the general chapter.[2] For a similar reason—that divergent customs could not be observed in different houses of the same order—the monks of Bec[3] refused to adopt liturgical changes proposed by the general chapter of the province of Rouen in 1282.[4] The abbots were, however, perfectly willing to attend the chapter and sometimes presided.

The claims of the lay patrons could not be brushed aside so rapidly. There is no space here to deal with the wide problem of ecclesiastical patronage in England, which is still largely an unworked field. But it may be suggested that the small alien priories were in a peculiar way dependent on their patrons: remote from the mother house, in territory that was to become a separate kingdom, they had to rely on the local patron for protection from violence and—especially as the fourteenth century advanced—royal exactions. Even so single-minded a reformer as Archbishop

[1] W. A. Pantin, op. cit. iii. 264 seq., prints the section of MS. Dom. A XI dealing with the whole of this dispute.

[2] The priors of Spalding, subject to St. Nicholas d'Angers, continued in spite of protests to be included among the contumacious. Ibid. ii. 18, 19.

[3] Not the abbot. Ymerius, when charged with neglect of the statutes, 'respondit se velle libenter quantum ad ipsum pertinebat observare statuta memorata'. MS. Dom. A XI, ff. 121–121*v*.

[4] Ibid. ff. 120–3*v*.

Pecham could write to the abbot of Cluny urging him, in his own interest, to placate the earl of Warenne, patron of Lewes priory 'for if you offend such a worthy magnate, you will offend all the princes and prelates of England'.[1]

Until the Clare estates were broken up in 1314 the head of the house of Clare was patron of St.Neot's, Stoke-by Clare, and Goldcliff. A charter of Richard of Clare to the prior of St. Neot's shows that he reserved to himself the guardianship of the property during vacancies or when the prior had crossed the sea.[2] Consequently desire for financial profit may have caused Gilbert of Clare to prolong the 1264 vacancy on technical grounds;[3] and again in 1292 to hold up the appointment of a prior for a long while before giving his consent.[4] Newly appointed priors of all three cells had to bring with them letters of presentation from the abbot to the patron, and the formulary contains examples; two versions similar to those sent to the diocesans were provided, the first reading *mittimus* and the second *presentamus*. The earl might claim a voice in the appointment of any prior;[5] thus Gilbert of Clare claimed that one prior of Goldcliff had been removed from office and later, at his intercession, sent back to Goldcliff.[6] On occasion, even when a priory was not vacant, he laid hands on its property or liberties. In 1289 there was strife and bitterness between the priory and its patron, for the formulary records that Gilbert of Clare had held the liberties of the priory in his hand for a year and more, 'asserting that the prior and monks of the place had abused these liberties to his detriment'.[7] The prior had, however, a powerful defender in Edward I, who was always

[1] *Reg. Epist. Joh. Peckham*, iii. 904.

[2] Porée, ii. 213, n. 3. The king guarded the temporalities during the minority of the earls of Clare.

[3] Gorham, op. cit., p. cxli.

[4] Ibid., p. cxlii, note *h*: 'Verum quia dominus comes Gloverniae, patronus domus de Sancto Neoto, medio tempore se opposuerat provocando et appellando ne absque ipsius consensu admittetur presentatus predictus . . . presentatus, prefatum dominum comitem adiens, post multum temporis ad episcopum rediit, exhibens sibi literam dicti domini comitis. . . .'

[5] Cf. the allegation of Giraldus Cambrensis that alien priors who did not wish to be recalled would induce their patrons to have their stay in England prolonged; a statement which, whether true or untrue, would not have been plausible unless the patrons were able to influence appointments. *Opera*, iv. 32.

[6] P.R.O. Plea Rolls, K.B. 27/137.

[7] MS. Dom. A XI, f. 137.

ready to whittle down Marcher custom;[1] and by 1291 he had countered the arbitrary behaviour of his patron by bringing the case into the King's Bench and making the king a party to the suit.[2] He claimed that he held his possessions in chief by gift of Howell of Caerleon, and could be impleaded only by writs of the royal chancery; whereas Gloucester was trying to implead him in the court of Caerleon by his own writ of *Quare impedit* over the advowson of Undy church. During the course of the case Gloucester claimed suit of court from the prior of Goldcliff as his tenant,[3] and the evidence produced illustrated Gloucester's relationship with the prior of Goldcliff as well as the exact status of the prior. But in spite of the king's interest, the proceedings were suspended for a time and finally cut short by Gloucester's death. The patronage of Goldcliff remained a constant cause of dispute; in its early days the priory had changed hands several times by conquest,[4] and the descendants of the original donors tried to revive their claims. Among these was Philip de Columbers, who raised his claim in 1321 and again in the time of Edward III;[5] but for a time in the early fourteenth century the priory was certainly under the royal patronage.[6]

The Courtneys were the patrons of Cowick priory; they too insisted on receiving letters of presentation from each new prior,[7] but during vacancies the bishops of Exeter claimed some control. The lay patrons showed a proper interest in the right direction of the monastic revenues; and when during the fourteenth century all profits from alien

[1] Cf. his dramatic humbling of Gloucester and Norfolk for waging private war. J. E. Morris, *The Welsh Wars of Edward I*, chap. vii.

[2] P.R.O. Plea Rolls, K.B. 27/129, 27/131, 27/137.

[3] 'Et quo ad advocacionem prioratus de Goldclive, dicit quod Ricardus comes Gloucestrie pater eius obiit seisitus de advocacione predicta. Et mater comitis qui nunc est similiter, per quod idem comes petit curiam suam de predicto priore ut de tenente suo, scilicet in Wundi et villa Sancte Brigide et Carliun, que sunt de libertate et honore de Carliun. Et in Goldclive racione advocacionis prioratus eiusdem loci, de qua advocacione Ricardus comes Gloucestrie pater comitis qui nunc est obiit seisitus. Et in Coudrey, Frene et Christi Ecclesia que sunt de commoto de Lamberyth qui quidem commotus est de honore de Carliun ab antiquo.'

[4] Dugdale, *Monasticon*, vi. 1023.

[5] *Rot. Parl.* i. 398*a*–*b*; ii. 415*a*.

[6] *C.F.R.* iv. 86. Priors were also presented to the king as patron in 1313 and 1318 (P.R.O., Ancient Correspondence, S.C. 1, 33/25, 33/29).

[7] MS. Dom. A XI, f. 115.

priories were being paid into the royal exchequer, Hugh Courtney secured the diversion of £18 annual revenue for the support of a chantry in Cowick priory, which he had first endowed with a grant of £100.[1] Wilsford, Steventon, and Ogbourne, not being properly conventual priories, were even more independent: an inquisition taken in 1315 showed that the abbot of Bec held Wilsford priory of Thomas Wake in frankalmoign, and that Thomas's ancestors had never received any profits during vacancies, or the fealty of the monk whom the abbot appointed prior at his will.[2] Steventon was a royal gift, but the king put forward no claims as patron. It was Ogbourne that brought most profit into the royal coffers; the manor had been given by Maud of Wallingford, after whose death the honour of Wallingford escheated to the Crown; and though it was granted first to Richard of Cornwall and later to Piers Gaveston, it was for long periods in the royal hands.[3] The priors administered the English estates of the abbey, which were taken into the king's hand on the death of each abbot; gradually as the thirteenth century advanced the priors formed the habit of paying £200 to the king to keep the custody of the property during vacancy.[4] They were in any case presented to him as proctors of the abbot, and it is not always easy to separate the prior from the attorney.

We do not know if the patrons of the priories used pressure to secure the presentation of their relatives to churches in the priors' gift, as they did in their own parish churches.[5] They showed, however, a scrupulous insistence on the exact terms of the foundation and refused to allow their ancestors to be defrauded of their debt of prayers. In particular the Norman patrons rose in a body when Clement V gave the priory of Ogbourne in commendation to his

[1] P.R.O., E. 159/179.
[2] *C.Cl.R. 1313–18*, p. 139.
[3] Cf. Edward II's reference to the 'priory of Ogbourne of the royal patronage' (*H.M.C.* iv, Appendix, p. 384).
[4] *C.F.R.* i. 163, iv. 64.
[5] Cf. *Reg. Joh. de Pontissara*, p. 202: 'Item cum Comites, Barones et alii nobiles Regni Anglie plures ecclesias fundaverint, dotaverint ac earum fuerint patroni, et ad eas presentaverint filios, nepotes et propinquos . . .' This, however, is a general statement of the action of patrons in parish churches of their foundation, and they may not have sought the same advantages from the churches they bestowed on the priories in their patronage. The history of ecclesiastical patronage in England is still unwritten.

nephew, Raymond de Got. They pointed out that the goods and revenues of the priory had been given by their ancestors to the abbey of Bec 'to perform the divine office, and pray for them and for us, and maintain hospitality and charity in the abbey, and give alms', adding, 'We should be deeply grieved if these goods were converted to the advantage of one person; for our ancestors gave them to the abbey and the monks there serving God for the purposes we have stated; and if we or our heirs learned that these goods had been so converted, by the custom of the land we might take them back and hold them.'[1] And there are cases of investigations in England about the due administration of alms in the manors of Preston, Hooe, Ogbourne, and Ruislip.[2]

(iv)

The priors themselves steered a middle course between the local powers, hungry for authority over them, and the abbots of Bec, who steadfastly and moderately demanded subjection and obedience. They were opportunists—amphibious beings, making the best of two worlds—and it would be as misleading to accept the truth of their general statements as to attempt to classify them as dative or conventual priors and then deduce their duties. When the English abbots summoned them to a general chapter they openly announced that they were members of the order of Bec; and the abbot supported them, though he insisted that they were to pay their share of the costs of litigation.[3] In lawsuits they treated their dependent position as a device of pleading, announcing or suppressing it at will; and the royal justices were inclined to use the measuring-stick of precedent rather than investigate the strictly legal position of the priors. Their attitude was justified in the event for the abbot of Bec never tried to reverse an unfavourable verdict on the grounds that the prior who had lost the case was not authorized.

During the *quo warranto* inquiries of Edward I the prior of St. Neot's once began his defence by saying that he was a monk of Bec, amovable at the will of the abbot, unable to defend his liberties without him; and at the next session he

[1] Porée, ii. 63.

[2] *C.P.R. 1330–4*, p. 504; *1338–40*, p. 146; *C.Cl.R. 1330–3*, pp. 406, 419.

[3] *Supra*, pp. 27–8.

brought the abbot's attorney. But in the time of Edward III another prior defended his liberties himself. When Richard of Aldborough, the king's representative, protested that as a dative prior he could not do so, the prior replied that he and his predecessors had sued and been sued in all pleas, real and personal, since time immemorial. Richard of Aldborough reserved his objection, and the case went on.[1] One of the earl of Gloucester's exceptions in his suit against the prior of Goldcliff was that he could not be compelled to answer the plaintiff, who was only a bailiff of his abbot and not a legal person;[2] finally it was overruled because he had already cited the prior to his court of Caerleon and had on other occasions treated him as a legal party to a suit. First, however, there had been a passage of arms between the two: Gloucester maintained the strict legal rights of the abbot of Bec, insisting that any infringement of them was *de facto*, not *de jure*. The prior confined his defence to a statement of the acts he had performed; he and his predecessors had given lands, gifts, and annual pensions, and freed villeins, and no act of theirs had been revoked by any abbot of Bec. He had a convent in his priory and a common seal and he presented clerks to churches in the patronage of the priory. At his creation he had been presented to the bishop of Llandaff and admitted as prior, and the spiritualities of the priory had been entrusted to him. And all lands, tenements, advowsons, and possessions of the priory had originally been given to God, and the prior and monks of Goldcliff.[3] There are no other statements as full as this, but the priors of Stoke and St. Neot's not infrequently pleaded in their own names.[4]

Letters of the abbots, tirelessly repeating the same instructions, show that they felt the English priors slipping from their authority and were unwilling to permit it.

1 *Placita de Quo Warranto*, pp. 9, 55–6.

2 Cf. Bracton: 'Sunt etiam quidam priores et procuratores, qui sunt amotibiles, qui nec dare possunt nec alienare, sicut nec rem in judicium deducere, nec permutare, nec cum consensu superioris nec sine consensu abbatis vel prioris, . . . vel alterius talis, quia amotibiles sunt et non perpetui, nec generalem nec liberam habent administrationem' (R.S. i. 96).

3 P.R.O. Plea Rolls, K.B. 27/129.

4 See *Abbreviatio Placitorum*, pp. 46, 190, 254; P.R.O. Plea Rolls, K.B. 26/37, rot. 5; Lambeth MS. 244, ff. 3*v*, 4*v*, 41*v*, 68*v*, 72*v*, 89, and *passim*.

Richard of St. Léger, Peter de la Cambe, and Ymerius were all obliged to forbid the alienation of property,[1] in spite of the written promise given by the priors in 1215. Ymerius forbade the reception of visitors from the general chapters of the province of Canterbury, and warned the priors against rashly granting the right of preaching in their chapter since the unscrupulous might base a claim to visitation on such a concession. He also rebuked them for not paying in full the pensions that they owed as a sign of subjection and obedience, and commanded them in future to pay their pensions to the general proctor in England. Renewed insistence on attendance at the general chapter of Bec was another method of reminding the priors that their abbot still held the reins of authority, and by demanding to see the *status* of each priory at regular intervals Ymerius applied a curb. After his death the priors still continued at times to attend the chapter; we know that the prior of Goldcliff either came in 1313 bringing his *status domus*, or sent it;[2] and in 1331 the priors of Stoke and St. Neot's received permission to cross the Channel in order to be present at their chapter at Bec.[3] Another measure to secure prompter obedience from the monks in English priories was adopted in the general chapter of 1304; they were to be recalled to Bec or one of the French priories after six years' absence at the most, and each monk was to bring with him a certificate of good conduct.[4]

The abbots of Bec never appointed a vicar-general in England; but it is not surprising that the prior of Ogbourne, already encumbered with many duties in the thirteenth century, became during the fourteenth century something resembling a vicar-general. To the prior of Ogbourne, not to the abbot of Bec, the bishop of Exeter announced his dissatisfaction with the prior of Cowick.[5] On one occasion he is mentioned as the abbot's visitor in England.[6] Finally, when the Schism and the French wars had cut off communications with Bec, the pope sanctioned an arrangement that had never been permitted by the abbots of Bec; in 1393

[1] Porée, ii. 210; MS. Dom. A XI, ff. 112–13.
[2] Porée, ii. 55–6.
[3] *C.Cl.R. 1330–3*, p. 319.
[4] Porée, ii. 566–7.
[5] MS. Lat. 13905, f. 12.
[6] *C.F.R.* v. 161; *C.Cl.R. 1341–3*, p. 92.

he empowered the bishop of London and the priors of Ogbourne and Cowick to convoke to a fit place a chapter-general of the religious of the order of Bec in England; and also to receive fit persons as monks, to institute and deprive 'priors, provosts and deans' of dependent houses, and to do all things which the abbot could do by custom or right.[1]

Indeed the French wars were, from the time that they became chronic, the final test of dependence on the abbey of Bec. In 1295, when Edward I seized all priories subject to French abbots, every priory with a convincing case claimed to be independent. Not one of the priors of Bec attempted to secure exemption; even though some paid only nominal pensions, their spiritual dependence was too manifest. Only after a hundred years and more had passed did the priors of Stoke and St. Neot's seek and obtain letters of denization, and the priories of Cowick and Goldcliff remained dependent for several decades longer.

During the centuries of their dependence the priories cannot have seemed ideally placed to any abbot. The dependent cell was a standing problem in monastic history; the Benedictine ideal was not a life of solitude, yet the monks in remote cells were condemned to live in tiny communities—often in twos and sometimes, in spite of episcopal and abbatial protests, alone. Worse, there is no reason to doubt that abbeys sometimes ridded themselves of *mauvais sujets* by banishing them to distant dependencies; for even setting aside the stories of Giraldus Cambrensis, prince of gossips,[2] we have the sober testimony of the reforming bishops. Grosseteste, for example, was obliged to tell the abbot of Fleury that he ought not to send monks who were vicious or insane into remote cells.[3] Nevertheless these are insufficient grounds for asserting dogmatically that 'the discipline in these priories seems to have been much inferior to that of the native houses'.[4] The weakness of the 'alien priories' was that they were dependent cells, mostly very small, and that—

[1] *C.P.L.* iv. 412. Cf. E. Perroy, *L'Angleterre et le Grand Schisme d'Occident*, pp. 91–2.

[2] *Opera*, iv. 29 seq., 45.

[3] *Epistolae*, no. liii. Cf. also *Reg. Epist. Joh. Peckham*, iii. 786–7.

[4] C. H. New, op. cit., p. 46.

in spite of the remarkable mobility of medieval society—the Channel was a barrier to rapid communication. It was not that they were alien, in spite of all that their contemporaries, such as Giraldus might say. Contemporaries, after all, were not unbiased, and the pages of Matthew Paris show that even in the thirteenth century cultured Englishmen were capable of showing dislike for aliens as aliens—a dislike that was likely to be at least as old as the loss of Normandy in 1204, and long afterwards found ready sympathizers in a more nationalist age.

In general, the monks of Bec in England led obscure lives, undistinguished by fame or notoriety. Occasionally one rose to more than local eminence: Hugh, prior of St. Neot's, was one of the three *extranei* suggested by the monks of St. Edmund's as candidate for the abbacy in 1182;[1] Osbern, prior of Goldcliff, became bishop of Llandaff in 1219;[2] and one prior of Goldcliff served Archbishop Hubert Walter as judge delegate in an appeal to Canterbury.[3] Occasionally, particularly at Goldcliff in the turbulent Welsh marches, contemporaries caught the rumour of scandal.[4] That the abbots of Bec were alive to the difficulties of governing a number of small dependencies is certain. They included in the thirteenth century moderate and patient men and wise administrators, in particular Richard of St. Léger and Ymerius of St. Ymer; and Ymerius' concern for the English cells has left record in his statute requiring the recall of monks from England after not more than six years' absence. Rigaud's register shows that the monks in French priories had been changed fairly often, and possibly the system worked well enough to induce Ymerius to extend it to England; disturbing as it may have been to the administration of the priories, it would help to keep the monks in closer contact with conventual life. There are no lists of monks in England, but the priors, with the

[1] *Memorials of St. Edmund's Abbey* (R.S.), i. 228. Jocelyn of Brakelond's praise, however, is faint if not forced; he describes him as 'virum admodum religiosum et in temporalibus et spiritualibus admodum circumspectum'.

[2] W. de Gray Birch, *Memorials of the See and Cathedral of Llandaff*, pp. 287 seqq.

[3] Canterbury, Dean and Chapter Muniments, Sede Vacante Book I, p. 132.

[4] *C.Cl.R. 1318–23*, p. 133; R. Graham, 'Four Alien Priories in Monmouthshire', *J.B.A.A.* xxxv (1929), p. 112.

exception of the prior of Ogbourne, were generally changed every few years.

Taken as a whole, then, the records give very little indication of the real state of discipline in the English priories. Visitation by the bishop was rare. The only recorded injunctions are those of Archbishop Pecham to Goldcliff, and he merely urged the adoption of certain financial devices he was recommending to most English monasteries—a treasury and a central audit. As they stand, the facts give no solid support to the sweeping condemnations made by biased and irresponsible contemporaries, and any judgement should make distinction rather between conventual priories and granges than between alien and native cells. Certainly the abbots knew the dangers to discipline and struggled to overcome them. Nevertheless the existence of small and remote granges whose *raison d'être* was temporal administration could not fail to be a source of weakness to any monastery, and no amount of careful legislation could do more than ensure the financial welfare of the priories and—to a limited extent—the moral welfare of the monks; it could not convert fortuitous growths, which were a drain on the strength of the mother house, into vital centres of religious life.[1]

[1] Cf. Dom Knowles, *The Monastic Order in England*, pp. 135–6.

PART II
THE BAILIWICK OF OGBOURNE
(I)
ADMINISTRATION
(i) *Estate Organization*

THE English manors subject to the abbey of Bec formed, by the circumstances of their donation, a group of a peculiar type. As we have seen, any substantial gift was usually accompanied by the foundation of a small conventual priory; isolated manors, slowly acquired from various benefactors, lacked the focal point which would have been provided by a monastery or the residence of a bishop or lay lord. The estates of the Knights Templars offer some points of comparison; but the Templars' manors, which were numbered by hundreds rather than tens, were administered by several local preceptories, whereas there were only twenty-four manors in the bailiwick of Ogbourne and so, in spite of their sparseness, they became for a time very closely linked together.

Legally and theoretically these manors were, to a remarkable degree, cut off from their local setting and united to one another. Many of them were conterminous with the vills of the same name, so disputes with neighbouring landholders were reduced and the abbot had much greater control over agricultural arrangements than if the interests of other territorial magnates had had to be considered. Bledlow and Dunton were among the exceptions, but exceptions were few. And as the abbot's tenants were exempt from suit of shire and hundred, most of their ordinary legal needs were met in the abbot's courts. Practically, however, geography and convenience were working against this theoretical isolation. Communications were difficult: and, though over half the manors of Bec lay on or very near Roman roads still in use and these were supplemented by unmapped medieval trackways, distances stood in the way of very close supervision. The higher officials could visit some manors only once or twice in a year, and the manorial court might meet in full session only when they came. Between these visits much administration was in the hands of local men, brought up in local methods and imbued with the conservatism of the country-side. And even if no formal suit of court was owed, free men at least could plead and be impleaded in the public courts. Isolation from the district was much slighter than a casual perusal of the abbot's charters of immunity might lead one to suppose; and, as the centralized administration could not overcome the great distances sufficiently to organize central stock-farms or sheep-runs, each manor was also thrown back economically on its own district in many ways.

The pivot of English administration was the man described as the 'prior, proctor or administrator of the priory, place, bailiwick or prebend of Ogbourne'.

On the one hand he was the abbot's representative in England; as his letters of proxy stated, he was to represent the abbot and convent in all suits, temporal or ecclesiastical, touching the abbey or its property in England or Wales; to present suitable persons to churches in the patronage of Bec, and to collect the abbot's multifarious revenues, including apports due from the other priories: he might whenever necessary appoint proxies to act in his place.[1] On the other, he had duties of steadily increasing importance in the bailiwick of Ogbourne. His position in monastic history is indeed remarkable; he conformed to the canons of reforming popes by not living alone, but at the same time, although he was not exactly *monachus vagabundus*, his duties involved much travelling about. Lawsuits took him to London and elsewhere, and together with his companion monk he made periodic progresses round the estates in his bailiwick. Presumably he recited the monastic offices wherever he happened to be; but, unlike the monk-wardens of Christ Church, Canterbury, whose duties as estate managers resembled his own, he was not obliged to spend part of the year in the choir of his own monastery. In fact general proctors, once appointed, spent long years in England, and sometimes settled down there for life.

[1] MS. Dom. A XI, ff. 135*v*–6*v*.

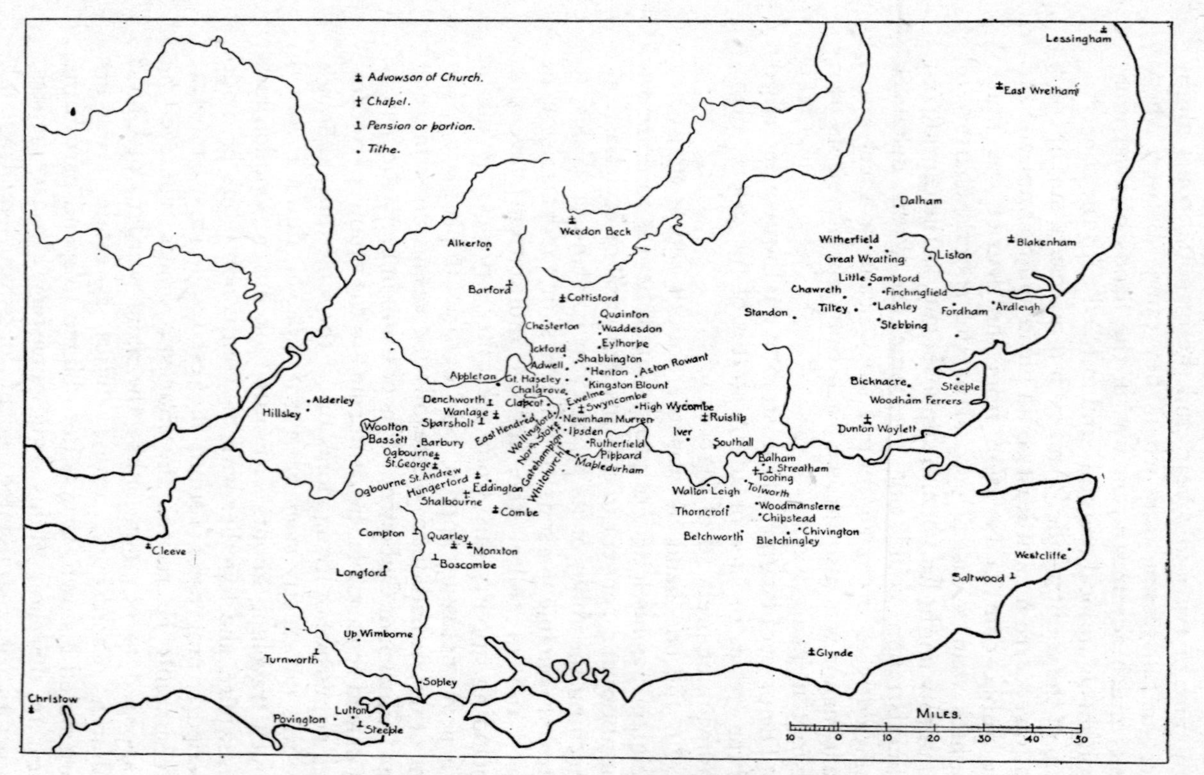

Ecclesiastical Possessions in the Bailiwick of Ogbourne

Before the appointment of the proctor-general the history of the English manors is almost a blank. There is a record of the manor of Dunton being leased for life in 1149.[1] Of the abbot's charters granting land in the manors two only remain: Osbern, abbot of Bec from 1179 to 1187, granted a cottage and a virgate of land in Ogbourne to Roger Offechot, his servant;[2] and Roger II, 1187–94, granted to Gilbert Franklyn and his heirs three virgates in Ruislip, which were released from their common services in 1226.[3] From these fragmentary facts it is impossible to tell how the abbot administered his manors during the twelfth century, and whether he held them in demesne under the charge of his monks or—like the abbess of Caen—first leased them out to wealthy laymen and later sublet the demesne to the tenants.[4]

In the thirteenth century we are on surer ground. The presence of two administrators, the priors of Ogbourne and Ruislip, has already been proved;[5] and it seems highly probable that their authority was territorial. Thus Richard, monk of Ruislip, who presented a vicar to Dunton church in the late twelfth century, is spoken of as 'administrator of the property of Bec in the diocese of London'.[6] The assumption is borne out by the payment of dues from the west at Ogbourne and from the east at Ruislip. Finally, the rolls at King's College contain the customs of all the manors in the south-west, and so are very likely to represent the customs of manors in the custody of the prior of Ogbourne before the estates came under one control.

The method of farming was governed by the function of the estate. Bec was sufficiently richly endowed with French manors for the feeding of the monks. Since the tiny river Risle was not navigable, any produce sent from England must have been carried overland from Rouen; and as transport on the English side and the navigation of the Channel had also to be considered, it seems improbable that

[1] MS. Cinq Cents Colbert 190, p. 61: 'Bail à vie du manoir de Donthon par l'abbaye du Bec en l'an 1149.'

[2] King's College, Dd 20.

[3] King's College, Q 2.

[4] See Miss Jean Birdsall, 'The English Manors of La Trinité at Caen', in *Haskins Anniversary Essays*, pp. 25–44; and Professor Postan's important article on 'The Chronology of Labour Services', *T.R.H.S.*, 4th Series, xx (1937), 169–95.

[5] *Supra*, pp. 23–4.

[6] Newcourt, *Repertorium*, ii. 230, note *a*.

Bec would at any time wish to draw a regular food-farm in grain from the English manors. Nevertheless there is no inherent impossibility in this. Cheese and wool were a different matter: the high quality of English wool is one of the basic facts of English trade, and there is ample evidence that English cheeses were highly prized in Normandy. In the fourteenth century the customs books of Rouen and Dieppe had a special tariff for cheeses coming from England;[1] and many Norman abbeys received part of their English revenues in cheeses. By the beginning of the thirteenth century the abbot of Bec had defined the goods due from the prior of Ogbourne in detail: he owed annually at Michaelmas two leather garments and a blanket to the abbot and a garment to the prior of Bec; at the feast of St. John the Baptist two marks, and knives to the convent; and annually for the use of the convent, twenty lengths of woollen cloth (*telas staminarum*), thirty leather garments (*pelliceas*), and thirty-two weys of cheese.[2] There is one licence for the year 1224 permitting the prior to cross the seas with cheeses, woollen cloths, and leather goods, which he was taking to his abbot of Bec.[3]

Apart from discharging this obligation—which cannot have weighed very heavily on an estate with extensive downland pastures in Wiltshire and Hampshire—the prior of Ogbourne was expected to manage the estate as a profit-making concern. Had he been the steward of estates in France or the Low Countries there seems little doubt that he would have leased out most of the demesne in small parcels, assuming the functions of a rent-collector, and swelling his annual revenue by investing in rents.[4] No

[1] *Coutumier de la vicomté de l'eau de Rouen:* 'Pour chacun chef de fourmage v deniers, pour le demy chef iij deniers, se il vient d'Angleterre; et le chef de fourmage sont de ccl livres.' *Coutumier de Dieppe:* 'Acquis de fromages venants d'Oultre-mer. Tu dois savoir que de XXV fromages d'Engleterre venans en aucune nef, l'en doit j fromage, ne le pire ne le meilleur, et se en la nef n'est trouvé la value de xxv fromages, l'en doit paier de coustume le xxve denier de la valeur des diz fromages vendus.' Cited, Delisle, *La Condition de la classe agricole en Normandie*, p. 250.

[2] MS. Add. 24316, f. 31*v*.

[3] *Rot. Lit. Claus.* i. 624*b*, 649*b*.

[4] Cf. the action of Abbot William of Saint Trond, *Le Livre de l'abbé Guillaume de Ryckel* (*1249–72*), ed. H. Pirenne (Ghent, 1896), pp. xxiv seqq.; and the review of R. N. Sauvage's 'Histoire de l'Abbaye de Saint Martin de Troarn', by K. Génestal in *Vierteljahrschrift für Social- und Wirtschaftsgeschichte*, xi. 274.

clearer proof of the strength of local influence could be given than the fact that, by the mid-thirteenth century, demesne farming was in full swing on the abbot of Bec's English estates.

The first administrator to make his mark on the estates was brother William de Guineville.[1] The names of two earlier representatives are known: William of Wantage was proctor of the monks of Bec in 1218, and brother Michael de Turnebu in 1232;[2] but their activities are shadowy. William de Guineville may possibly have been the first official to have charge of both eastern and western custodies on the estates. His name is associated with agricultural changes, such as assarting in various royal forests,[3] and the purchase of pasture lands in the manor of Combe;[4] and with administrative activities, including the lease of Christow at perpetual fee farm to the prior of Cowick in 1244 and the inquisition into manorial customs embodied in MS. Add. 24316.[5] Whilst he held office the earliest surviving court rolls began, though there is no means of knowing how long manorial courts had been held and their records kept. His legal duties naturally involved him in a number of compromises defining the exact rights of the abbey;[6] one of these, concerning the hunting-rights of proctors of Bec, shows that he did not view the relaxation of the chase with the austere aloofness of Abbot Samson of Bury. After his fifteen or more years of energetic service it must have been difficult to dislodge him from the English estates; and in 1254, when a new proctor-general was appointed, he was granted for life *ad sustentacionem suam* the manors of Povington with Lutton, Milburne, Wantage, Bledlow, Brixton-Deverill, Chisenbury, Combe, Quarley, and Monxton, which he held until his death in 1258.[7] No other proctor-general of the abbey is known to have retired on so substantial a pension.

[1] The letter nominating him attorney was dated 1242 (*C.P.R. 1232–47*, pp. 272, 291); he was, however, already proctor-general in 1239 (Porée, ii. 216).

[2] Eton, C 14, Cottisford charters.

[3] *C.Ch.R.* i. 331.

[4] King's College, L 65, 66, 66*a*.

[5] *Supra*, p. 5.

[6] Porée, ii. 214 seq.

[7] *Close Rolls 1256–9*, p. 345. The only records of this transaction are royal letters to the escheators who had mistakenly seized the lands, ordering them to give seizin at once to John de Plessac, the new proctor-general.

The records accumulated in the course of brother William's administration leave no doubt that demesne farming was well established on the manors. The court rolls from the beginning show society organized for the cultivation of the lord's land; they contain frequent entries of fines for failure to perform labour services properly, and for trespass not only in the lord's woods and pastures but also in his corn: domanial offences are more numerous in these rolls than in the records of the courts of St. Albans.[1] If the demesne had not been extensive, the labour services would almost certainly have been lighter. Carrying services too include the transport of corn to neighbouring market towns, and as the juries were stating past customs, conditions described by them were likely to be some years older than the surveys. But the actual size of the demesne and the number of animals it could support are given in the custumal for two manors only: Ogbourne St. George and the small outlying manor of Lessingham.[2] The outlines of manorial administration in this period are dim, but from the custumal comes the first reference to an estate steward, Andrew;[3] and it is at least possible that this is Andrew of Croydon, clerk, who acted as the prior's attorney in several cases between 1229 and 1236,[4] and was witness to numerous charters in the Cottisford series.

There was always one alternative to demesne farming, which the abbot adopted from time to time. Just before the time of brother William de Guineville, in 1231, the Norfolk

[1] A. E. Levett, *Studies in Manorial History*, p. 94.

[2] MS. Add. 24316, f. 31 [32]: 'Sciendum est quod apud Maiorem Ockeburn sunt septem caruce in dominico. Et est ibi . . . pastura sufficiens ad sustentacionem quingentarum ovium et ducentorum multonum et aliorum animalium ad sustentacionem domus necessariorum.' Ibid., f. 55*v* [56*v*]: 'Iurati presentant quod apud dictum manerium habentur due caruce terre in dominico, et quod probabiliter poterit carucis propriis, scilicet duabus, tota dominica terra arari et excoli sine consuetudinibus, et quod manerium sustentare potest per annum inter equos et boves et vaccas xxvj, unde nutriri poterunt viij^to^ vacce cum totidem vitulis, xxx porci, centum oves.'

[3] Ibid., f. 26: 'Item sciendum est quod Alexander prepositus et Rogerus Hudemann' tenent dimidiam virgatam terre pro duabus solidis et sex denariis et pro communibus operibus, quam quidem terram receperunt a domino Andr' senescallo ad terminum decem annorum sequencium, et pro qua non plene operantur sicut alii semivirgatarii.'

[4] P.R.O. Feet of Fines, Suffolk, 213/14, no. 79; Wilts., 250/8, no. 46.

manors of Wretham and Lessingham had been leased for life to Peter Rex, chamberlain of Bec, on the express understanding that his heirs were to have no claim to them.[1] In 1251 Peter Fountain received the important manor of Ruislip at fee-farm for life for one mark annually;[2] and as a year or two later nine of the manors were assigned to William of Guineville for his support, the estate must have been only partly under the supervision of the prior of Ogbourne for a few years. But leasing seems to have been unusual during this period, and demesne-farming remained the norm to which the administration reverted. Court rolls, which begin again in 1269, show officials going on regular circuits round the manors; and part of a pipe roll, containing enrolled bailiff's accounts for fifteen manors from Michaelmas 1288 to Michaelmas 1289, prove that the abbot's demesne farming was on no mean scale. Rents and court dues brought in a handsome revenue; but the outstanding item was sale of corn, which totalled over £275; wool sold, though considerably less in value, amounted to nearly £90, and probably did not include the whole receipt from the clip.

Manorial Receipts, 1288–9

Manor	*Rents (including forinsec rents)*			*Court dues and tallage*		
	£	*s.*	*d.*	£	*s.*	*d.*
Cottisford	4	15	9	1	12	0
Atherstone	8	0	3	7	5	8
Weedon	18	7	1	55	14	7
Swyncombe	21	8	7½	1	4	0
Wantage	17	5	9		17	3
Bledlow	14	2	6	10	16	0
Ruislip	22	16	0	21	2	8
Wretham	7	7	4	3	8	3
Lessingham	5	5	2½	11	2	9
Blakenham	5	5	4¾	1	14	3
Combe	9	18	1	3	13	10
Hungerford	5	15	3		6	8
Quarley	4	15	1	2	0	9
Monxton	3	18	2	2	3	7
Povington	4	7	5	2	4	4
TOTAL	153	7	10¾	125	6	7

[1] Porée, ii. 212; MS. Lat. 12884, f. 316*v*.
[2] Porée, ii. 214; MS. Lat. 12884, f. 351*v*.

Manorial Receipts, 1288–9 (cont.)

Manor	Sale of wool and fleeces £	s.	d.	Sale of corn £	s.	d.
Cottisford	19	18	6½		11	8
Atherstone	1	2	3	3	13	1
Weedon	10	15	7	16	9	11½
Swyncombe	5	16	11	1	10	9¼
Wantage	3	5	4	59	5	10¾
Bledlow		2	2	30	11	4¾
Ruislip	4	1	2½	31	7	11
Wretham	9	6	1¼	19	5	8
Lessingham		12	1	8	12	6½
Blakenham		1	6	21	6	9½
Combe	10	15	9	21	12	6
Hungerford	1	1	11½	10	18	6
Quarley	12	8	6½	24	0	10½
Monxton	8	9	10	16	5	8
Povington	2	1	10	10	0	0
TOTAL	89	19	7¼	275	13	2¾

Further evidence is provided by figures in the royal extents, which were taken in the summer of 1294, a year before the first seizure of the alien priories. Extents exist for fourteen manors in Wiltshire, Oxfordshire, Berkshire, Hampshire, Middlesex, Buckingham, and Warwickshire; and include the important manors of Ogbourne and Brixton-Deverill which are not on the pipe roll. They indicate traces of one farm only: at Swyncombe the demesne had been let to John Romayn of Chinnor, evidently later than 1289.[1] These extents give the following figures (p. 47) for acres in demesne and sheep on the manors.[2]

These figures are not surprising since the period was the hey-day of demesne farming in England. Scattered as the estate was it could be held together by an administrative system typical of the century and the country, which preserved a nice balance between local initiative and tightly centralized control. Numerous local markets, a flourishing wool-trade, a class of officials ready to take up administrative duties, and a highly developed method of accounting made possible the adequate supervision of the estate under one

[1] Exch. K.R., E. 106, 2/6: 'Terra de Swinecumb' dominica dimittitur ad firmam Iohanni Romano de Chinnor, cum redditu eiusdem, pro x *li*.'

[2] Exch. K.R., E. 106, 2/1–2/6.

Manor	*Total arable acres*	*Acres sown*[1]	*Acres of meadow*	*Pasture*
Ogbourne St. George	871	558	8	For 1,000 sheep, 108 cattle
Ogbourne St. Andrew	352	..	8	For 700 sheep, 16 avers
Brixton-Deverill	717	..	6	Value, £2. 1*s.* 0*d.*
Chisenbury	253	..	8	For 300 sheep and 20 oxen
Cottisford	128	126	5	..
Swyncombe	300	..	5	100 acres
Wantage and Charlton	269	104	22	Worth 6*s.*
Hungerford	80	115[2]	4	Worth 3*s.* 4*d.*
Combe	160	120	..	For 1,000 sheep; and pasture for cattle worth 10*s.* 4*d.*
Quarley	400	223	..	For 160 sheep
Monxton	327	149	2	For 400 sheep
Ruislip	907	675	45	14 acres separate, 80 acres in park
Bledlow	317½ 1 r.	225 2 r.	37½	19 acres
Atherstone	..	280	..	..

Manor	*Sheep*	*Total*
Ogbourne St. George	600 ewes, 350 wethers, 500 lambs	1,450
Ogbourne St. Andrew	569 ewes, 400 wethers	969
Brixton-Deverill	465 ewes, 250 wethers, 178 hoggetts, 250 lambs	1,143
Chisenbury	224 sheep	224
Cottisford	195 ewes and hoggetts, 220 wethers, 100 lambs	515
Swyncombe	220 ewes, 159 wethers, 100 hoggetts, 100 lambs	579
Wantage and Charlton	79 wethers, 26 hoggetts	105
Hungerford	36 ewes, 39 wethers, 22 lambs	97
Combe	541 ewes, 456 hoggetts, 120 lambs, 10 rams	1,127
Quarley	275 ewes, 306 wethers, 137 lambs	718
Monxton	244 ewes, 217 wethers, 84 lambs, 4 rams	549
Ruislip	89 sheep	89
Bledlow	4 sheep	4
		7,569

[1] These statistics seem not to have been taken on the same principle in each county: thus at Cottisford the total assessment appears to include only acres sown with corn, not land in fallow. The number of acres sown is, however, given here as a check on the total acreage, to indicate whether all the demesne land was included or only the land under cultivation that year. The comparatively small amount of land under cultivation at Monxton and Quarley seems to point to a two-field system.

[2] These are the figures. I cannot explain the discrepancy.

man, and that man a French monk. The administrative system may be understood by studying first the organization of farming, with its emphasis on local amenities; secondly the hierarchy of officials, rooted in each individual manor; and lastly the central control that directed the manors for the profit of the abbey of Bec.

On many monastic estates the manors were treated as a group for the organization of stock-farming, and central sheep-runs or dairy farms were developed.[1] The manors of Bec, however, showed no such interdependence. Sheep apart, the rearing of animals was unimportant; each manor supported its own plough beasts, occasionally, if pasture proved inadequate, with the assistance of a neighbouring manor:[2] otherwise stock-farming combined the avoidance of waste with the absence of enterprise. Where there were woods, pigs were turned into them and fattened either for sale or food for the higher manorial officials; where there were meadows, cows were reared, unless it seemed more profitable to lease the pasturage.[3] Even in the peak period of the late thirteenth century numbers were never very large: 22 cows and 80 pigs at Ogbourne St. George, 25 cows and 110 pigs at Ruislip,[4] 24 cows and 37 pigs at Wretham,[5] 68 pigs at Cottisford,[6] and about 25 pigs at Brixton-Deverill and Bledlow[7] are the highest figures. The total receipts from the sale of stock in the pipe roll were £37. 5*s*. 8*d*; and this included the 'crones' weeded out from the sheep and plough beasts each year and replaced by the young stock. Even this half-hearted stock-farming showed a falling off in the early years of the fourteenth century.[8]

[1] Cf. M. Wretts Smith, 'The Organization of Farming at Croyland Abbey', in the *Journal of Economic and Business History*, iv (1932).

[2] In 1304–5 the oxen of Cottisford were pastured at Weedon (Weedon Account Roll, 1304–5, Eton B 11: 'In stipendio j garcionis custodientis bovectos et boviculos de Wedon' et Cotesford xx *d*.').

[3] Sometimes even the sheep's pasture was let out for a period; at Blakenham from 1297 to 1303 only about a dozen sheep were reared on the manor, and foreign sheep were admitted to the lord's pasture; the one shepherd is described as 'bercarius custodiens bidentes extraneorum iacentes in faldo domini' (Eton, D 5/8).

[4] Exch. K.R., E 106, 2/1, 2/3.

[5] Eton, A 20, 1303–4 account roll.

[6] Eton, C 14, 1292 account roll.

[7] Exch. K.R., E 106, 2/1, 2/3.

[8] At Wretham no pigs were reared after 1336; at Cottisford pigs disappear between 1292 and 1316 and cattle after 1316; at Blakenham the last pigs were sold in 1335–6 (Eton, account rolls, A 20, C 14, D 5).

There was too a change of method in dairy-farming; where cows were still kept they were, as a rule, farmed out to the dairyman for a fixed price yearly.[1]

The emphasis was, in fact, on corn and wool; each manor individually might produce these to the utmost of its ability, and a good market lay to hand. Corn could be sold in almost any little country town, either for consumption on the spot or for transport down the rivers to larger centres. Carrying services of tenants in the custumal suggest some of the obvious markets for the sale of corn produced on the manors of Bec. The corn of Blakenham was to be taken to market at Ipswich and seed brought back;[2] Norwich and Yarmouth provided markets for Lessingham,[3] and Shaftesbury for Deverill;[4] London was of course one of the markets for Ruislip,[5] and probably also for Tooting. The cheeses and wool of Povington were taken to Wareham,[6] and probably its corn went at times to feed the population there, though the duty of tenants was simply to carry corn to some market within the county; and this indeed is the formula most common on other manors in the custumal. It would be unsafe to assume that, even when a market was named, corn and produce were always taken there; the bailiff would presumably choose the market offering the best price within a reasonable radius. The account rolls of Combe give the expenses of the bailiff in taking corn to the nearby markets of Andover and Newbury.[7] And the movements of the bailiff of Ogbourne St. Andrew are even more suggestive; with Marlborough less than 4 miles away he took corn nearly 20 miles to Newbury, most probably in search of a better market.[8] Of the towns actually named in the custumal, three were East Anglian coastal towns, from

[1] At Blakenham the farming out of cows began between 1303 and 1331; at Wretham between 1308 and 1336, though in 1337–8 the old method of cheese-making was tried and proved less profitable. In both cases the farm included, as well as the milk, all but six of the calves born (Eton, A 20, D 5, account rolls).

[2] MS. Add. 24316, f. 40 [41].

[3] MS. Add. 24316, f. 51 [52].

[4] King's College, Dd 33, m. 9.

[5] MS. Add. 24316, ff. 1–1*v*.

[6] King's College, Dd 33, m. 8.

[7] King's College, Combe Account Rolls: 'In expensis prepositi quando vendidit xxiij onera bladi apud Andevere et apud Nuburi, ij*s*. ix*d*. *ob*.'

[8] King's College, Ogbourne Account Rolls: 'Et in expensis ballivi carientis xiiij quart' bladi apud Nywebery ad vendend' una cum expensis ij carettarum et vj equorum . . . xiij*d*.'

which sea-borne trade to London or even the continent may have helped to maintain a high price-level;[1] frequent sales in these towns would account for their mention in the custumal, although later the bailiff would regard himself as free to send the corn elsewhere. At Atherstone, which had a market of its own, corn could have been disposed of on the spot; certainly there are no carrying services to other markets in the custumal.

The principal cash crop was wheat, which was grown whenever possible; at Wretham, where the soil was too poor, rye was the winter crop. Barley too was grown for the market as well as for home brewing. Oats, mixed corn, and leguminous crops were produced primarily for the staff of permanent servants, and as provender for the beasts, but the surplus was sold; and the sale of corn was the chief single source of the abbot of Bec's income.

Corn Grown, 1288–9

Manor	*Yield*	*Acquired*[2]	*Sold*
		WHEAT	
Cottisford	34 q. 3 b.	..	..
Atherstone	109 q. 4 b.	..	23 q.
Weedon	150 q. 2 b.	1 q. 4 b. (*b*)	55 q.
Swyncombe	87 q. 6 b.	..	16 q.
Wantage	416 q. 4 b.	..	344 q. 5 b.
Bledlow	252 q. 1 b.	..	191 q. 7 b.
Ruislip	961 q. 5 b.	..	202 q.
Wretham	4 q. 7 b.	..	..
Lessingham	12 q. 6 b.	..	8 q.
Blakenham	71 q. 1 b.	38 q. 2 b. (*r*)	95 q. 2 b.
Combe	99 q. 7 b.	..	64 q. 2 b.
Hungerford	81 q. 2 b.	..	54 q. 2 b.
Quarley	89 q. 7½ b.	..	67 q. 2 b.
Monxton	58 q. 2 b.	..	43 q. 5 b.
Povington	82 q. 3 b.	..	48 q.
Milburne	8 q. 1 b.	1 q. (*b*)	2 q. 4 b.
		RYE	
Cottisford	70 q.	..	..
Atherstone	9 q. 2 b.	6 q. (*b*)	..
Weedon	120 q. 2 b.	3 b. (*r*)	56 q. 1 b.
Wretham	108 q. 2 b.	49 q. 4 b. (*r*)	97 q. 4 b.
Blakenham	68 q.	..	15 q. 6 b.
Povington	3 b.	..	..

[1] Gras, *The English Corn Market*, pp. 62–4. For the coastal corn-trade of E. England see *Cartularium Monasterii de Rameseia*, iii. 141–57; Ballard, *British Borough Charters*, p. lxxi.

[2] (*b*) = bought; (*r*) = remaining from the previous year; (*n.g.*) = new grain.

Manor	*Yield*	*Acquired*	*Sold*
		DRAGE	
Cottisford	51 q. 4 b.	..	..
Atherstone	9 q.	..	..
Weedon	180 q.	..	66 q.
Swyncombe	9 q. 3 b.	..	..
Ruislip	3 q.	..	3 q.
Hungerford	13 q. 6 b.	..	9 q. 4 b.
Quarley	59 q. 5 b.	..	38 q.
Monxton	25 q. 5 b.	..	12 q. 4 b.
		MANCORN	
Swyncombe	48 q. 6 b.	9 q. 6 b. (*b*)	2 q. 4 b.
Bledlow	23 q. 1 b.	..	9 q. 5 b.
Quarley	19 q. 6 b.	..	15 q. 7 b.
		BARLEY	
Atherstone	9 q. 4 b.	..	..
Swyncombe	71 q. 6 b.	..	15 q. 4 b.
Wantage	216 q. 2 b.	12 q. 6 b. (*r*)	153 q. 2 b.
Bledlow	43 q. 7 b.	..	9 q. 4 b.
Ruislip	6 q. 4 b.	..	6 q. 4 b.
Wretham	149 q. 3 b.	..	27 q. 4 b.
Lessingham	143 q. 5 b.	..	52 q. 1 b.
Blakenham	59 q. 1 b.	..	36 q.
Combe	134 q. 1 b.	..	86 q. 4 b.
Hungerford	47 q.	..	15 q. 6 b.
Quarley	156 q.	..	63 q.
Monxton	103 q. 2½ b.	..	51 q. 6 b.
Povington	97 q. 4 b.	..	27 q. 4 b.
Milburne	18 q.	..	8 q. 1 b.
		BERE	
Combe	103 q. 1 b.	..	41 q.
Hungerford	40 q. 1 b.	..	32 q.
Quarley	10 q. 3 b.	..	10 q. 3 b.
Monxton	6 q. 3 b.	..	1 q. 7 b.
Milburne	11 q. 4 b.	..	4 q. 4 b.
		OATS	
Cottisford	50 q.	..	..
Atherstone	128 q. 6 b.	..	39 q.
Weedon	172 q. 7 b.	..	13 q. 4 b.
Swyncombe	72 q. 4 b.	70 q. 5 b. (*b*)	..
Wantage	49 q. 4 b.	..	..
Bledlow	78 q. 6 b.	25 q. 4 b. (*b*)	..
Ruislip	912 q. 5 b.	..	..
Wretham	79 q. 1 b.	4 q. (*b*); 8 q. 4 b. (*n.g.*)	..
Lessingham	61 q. 2 b.	..	5 q. 4 b.
Blakenham	74 q. 7 b.	..	..
Combe	78 q. 7 b.	4 q. 4 b. (*b*)	5 q. 4 b.
Hungerford	34 q. 6 b.	..	5 q.
Quarley	97 q. 5 b.	..	..
Monxton	55 q. 4 b.	13 q. 5 b. (*b*)	..
Povington	56 q. 2 b.	..	21 q. 2 b.
Milburne	15 q. 7 b.	..	1 q. 4 b.

Corn Grown, 1288–9 (cont.)

LEGUMINOUS CROPS

Manor	*Species*	*Yield*	*Acquired*	*Sold*
Atherstone . .	Peas	21 q. 2 b.	..	2 q. 6 b.
Weedon . .	Peas and beans	19 q.	8 q. (*n.g.*)	3 q.
Swyncombe .	Peas	2 q. 6 b.	..	..
,, .	Vetches	2 q. 1 b.	..	..
Wantage . .	Beans	44 q.	7 q. 2 b. (*r*)	23 q. 7 b.
Bledlow . .	Beans	9 q. 7 b.	..	..
Ruislip . .	Peas and beans	190 q. 3 b.	..	10 q.
Wretham . .	Peas	7 b.	4 q. (*b*)	..
,, . .	Vetches	1 b.	..	..
Lessingham .	Peas	36 q. 1 b.	..	20 q. 4 b.
,, .	Beans	2 q. 5 b.	..	1 q. 1 b.
Blakenham .	Peas	6 q. 7 b.	..	2 q.
Hungerford .	Beans	3 b.	..	..
,, .	Peas	2 q. 1 b.	..	1 q.
Quarley . .	Peas	5 q. 6 b.	..	3 q.
,, . .	Vetches	7 q. 4 b.	..	4 q. 4 b.
,, . .	Lentils	5 q. 2 b.	..	4 q.
Monxton . .	Peas	4 q. 5 b.	7 q. 4 b.	8 q. 7 b.
,, . .	Vetches	6 q. 6 b.	..	4 q. 6 b.
,, . .	Lentils	5 q. 6 b.	..	4 q.
Povington . .	Beans	5 q. 6 b.	..	1 q. 7 b.
,, . .	Peas	1 q. 5 b.	..	..

The disposal of wool was made easy by the high organization of the wool trade. A lord of wide pastoral acres might contract to sell the whole of his clip to a single merchant, or it might be disposed of in a number of small deals with local men.[1] Since some receipts from the clip are included in each bailiff's account in the 1288–9 pipe roll and in the separate accounts of Combe, Ogbourne St. Andrew, and Wretham, it is possible that the wool was sometimes sold separately on the Bec manors. However, it seems unlikely that the bailiff's figures in the pipe roll cover all the wool sales, since they do not bear a reasonably close ratio to the numbers of sheep given in the 1295 extent; to take one example, the wool sales at Monxton were only £2. 5*s*. 11*d*. less than at Combe, but the number of sheep was over 500 less. And again, the expenses of the merchants coming round to supervise the shearing of their fleeces are often coupled with those of a

[1] See Eileen Power, *The Wool Trade in English Medieval History*, pp. 42–5.

manorial official or even the lord himself,[1] and suggest that sometimes the wool of a group of manors was sold collectively. At Cottisford certainly, from 1316 to 1322 the wool was sold over the head of the bailiff; receipts for it are not recorded, and it was sent, sometimes with the wool of Weedon, either to Bledlow or to the town of Henley.[2] Otherwise the movements of wool can only rarely be traced. In 1294 wool from Povington was found at Brixton-Deverill;[3] one entry in the Combe accounts mentions the carriage of wool from Combe to Wycombe which, at that period, was encouraging a small cloth industry;[4] and in 1342–3 the wool of Weedon and Cottisford was sent to Ruislip, possibly to meet the needs of the king.[5] But these examples are too isolated to prove the normal method of disposing of the wool-clip.

(ii) *Manorial officials*

The staff of servants on each manor was provided by the manor itself, as was usual at the time. Reeve and hayward were chosen from the tenants by election or at the lord's will, or by compromise between the two; shepherds and ploughmen and other skilled *famuli* were more likely to be appointed directly by the lord. The jurors of Lessingham were most explicit about the appointment of reeve and hayward;[6]

[1] King's College, Combe account rolls, 1306–7: 'In expensis Iohannis de Wanetyng' mercatoris lane et Roberti de Querle ballivi pro lana ponderanda et saccanda'; 1311–12: 'Item computat in expensis domini iiij *s.* Item computat in expensis fratris Radulfi socii domini et mercatorum lane cum supervenientibus, vij *s.*'

[2] Eton, C 14 (Cottisford), 1316–17: 'In expensis ij hominum cariancium lanam apud Bled', ij *d.*'; 1318–19: 'In expensis ij hominum cariancium lanam de Wedon et Cotesford apud Bled', ij *d.*'; 1320–1: 'In expensis ij hominum iiij equorum cariancium lanam apud Enle, ij *s.* j *d.*'; and in the oats account for the same year: 'In prebendis ij equorum de Wedon', ij equorum domus per i noctem apud Codesford tempore quo cariaverunt lanam apud Enle ij busselli, et lib' ad prebend' eorum per alteram noctem versus Enle, ij busselli.'

[3] Exch. K.R., E. 106, 2/2.

[4] King's College, Combe account rolls, 1316–17: 'In expensis carettarum et equorum cariancium lanam apud Wycombe, xviij *d.*' Cf. *V.C.H. Bucks.* ii. 128. In the early fourteenth century the governing body of Wycombe tried to encourage the cloth industry by remitting a tax on looms.

[5] Eton, C 14 (Cottisford), 1342–3 account: 'Et in lanis duorum annorum cum lanis de Wedon' packand' et cariand' usque Risshelep' cum stipendiis packatorum, ix *s.* iij *d.*'

[6] MS. Add. 24316, f. 56 [57]: 'Dicunt iurati quod tota soccha eligere debent unum messarium de se ipsis, et domini de ipso electo poterunt facere prepositum

customs on the other manors have to be deduced from the court rolls. At Ogbourne St. George the hayward, elected by the tenants, had to be presented to the bailiff;[1] the men of Ogbourne St. Andrew chose their own reeve:[2] the men of Combe presented four names which later, probably by the lord's choice, were reduced to one.[3] These officials and the skilled labourers—shepherds and ploughmen—were at first on many manors men of substance, holding a virgate or half a virgate;[4] their duties could best be performed if they held office for several years, and the court rolls have preserved at least one echo of a reward to a shepherd for long and faithful service.[5]

But the tenantry provided more than the lowest grades of manorial servants, the reeves whose very office might be held to carry a stigma of villeinage.[6] Bailiffs too were drawn from the abbot's tenants, and like the bailiffs of the Ramsey manors they might be 'strangers' to the manor on which they were placed.[7] Sometimes their names announce their place of origin: Henry of Ogbourne was bailiff of Cottisford in 1292, Robert Deverill bailiff of Blakenham in 1331–5; William Wylemot of Ogbourne bailiff of Blakenham and Wretham in 1335–9.[8] Sometimes there is other evidence: in 1350 the chattels of a dead tenant of Combe were seized

vel permittere ipsum esse messarium, et si transigerit, emendabunt pro eo; vel domini eligent si voluerint, et si domini elegerint nondum obligabuntur ad emendacionem pro eo.'

[1] *Select Pleas*, p. 36 (1290): 'Tota villa, exceptis Ada Russel, Johanne Druet, Johanne Butery, Willelmo preposito et Petro messore in misericordia quia elegerunt sibi communem messorem et non presentaverunt illum ballivo loci prout moris est.'

[2] King's College, C 6 (1275): 'Tota decena minoris Ockeburn' elegit sibi prepositum, Johannem de Ponte.'

[3] King's College, C 21 (1349): 'Omnes tenentes elegerunt ad officium prepositi Johannem Baggemere, Ricardum ate Hethe, Henricum ate Hethe, et Johannem Kempe. Et dictus Johannes Baggemere remanet.'

[4] For the position and work of the *famuli* see *infra*, pp. 87 seqq.

[5] King's College, C 10 (Ogbourne, 1290): 'Walterus bercarius seisitus est tenemento quod tenuit Agnes la Muchele, et habet ingressum ex dono . . domini, quia bene et fideliter semper se habuit et habet in servicio . . domini.'

[6] Cf. the report of an inquisition taken at Ogbourne in 1332 (*Cal. Misc. Inq.* ii. 1269): 'The men of the abbot of Bec Herlewin of Great and Little Ogbourne are his villeins and subject to tallage yearly at his will, and have been so from time immemorial, by taking from them ransom of flesh and blood and making them reeve or hayward.'

[7] W. O. Ault, *Court Rolls of the Abbey of Ramsey and the Honor of Clare*, pp. l–li.

[8] Eton, Account Rolls, C 14, A 20, D 5.

until his widow should render account for the time he had been bailiff of Bledlow;[1] and in 1308 the bailiff of Preston was Richard Rouce of Tooting.[2] Not every manor had a separate bailiff; in 1288–9 the manors entered on the pipe roll were grouped as follows:

Swyncombe, Wantage, and Bledlow;
Wretham, Lessingham, and Blakenham;
Combe and Hungerford;
Quarley and Monxton;
Povington and Milburne;

and there were separate bailiffs on each of the manors of Cottisford, Atherstone, Weedon, and Ruislip.[3] There might or might not be a reeve on each manor under the group bailiff; thus from 1303 to 1305 William Sorel, bailiff, himself rendered account for Wretham and there was no reeve; from 1305 a reeve, Henry Foc, held office and rendered the accounts, though William remained bailiff and visited the manor at frequent intervals.[4]

Above these local or semi-local officials the influence of the manor still showed itself. The Combe account rolls constantly mention an itinerant bailiff, Henry Butery, who came to hold the courts; although called bailiff he was fulfilling the duties of a steward of the courts. He had the name of a family of virgate holders at Ogbourne St. George, to whose continued presence on the manor throughout the thirteenth and early fourteenth centuries the court rolls bear constant witness. Although this points to Ogbourne as the native vill of Henry Butery, it would be fanciful to assume that he, like his namesakes, was humble in status; he had his own seal[5] and very probably enjoyed full legal liberty: and James Freysel, another itinerant official men-

1 King's College, C 21: 'Item dicunt quod de pannis aut aliis bonis Johannis le Tal [*hole in MS.*] defuncti nichil remanet infra dominium istum nisi una vacca et unus lectus qui fuit pro usu suo proprio. Ideo preceptum est arrestare illa et retinere in manus domini quousque Johanna que fuit uxor eius et alii executores inveniant domino securitatem de compoto suo reddendo de tempore quo fuit ballivus domini prioris apud Bledel'.'

2 King's College, C 12.

3 Eton, C 14.

4 Eton, A 20, Wretham account roll, 1306–7: 'In expensis Willelmi Sorel ballivi manerii per adventus suos, xxix *s*.'

5 King's College, Dd 28 is a quitclaim to the abbot of Bec of land in Ogbourne, sealed by Henry Butery.

tioned in the later account rolls, was a knight of the shire. He too was directly connected with the abbot's property and held land in Bledlow.[1] If the base of the administrative pyramid was made up of villeins and prosperous peasants and the apex of lesser gentry, it was not always easy to tell where one class ended and another began: all, however, were united in one thing, that they knew, and lived by, the land.

The highest official on the estates of Bec was the chief steward. By chance during the three and a half decades when the records are most informative one man continuously held this office; he was William of Harden, knight. He was not a tenant of the abbey, but held an estate in chief by serjeanty in the county of Wiltshire.[2] In 1279 he made his first appearance as the abbot's attorney during the *Quo warranto* inquiries,[3] and a year later he obtained a quitclaim from John of Lovetot for homage and suit of court for a tenement in Blakenham.[4] In 1289 he was called steward,[5] and was named over and over again in the court rolls for the next thirty years; in 1324, as steward of the prior, he received charge of some manors after the seizure of alien property.[6] This record of forty-five years' steady service shows that he was not an ambitious steward of a type common at the period, using the experience gained in his first offices to climb to higher dignities,[7] and it leaves the impression that he fulfilled the first and greatest requirement of much earlier stewards, 'that a man be found faithful'. His duties were closely parallel with the duties of the prior of Ogbourne, namely, legal representation of the abbot and general supervision of the estates. As attorney he incurred in one year expenses before the justices of the forest, and before other justices for pleas concerning Ogbourne and a parcel of land called 'Goldhord'.[8] As estate-manager he went on progresses round the manors, held the courts, and settled

[1] For his career see *infra*, pp. 115–16. He and Henry Butery are repeatedly mentioned in the accounts of Cottisford and Wretham at the same period.

[2] *Inq. Post Mortem*, vii. 242.

[3] *P.Q.W.*, p. 759.

[4] Feet of Fines for Suffolk, 215/34, no. 19.

[5] Eton, C 14.

[6] Exch. K.R., E 106, 8/9.

[7] See N. Denholm-Young, *Seignorial Administration in England*, pp. 69–71.

[8] King's College, Combe account rolls, 1309–10.

specially difficult suits;[1] when the time for accounting came, he heard the accounts of the manorial officials.[2] His successor was probably John Broughton, who is mentioned in all the accounts from 1333, and fulfilled the usual duties of a steward. He was a man of a different type, a clerk who became rector of East Wretham and Dunton.[3] Almost certainly he is to be identified with John Broughton, king's clerk, who held a succession of offices in the royal administration at this period.[4] There are almost no account rolls after 1340 to indicate the length of his tenure of office.

(iii) *Council, audit, and courts*

From the persons employed in the prior's service we must turn to the machinery of administration: the prior's council, the audit, and the manorial courts. Of the first two, unfortunately, we have very little knowledge. The general duties and composition of estate councils have been described by Professor Levett; normally including the steward and higher administrative officials, together with legal experts, they were competent to deal with difficult cases and disputes between two or more lords; and as the fourteenth century advanced they often became courts of appeal above the manorial courts, sometimes even cutting across the custom of the manor.[5] But the prior of Ogbourne's council is no more than a shadow. It is expressly mentioned in two entries on the court rolls, when cases concerning refusal of tallage and a purpresture made by the tenant of another manor were referred to it.[6] We may safely assume that it would include

[1] *Infra*, p. 61.

[2] Cf. pipe roll, Eton, C 14; also King's College, C 10 (Deverill, 1291): 'Et sciendum est quod computatum est de tota ista pecunia prescripta, videlicet de fine W. Ridegrom et H. Porker, in compoto anni preteriti coram Willelmo de Hardene reddito.'

[3] *C.Cl.R. 1343–6*, p. 642; and Blakenham Charters (Eton, D 5).

[4] *C.P.R. 1338–40*, p. 249; *C.Cl.R. 1343–6*, p. 620 and *passim*.

[5] 'Baronial Councils and their relation to Manorial Courts', in *Studies in Manorial History*. Cf. also F. M. Page, *The Estates of Crowland Abbey*, pp. 45–9.

[6] King's College, C 14 (Atherstone): 'Loquendum est cum domino et suo consilio de communi tallagio deducto et detento.' C 13 (Monxton): 'Ricardus le Pottere capitalis decenarius cum sua tota decena presentat quod Johannes de Anna Port fecit unam purpresturam super dominum apud Dongere, et chaciam domini et tenencium suorum de Anna Bec iniuste impedit et deforciat etc. Distringatur etc. Loquendum est inde cum domino et suo consilio.' This case would involve the lord of Amport.

the chief steward, and perhaps manorial officials of the type of Henry Butery and James Freysel; a legal element may well have been present, for the prior had to maintain a large number of professional pleaders. One letter speaks of his expenses 'pour sa mesnie et pour sa gent, pledeours et autres, dont il esconvient que il ait grant foison a robes et a despens pour la deffense des biens de ladite baillie . . .'.[1] But there is no proof of this.

The scarcity of central records partly obscures the financial organization of the estate. Each manor was a distinct financial unit, and in addition to being responsible for temporal profits was the place of receipt for spiritualities and forinsec revenues from the surrounding district. If Ogbourne and Ruislip were the most important centres for the payment of large pensions and fee-farms, convenience demanded that small pensions and portions should be collected as far as possible on the spot. Occasionally the proctor himself is mentioned as receiver; in 1244, when the religious of Bec leased a mill and a meadow to the abbot of Lyre, they stipulated that the payment of 50*s.* annually was to be made to their proctor in the manor of Povington;[2] but in practice this would mean that the reeve or bailiff of the manor collected the rent and rendered account for it to the proctor.[3] A particularly large number of forinsec tithes —due from the demesne of Miles Crispin—were payable at Swyncombe and Wantage, as the pipe roll shows.[4]

There was no centralized receipt. The reeve or bailiff of each manor had first to meet the special expenses incumbent on the manor, which included ecclesiastical tenths and, at Combe, a small contribution towards the expenses of the clerical proctor in parliament:[5] then to transfer the profits

[1] Porée, ii. 62. The names of two of his attorneys, John de Stokes and Henry de Greneford, occur in cases in Lambeth MS. 244, ff. 78, 78*v*, 90, 90*v*, 101. Henry de Greneford was almost certainly a professional advocate, since he appeared as proctor for various other litigants. Ibid., ff. 102, 104, 120*v*.

[2] Porée, ii. 214.

[3] Cf. MS. Add. 24316, f. 44 [46] (Cottisford): 'Et sciendum quod debet quolibet anno serviens manerii recipere de persona de Cestr' ad festum Sancti Michaelis xv sol' et de persona de Bereford vij sol' ad duos terminos'; f. 66 [67] (Bledlow): 'Decime spectantes ad custodiam manerii: De Wycumb', De Estona, De Henton', De Wottesdon', De A'thropd', De Quenton.'

[4] Eton, C 14.

[5] King's College, account roll, 1306–7: 'Et liberat' ad expens' clerici decanatus

as required to the lord or steward, either in person or by the hands of one of the administrative officials. Money urgently needed by the steward for legal expenses could of course be levied at any moment from one of the manors. The Combe account rolls for 1306–7 contain the following liveries to the prior of Ogbourne: £5 by Henry Butery, £10 at Ogbourne, £9 by Henry Butery in July, and £12 at Ogbourne at Michaelmas. In 1309–10 several payments were made to William of Harden whilst he was at the manor for his judicial expenses, and in 1316–17 James Freysel appears as one of the officials who received money for the lord. In the Ogbourne account rolls the same method appears; small sums were paid to the lord through Simon of Ruislip, John Broughton, and William of Cothull, or given to meet expenses incurred by William of Ramshill; and the same method is illustrated in other manorial accounts, though after the first quarter of the fourteenth century there was a marked tendency to pay profits at Ruislip.

Local expenditure was checked by the centralized audit. This was held at Ruislip; the account rolls of Combe contain regular entries of the reeve's expenses in going to Ruislip to render account, and there are similar entries for the bailiffs of Ogbourne St. Andrew, Wretham, and Blakenham. Ogbourne was the only other manor that might have seemed a likely centre for auditing, and the fortunate survival of its account rolls shows that it was not one. In the late fourteenth century the court rolls of Ruislip still contain notes of the expenses of steward and auditors for several days hearing accounts.[1] An inventory of the manor-house at Ruislip, made in 1435–6, mentions a counting house and a counting board, which were probably in existence at least for the late fourteenth-century audits;[2] and plainly,

euntis ad parliamentum apud Carliel, v *d*.'; 1308–9: 'In expensis j clerici euntis ad London' ad parliamentum x *d*. pro qualibet marca quadrig'.' For similar expenses see E. Clark Lowry, 'Clerical Proctors in Parliament and Knights of the Shire, 1280–1374' (*E.H.R.* xlviii (1933), 443–55); A. E. Levett, op. cit., p. 48; and F. M. Page, op. cit., p. 63.

1 King's College, Q 45 (Oct. 1396): 'Expense senescalli, auditorum et aliorum existencium ibidem per v dies, pro curia ibidem tenenda, compot' audiend' et manerio supervidendo. . . .' Also Q 49 (1395). Possibly, however, the auditors were concerned with the account of the manor of Ruislip only.

2 Ministers' Accounts, S.C. 6, 917/27. The estate had been farmed to the duke

though Ruislip ceased to be a separate priory in the early thirteenth century, it remained an administrative centre as important as Ogbourne until the estates were broken up under royal pressure two hundred years later. Of the officials who heard the accounts in the early years we can be certain only of the steward, who heard accounts from October to December 1289[1] and is mentioned on other occasions;[2] professional auditors may not have made their appearance until later. Although one pipe roll only has survived in part, it seems likely that normal practice in the late thirteenth and early fourteenth centuries was to enrol the manorial accounts in an abbreviated form after the audit. The further stages of accounting and the assessment of the prior of Ogbourne's total revenue and expenditure—if there were any—have left no surviving records. There is only one hastily scribbled memorandum at the end of a roll of transcripts of acquittances for the crusading tenth, from 1275 to 1279:[3]

'For the fine at the time of vacancy, and the arrears from Stoke, St. Neot's, Goldcliff and Wilsford, and the money given at the lord abbot's command to the prior of St. Neot's, and the pension of Ralph, clerk of the lord king, and the allowance of tenth to the abbot of Cleeve, and the payment of cash to Master R. of Thurlow and Ralph Blond and Master Bartholomew Lard, £406. 5*s.* 8*d.*

'Also to Master Ralph of Framingham, 10 marks.

'Also for the tenth granted to the lord king £100.'

Indeed, it is impossible to tell if the prior of Ogbourne ever kept more developed accounts than the pipe rolls, or presented a *status domus* to his abbot; unless this was contained in the 'parchment roll in which are inscribed the revenues of Great Ogbourne'.[4]

Together with the audit, the courts provided an efficient check on the administration of the manors. They were held by the prior of Ogbourne himself, the steward, or the itinerant bailiff, who might well be called a steward of the courts. The Combe account rolls sometimes state the holders of the courts; in nine years the prior of Ogbourne is named

of Bedford for the previous thirty years; but the mention of a *camera prioris* in the inventory suggests that the manor-house was still as the prior had left it. In any case the duke of Bedford's audit was probably held elsewhere.

[1] Eton, C 14.

[2] For instance, *supra*, p. 57.

[3] King's College, Dd 32.

[4] *Supra*, p. 7.

once, William of Harden once, Henry Butery seven times, and for the remaining nine courts no names are given. Each manor was visited once or twice a year and sometimes more; as a rule the steward's busiest periods were between Michaelmas and Christmas, and in May and June; but sometimes he went on a small circuit in Lent or continued his work right through the summer.[1] Ruislip had a particularly large number of courts, possibly because its importance as an administrative centre made it one of the residences of the lord and a court could conveniently be held whenever he was there, and because the size of the manor necessitated the transaction of an unusually large amount of business.[2] At the end of the year or later[3] the court rolls were written up by a scribe, and the perquisites, fines, and tallage added up for the greater convenience of the steward who would hear the reeve's accounts. Other courts may have been held under the supervision of the local bailiffs, but if so there were probably no perquisites,[4] and little business except the completion of suits between tenants can have been transacted.[5] Particularly difficult business was always reserved for the courts held by the steward or the lord.[6]

1 The roll for 1311–12 (King's College, C 13) is complete, and gives the following circuit: Wretham 7 Oct., Lessingham 9 Oct., Chisenbury 8 Nov., Deverill 10 Nov., Povington 12 Nov., Milburne 13 Nov., Monxton 15 Nov., Quarley 15 Nov., Combe 16 Nov., Hungerford 17 Nov., Atherstone 27 Nov., Cottisford 1 Dec., Ruislip 6 Dec., Preston 10 Dec., Dunton 14 Dec., Bledlow 20 Dec., Swyncombe 21 Dec., Ogbourne 18 Jan., Tooting 4 Feb., Preston 1 May, Atherstone 14 Aug.; *dorse* Wantage [*MS torn*], Ruislip *c.* 12 March, Ruislip 6 May, Dunton 20 June, Bledlow 22 June, Swyncombe 23 June, Ogbourne 26 June, Chisenbury 28 June, Deverill 29 June, Povington 1 July, Monxton 3 July, Quarley 3 July, Combe 4 July, Hungerford 5 July, Wantage 7 July, Wretham 24 July, Lessingham 26 July, Tooting 1 Aug., Cottisford 16 Aug.

2 In the summer of 1290 courts were held at Ruislip on 22 June, 16 July, and 3 Aug. (King's College, C 9).

3 Cf. *Select Pleas*, p. 35, for evidence of proceedings in the Easter and December courts of Combe (1290) being written up at the same time.

4 The Combe account rolls tally with the court rolls for a number of years, and the perquisites are always exactly the same on both.

5 Cf. *Select Pleas*, p. 4: 'It is possible that they met . . . under the presidency of the local bailiff for merely formal business.'

6 Ruislip (King's College, C 11): 'Datus est dies operariis usque ad proximum adventum W. de Hardene senescalli ad respondendum quare non venerunt ad summonicionem domini.' Ogbourne (C 17): 'Adam le Muleward calumpniatus de eo quod non dat domino capitagium nec aliquem redditum racione recognicionis

Apart from their place in estate administration, the courts regulated relations with the central government and local lords, and their origin and growth were complex. Academically the abbot's jurisdiction was of two types: seignorial, in virtue of his tenure, exercised in the hallmote; and franchisal, by royal delegation, in the court leet. Academically the latter in its turn derived from both the view of frankpledge and the sheriff's tourn or leet,[1] but the amalgamation of the two was so complete that in the Bec records 'leet' is frequently used as a synonym for 'view of frankpledge' in Norfolk. In practice there was a single session of a court dealing indiscriminately with domanial and franchisal business. The historian's interest in the precise line dividing the two was probably not shared by contemporaries in the early thirteenth century; the early rolls of the Bec manors were concerned directly with the amount of fines, heriots, or other dues and the names of offenders and pledges, and only incidentally with the nature of the business and the procedure that brought it into court. They were meant to guide manorial officials in the collection of perquisites. Two things helped to produce greater detail and definition: the first was the increasing complexity of the centralized manorial administration with its need for precise and stereotyped local records; the second, the relentless pressure of the royal lawyers in repeated *Quo Warranto* inquiries. The wisdom of these inquiries is obvious: in a small community where one meeting of the court sufficed for all business and the same men might be reeves and chief pledges, private might have engulfed public jurisdiction, and the lords of Bec forgotten that they held their police jurisdiction merely in trust for the king. The confusion of the early records is a sign of underlying legal confusion.

There is no doubt that the abbot in practice exercised some franchisal jurisdiction from 1246 at least, the date of the earliest court rolls; amidst a mass of undefined entries

nayvitatis sue, qui dicit quod non est consuetudo istius manerii nec solebat esse quod nativi domini nec bundi darent capitagium nec alium redditum nisi tenementa tenuerunt. Et super hoc petit respectum de stando voluntati et ordinacioni domini seu senescalli in proximo suo adventu, alterius eorum qui citius venerit, et super hoc inveniat plegios.'

[1] See *Select Pleas*, pp. xxvj seqq. for the amalgamation of view and leet.

there are a few relating explicitly to public order and the assize of ale;[1] and by 1275 tithingmen had been mentioned in most of the manors. He had, however, nearly lost some rights by neglect, and in 1259 Henry III confirmed his right to infangthief, although by failing to use it he had run the risk of forfeiting it.[2] As Henry III and Edward I carried out their investigations into private liberties, the abbot of Bec was compelled to seek the basis of his. There were two charters justifying some of his claims: Henry II's great charter of liberties with the general privileges of sake and soc, tol and theam, infangthief and exemption from shire and hundred courts;[3] and Henry III's confirmation of this, which added the right to the chattels of felons and amercements of tenants before the royal justices.[4] Claims to view of frankpledge and the assizes of bread and ale were based on immemorial custom, to which local juries gave testimony. On the whole charters and precedents together maintained the abbot's liberties intact during the early stages of the *Quo Warranto* inquiries under Edward I.[5] Later zealous royal pleaders, among whom Gilbert of Thornton stands out for his subtlety, sometimes raised the issue of a special point, but failed to make it because usage was clearly proved:[6] once in 1329 the abbot incurred a small fine for not having claimed his liberties in the preceding eyre.[7] But except in Sussex, where the jury found that he had been paying suit to the sheriff's tourn and the hundreds of Ninfield and Totnore,[8] the abbot seems to have been successful in upholding all his liberties. Not unnaturally, however, the process of definition had left its mark on the court rolls; the business of the leet or view of frankpledge was entered separately from other

[1] e.g. at Ogbourne, 1249 (*Select Pleas*, p. 19), Deverill, 1247 (ibid., p. 13), Wantage (King's College, C 5, undated but early roll), 'Presentatum est quod Ricardus de Gardino percussit quamdam mulierem, que levavit hutesium.'

[2] *Close Rolls, 1256–9*, p. 406.

[3] Porée, i. 471–3.

[4] *C.Ch.R.* i. 430–1.

[5] *P.Q.W.*, pp. 815 (Combe, Monxton, Quarley, 1281), 780 (Atherstone, 1284–5).

[6] Ibid., pp. 234–5 (Dunton, 1285), 88 (Bledlow, 1286), 461–2 (London, 1321). In the last case objections were overruled; the end of the inquiry is lost in the printed version, but there is a full copy in King's College, Dd 31, showing that the abbot successfully upheld his claim.

[7] *P.Q.W.*, p. 583 (Weedon, 1329).

[8] Ibid., p. 759 (Preston and Hooe, 1279). This seems to be a case of losing a liberty through failure to establish it in practice.

business in the later rolls, though normally the two were still held together on the same day.[1]

There are two cases of the abbot's overlord preserving a vestige of control over the court. By a compromise with Simon de Montfort, view of frankpledge at Weedon was held by the steward of the honour of Leicester; and although the abbot received the profits he also bore the steward's expenses.[2] At Ogbourne, in the honour of Wallingford, the right to hold the view of frankpledge and receive the profits from it was confirmed in 1253 by Richard, earl of Cornwall, who then stipulated that his bailiff of Wallingford might be present once a year at the expense of the manor to satisfy himself 'that the king's peace was properly kept'.[3] Where other manors existed in the same vill the court was a useful meeting-ground; and at Bledlow Henry de Turri, a free tenant who also, it seems, held a manor of his own in Bledlow, presented his tenants at the view with the abbot's tenants and took a fifth of the proceeds. Occasionally pleas involving the tenants of other lords came into the court, but they were never settled as part of the routine business; at Combe a plea concerning a tenant in Amport was reserved for consideration by the lord and his council;[4] and at Ogbourne attachments of the men of William Longespee and Sampson Foliot were respited, possibly for the same purpose.[5] William Longespee, earl of Salisbury, held land around—though not in—Ogbourne:[6] and as Sampson Foliot held a carucate of land of the honour of Wallingford actually in Ogbourne, it is surprising that his men do not figure more often in the proceedings of the court.[7]

Each local court transacted all manorial business, judicial and administrative. One of its functions was to keep its sphere of competence free from encroachment, and it relentlessly fined suitors who took cases into the courts

[1] Cf. Vinogradoff, *Villainage in England*, pp. 364 seqq. In the fourteenth century occasionally the court was held without the view and dealt with domanial business and pleas between tenants only; Wretham and Lessingham had normally only one view a year.

[2] Eton, Weedon Charters, B 11; cf. Exch. K.R., E 106, 7/12.

[3] Porée, i. 462.

[4] *Supra*, p. 57, n. 6.

[5] *Select Pleas*, p. 9.

[6] *L.F.*, pp. 708–10, 719–22, and *passim*.

[7] *R.H.* ii. 269.

Christian[1] or exacted forinsec tolls without permission.[2] There alone could relations between lord and villein or between the villeins themselves be regulated, and although free tenants had recourse to the royal courts in civil cases, they owed suit to the manor court, swore fealty there, and were subject to its jurisdiction in agricultural matters. There inherited land was transferred, heriots and reliefs given, entry fines assessed, fealty sworn, exchanges of land between tenants arranged, tallage collected, licences to marry issued; in brief, the routine business of any manor court brought its usual train of perquisites into the lord's exchequer. Offenders too paid the penalty of their offences, mostly in cash. Fines were levied for trespass on the demesne or on the land of other tenants, for incompetent work or refusal of labour services, for unlawful purprestures. However, the reckoning between manorial officials and tenants was mutual, and rascally officials were brought to book. Take, for instance, the long indictment brought by the homage of Preston against its reeve and bailiff in 1308:[3]

'Inquisition made *ex officio* by the whole homage of Preston into the custody of the manor by Henry of Bereford, bailiff there. They say on oath that Henry took half an acre of Richard Paterick's land, half an acre and a rood of John Bishop's, half an acre of the miller's widow's land, a rood of John Palmer's and half a rood of Matthew Palmer's and gave them no land in exchange, as he had promised to do and had openly contracted with them. The plea is in respite until the coming of the chief steward.

'Also they say that Henry had the lord's land ploughed and failed to sow it within three weeks to the great loss of the lord. Also that Henry carried away many goods from the manor, as Matthew, now

[1] King's College, C 7 (Atherstone): 'Alanus Prior quia traxit dominum Robertum capellanum tenentem domini extra curiam domini ad curiam Christianitatis, etc., in preiudicium domini et ad dampnum ipsius domini Roberti xx *s.*; ideo in misericordia xij *d.*' King's College, Q 49 (Ruislip): 'Item per eandem inquisicionem compertum est quod Hugo Solyn liber et Ricardus le Fuller nativus domini traxerunt Ricardum Walrand' et Luciam Roger nativos ad curiam Christianitatis in preiudicium domini et curie huius, ad dampnum ipsorum Ricardi et Lucie viij *d.* et ideo consideratum est quod predicti Ricardus et Lucia recuperent dampna predicta, et quod dictus Hugo remaneret in misericordia per plegium Hugonis Bysouth iij *d.* et dictus Ricardus le Fuller per plegium sui ipsius iij *d.*' Also C 15 (Wretham).

[2] Lessingham (King's College, C 13): 'Willelmus Bisshop convictus est quod per ipsum Juliana Wimot districta fuit ad solvendum tolloneum contra libertatem domini.'

[3] King's College, C 12.

reeve, knows well. Also that John Malin stole a wether from the lord's fold, and Walter the shepherd and Richard Colin two of Henry's ewes from the same fold, and these were seized by Matthew the reeve after Henry's departure.

'Also that Matthew the reeve and Hugh Ploket sold before the arrival of Richard Rouce, bailiff, 2 quarters and 2½ bushels of wheat, for how much they could not say. Also that they sold a sow for 5/-.'

If law and order were kept in the manor by the lord's officials, it was none the less the duty of the whole body of tenants to report the misdemeanours of the men who were set over them.

How was this mass of business brought into the court? There is no clear order in the court rolls, nor are there any surviving instructions to the steward. But the idealized pictures of procedure in manorial courts, written in the thirteenth and fourteenth centuries for the instruction of stewards, give some clues. There is, for instance, the lively and detailed account of business in a manor court with view of frankpledge about 1340 which Maitland has printed.[1] There, after essoins of the common suit had been taken, the steward charged the chief pledges with the articles about which they should inquire. Whilst they retired to consider their presentations the essoins of pleas were called for, the hayward presented in writing his attachments and plaints, and private persons brought forward their grievances. A jury of twelve free tenants was chosen, and after the chief pledges had returned and made their statement this jury presented offences that they had omitted.

Whilst none of the courts of Bec conforms to this pattern, it provides a useful working basis for inquiry. Attachments often came into the court by the presentment of one or other of the manorial officials, commonly the hayward. These may have been written; there is one instance of the hayward's first statement being checked later by verbal cross-examination.[2] In a late court roll of Ruislip the reeve presented default of suit, the two foresters trespass in the woods,

[1] *The Court Baron* (Selden Society, vol. iv), pp. 93–101. See also F. J. C. Hearnshaw, *Leet Jurisdiction in England*, pp. 60 seqq.

[2] Combe, 1334 (King's College, C 19): 'Robertus messor in misericordia pro diversis conceleamentis in presentacione attachiamentorum suorum compertis per examinacionem sui ipsius.'

and the hayward trespass in the corn.[1] During years of murrain special officials appeared—the *cadaveratores*—who had to account for all deaths in the flock, and whose presentations were borne in mind when the account was audited.[2]

A mass of business arises from the complaints of individual suitors. 'Peter Kiwel complains of William Viner and says that he has grievously defamed him'; 'John of Bagmere demands against John son of Walter Wells one virgate of land'. Essoins of the common suit and of pleas were sent too by the parties concerned. It is when we come to presentations by jurors or chief pledges that problems arise. In the late thirteenth century, when the rolls were more detailed, the tithingmen were often named and their presentments occupied a section apart. They then included statements of those in tithing, hues and cries, harbouring of strangers, purprestures, unlicensed marriages, breaches of the assizes of bread and ale, and miscellaneous breaches of the peace.[3] Frequently the shortcomings of brewers were presented not by the pledges but by the ale-tasters. Unfortunately, particularly at an early date, the rolls are often less explicit. Entries which begin 'It is presented that . . .' may refer to the statements of the pledges, particularly when they concern nocturnal malefactors or the hue and cry.[4] Other vague expressions—'the whole vill presents', 'the homage presents'—suggest the entire body of tenants; but there must always have been a spokesman, and a late court roll of Dunton shows that the 'homage' might in fact mean the chief pledges.[5] It cannot even be proved that purely manorial

[1] King's College, Q 49 (1334–5).

[2] e.g. at Combe in 1334 (King's College, C 19): 'Henricus Sewall' et Henricus le Smyth, cadaveratores, presentant morinam xij hogastrorum xxiij multonum, xlj ovium matricium et xx hoggettorum qui moriebantur de communi morina citra proximam curiam et non alio modo. Postea per examinacionem compertum est quod j hurtard' devoratus fuit per canes, et vj hurtard' xx multon' et iiij oves matrices unde bercarii nichil ostendebant cadaveratoribus. Et quia predicti cadaveratores presentant id quod non sciebant, consideratum est quod ipsi remaneant in misericordia. Et de bidentibus loquendum est super compotum.'

[3] Cf. F. J. C. Hearnshaw, op. cit., pp. 57–8, for the type of article presented to chief pledges in some courts.

[4] e.g. *Select Pleas*, p. 19.

[5] King's College, M 8 (1377). The entry runs: 'Presentatum est per totum homagium, videlicet Willelmum Canoun, Thomam Lorchoun, Johannem Heyward, Johannem Betill' et Johannem Stace . . .', and the view of the same year proves that these men were actually the chief pledges.

business lying outside the scope of the view cannot have been presented by the chief pledges, since they were often seignorial officials too, and it is unlikely that they always drew a clear line between their two functions. Miss Page has shown that on the manors of Crowland abbey the chief pledges often formed a ruling official class,[1] and the same is true of Dunton and possibly some other manors of Bec. Though the early court rolls too rarely give the names of officials, it transpires occasionally that the chief pledge of a manor was also the reeve.[2]

Whatever interpretation we may put upon *tota villa*, *decena*, or *homagium*, there is no doubt that a body of men other than the chief pledges sometimes brought forward charges on some at least of the manors of Bec. The one error I have found in Maitland's admirable study of the courts is his statement that 'the rolls do not show us a regular jury of presentment like the "leet jury" of later times'. Juries of presentment existed certainly at Atherstone and Bledlow, and probably at Ogbourne. A half-obliterated statement in one of the early rolls for Ogbourne suggests that an omission of the hayward's was revealed by twelve jurors.[3] There is a clearer reference in the roll for 1282: 'It is presented by ten sworn men that Robert Crispin, Cristina White, Adam and William Westmost allowed their sheep to devour ten sheaves of John Pound's corn; therefore they are in mercy'.[4] At Atherstone and Bledlow a system existed very like that described in the treatise: sworn men heard the tithingmen's presentments and pointed out their omissions. In 1316 the statement of the chief pledges of Atherstone is followed by the entry, 'The twelve jurors present that Thomas of Baxtorle has defaulted at this view, therefore he is in mercy; and because the chief pledges concealed this default they are in mercy';[5] and in 1320 twelve jurors declared that four men were forestallers of salt.[6] At Bledlow in 1311 'John of

[1] *The Estates of Crowland Abbey*, pp. 68 seqq.

[2] In 1311 Walter Gentil was chief pledge and reeve of Brixton-Deverill, and Thomas Culbel chief pledge and reeve of Bledlow; Adam Rouce, chief pledge of Chisenbury at the same period, was reeve in 1317 (King's College, C 13, C 7).

[3] *Select Pleas*, pp. 19–20: 'Omnes carucarii Majoris Ockeburn convicti fuerunt per sacramentum xij [. . . . . .] domini male fuit arata. . . . Et Walterus Messor in misericordia quia predictam araturam concelavit.'

[4] King's College, C 8.

[5] King's College, C 7.

[6] King's College, C 14.

Grately and the other free tenants present that John Wyking made a purpresture on the hills which the chief pledges concealed; therefore John and the chief pledges are in mercy':[1] and they made similar statements in 1312 and 1321.[2] In 1317 chief pledges and free tenants together declared 'secretly' that eleven people were evil-doers in the corn-crops; no doubt because they wished to give the guilty ones no chance of escape before justice could be taken.[3] Both manors contained a large body of free tenants. At Quarley, where there were few free tenants, there is one case of tithing and tithingmen making separate statements and acting as checks on one another.[4]

An accusation backed by a sufficient number of reputable men was almost equivalent to condemnation, and nothing remained but to assess the fine. Affeerors appear in the later rolls; for the thirteenth century we are left uncertain whether the lord or representatives of his tenants estimated the amount of the fines. The earliest custumal of Ogbourne suggests that two methods were possible: 'And the inquisition says that he may not have any other animals within these pastures; and if he is found guilty in this respect he shall make amends either by the judgment of his peers or at the lord's will'.[5] Sometimes pleas arose out of the charges, particularly the attachments; the accused could defend himself against his lord who would be represented by the official making the charge.[6] And the grievances of private individuals naturally gave rise to a mass of judicial proceedings. These cases might be settled in several ways, and certainly compurgation was not unknown; at Cottisford a man found guilty 'by inquisition of the whole court', to which he refused to submit, made his law and acquitted himself six-handed in the next court.[7] Arbitration was possible if both parties were agreeable.[8] Occasionally the

[1] King's College, C 13.

[2] King's College, C 13, C 14.

[3] King's College, C 7. Cf. F. J. C. Hearnshaw, op. cit., p. 47, for secret presentations in the sheriff's tourn.

[4] King's College, C 4 (1270): 'Presentatum est per capitalem decenarium quod Thomas Market desurpavit quamdam foveam. Ideo dictus Thomas in misericordia iij *s.* et decena pro concelacione ij *s.*'

[5] King's College, Dd 33.

[6] e.g. *Select Pleas*, p. 43.

[7] Ibid., pp. 32, 37. Cf. also *Court Rolls of Tooting Beck*, p. 33.

[8] *Select Pleas*, p. 21.

method was by something like acclamation by the whole court, and in one case 'the whole court' is substituted in the rolls for 'twelve lawful men'.[1] By far the commonest method of settling disputes was, however, appeal to a jury of twelve, or sometimes six, lawful men. Maitland commented on the number of suits between tenants which were settled by a sworn jury, and printed a good selection of them; they were as common and as circumstantial in the later court rolls. It is not really remarkable that men paid to have the verdict of a jury; they paid to make compurgation, or to have arbitrators, or indeed for the privilege of going to law at all; but the growing popularity of juries is suggested by the refusal of the suitors of Atherstone in 1336 to give judgement except by sworn inquisition.[2] Sometimes in cases where a jury was required procedure consciously aped the procedure of the royal courts; and at Dunton it might be decided to settle a case *in natura assise nove dissesine* or *in natura brevis mortis antecessoris*.[3] But one fourteenth-century development cut down the work of the juries; copyhold tenure began to take shape, and often suitors appealed to the written record of the court rather than the memory of a jury in cases of land-holding.[4]

Any discussion of the work of the courts involves a consideration of how far the custom of the manor was a strong and abiding force, and how far it was softened and unified through the work of officials travelling on circuit over a wide area, some of them officials who served on commissions in the king's courts. And it is a question that, unfortunately, does not admit of a definite answer. In some things, such as rights of common, which were dictated by purely local agricultural needs, the custom of the manor was bound to be strong. Over such questions as heriots, where both lord and tenants would stand out firmly for their

[1] *Select Pleas*, p. 20.

[2] King's College, H 4: 'Omnes sectatores pro contemptu in misericordia eo quod dixerunt quod noluerunt reddere iudicium nisi per inquisicionem iurat'.'

[3] e.g. King's College, M 8 (Dunton, 1389–90), M 9 (Dunton, 1399–1400).

[4] Early cases of a tenant paying a fine 'pro rotulis curie querendis quos vocat ad warantum de seysina tenementi sui' occur at Lessingham in 1308 (King's College, C 12) and Ruislip in 1316 (King's College, C 7); but at earlier dates the court rolls were sometimes appealed to on points of fact (*Select Pleas*, p. 35).

own rights, it was unlikely to be overruled.[1] But the custom of the manor was consulted also over civil rights, such as the right of inheritance, or the right of a widow to hold land after the death of her husband. And on these matters the jurors' decision is commonly recorded without their reasons for giving it, so that it is rare to find a number of parallel cases dealing with the same problem. It has been shown of unfree tenants that 'in many respects the proceedings and the rules relating to their holdings were coming to be fashioned upon the model of the proceedings and the rules relating to freeholding', and that customary law was tending to uniformity;[2] and occasional glimpses of customary law in the manor courts of the Bec estates illustrate this tendency. Thus at Dunton in 1355 the homage presented that widows were to have by right of dowry a third part of the tenements held by their husbands;[3] and this third part was the same as the common-law dower.[4] There are variations, however; at Weedon a widow received half her husband's land as dowry,[5] and sometimes the whole tenement might be left to the widow as long as she remained unmarried[6]—a custom comparable with, though more generous than, the 'free bench' custom of some manors or the gavelkind of Kent.[7] Customs of inheritance must have been well fixed, since juries never found any difficulty in naming the next heir to any given tenement, but these customs do not appear in the court rolls. It is likely that descent was often to the younger sons; and there is a case of the lord using discretionary powers to grant one tenant the right of naming any one of her younger sons as heir.[8]

[1] Thus although on most manors villeins owed their best beast or the money equivalent as heriot, at Lessingham the second best beast only was given. This was stated by the jurors when the custumal was made (MS. Add. 24316, f. 51 [52], and repeated after an inquisition of the whole court in 1312 (King's College, C 13).

[2] W. S. Holdsworth, *A History of English Law*, ii. 282, 317.

[3] King's College, M 7.

[4] Holdsworth, op. cit., iii. 161.

[5] King's College, C 10.

[6] 1334, Brixton-Deverill (King's College, C 19): 'Walterus Gentyl qui de domino tenuit unum mesuagium et dimidiam virgatam terre de Akermanneslond obiit. . . . Et tenementa predicta remanent Cristiane que fuit uxor predicti Walteri tenenda secundum consuetudinem manerii dum se viduam tenere voluerit per servagium inde, etc. Sine fine.'

[7] Holdsworth, op. cit., iii. 154.

[8] Ruislip, 1317 (C 7): 'Et dominus de sua gratia et voluntate speciali concedit eidem Margerie ad hanc seysinam quod quemcumque puerorum suorum ipsa

But these sparse references may be misleading. The steward may, in his regular circuits, have been introducing practices drawn from the common-law procedure; other practices must have been the same in king's and lord's courts because of the common source of local custom from which both derived. Nevertheless, in the early fourteenth century manorial custom on the manors of Bec appears to be both strong and varied. These are conclusions, however, that can only very tentatively be put forward. On matters of procedure the issue is a little plainer: the period of subjection to Bec was not long enough to give a uniform stamp to all the manors. Before the 1320's, when the centralized administration began to break down, the courts had been under a single group of men for only eighty recorded years. And when the rolls start stewards were only beginning to be trained in the specialized technique of holding manor courts and keeping their records; they had certainly not learned to make them stereotyped, and very probably the routine of the courts was imposed by the varying structures and needs of the manors themselves. Methods must have varied according, for instance, to the relative number of free or villein tenants in any place; it is in the manors with most free tenants that the leet juries grew and became most active in the early fourteenth century. Just when the demands of efficiency and necessity alike might perhaps have produced more uniform procedure the estate began to break up. As the administration became less centralized manors were leased for a term of years and often the court was leased with the manor; after 1330 the court rolls, which were no longer composite but separate for most of the manors, began to show widening divergences in the times of holding the court and the business transacted.[1] For other evidence

Margeria nominare ante mortem suam voluerit excepto filio suo primogenito, quod ille per ipsam sic nominatus sit heres eius propinquior ad succedendum eidem Margerie in huiusmodi suo perquisito, et ad faciendum finem versus dominum pro ingressu habendo in eisdem terra et mesuagio more debito et in manerio de Risslep semper usitato.'

[1] At Atherstone the court was held almost every month, and generally no business was done for lack of suitors; the only really profitable session was the view and court held in November; at Lessingham the view and court were held about Michaelmas and one or two other courts during the year, and all were steadily profitable. Dunton had one court with view on 11 June and up to three other

of the comparative influence of the unit and the group, the manor and the estate, we must turn to an examination of the economic conditions of the abbot's tenants.

courts during the year, but at Combe, Quarley, Monxton, and Ruislip view and court were held together, as before, in the spring and autumn. Courts at Ogbourne were held about every two months, and it is not certain how often the view was held.

II
ECONOMIC CONDITIONS

WE know that the two units of medieval rural life—manor and vill—represented two types of social organization. The village community was originally bound together by the necessities of communal agriculture, and these in their turn were influenced by the social practices of successive groups of settlers as well as by the quality of the soil and the hills, woods, marshes, and downlands of the country-side itself. Under such influences village custom slowly developed, the size of the standard holding was established, and rights of common were determined. Simultaneously in many districts seignorial pressure was producing the manor and shaping it, at least in a small degree, according to the will of the lord. Within certain limits he could change his demands upon his tenants for rent and labour services; and if local conditions, such as the suitability of the country for pasture or arable farming, determined the type of service he would require, he had more control over the size of the demesne. And he could control it according to the purpose of the estate and the fluctuations of the local market. A large demesne would be desirable to supply a community with food or produce corn for a lucrative market; the demesne would be leased if administrative difficulties were too great or rents more profitable than sales. The balance might shift backwards and forwards between *Gutsherrschaft* and *Grundherrschaft*.[1] Many centuries of quiet agricultural development and two hundred years or more of fluctuating seignorial requirements combined to make up the thirteenth-century manor, whether or not it was conterminous with the vill.

And so to understand peasant conditions in any manor we must consider it both as part of a district and part of an estate. Here lies the peculiar interest of the bailiwick of Ogbourne. It enjoyed the solidarity and continuous administration of any great Benedictine estate, yet there

[1] See M. Postan, 'The Chronology of Labour Services', *T.R.H.S.*, 4th Series, xx (1937), 169–95.

was no community to feed and the manors were so scattered that no more than four lay in any one county. It illustrates a great range of local customs and tenures, and a single purpose—the enrichment of the Norman abbey. Professor Levett has shown that the attempt to interpret medieval economic documents must often be accompanied by the warning *Caveat lector*, and the warning must be borne in mind whilst studying a group of estates for which the most honest and detailed source possible, a good series of account rolls, is lacking. Nevertheless custumals, court rolls, extents, and the few surviving account rolls, if used with caution and compared with the records of adjacent manors, may illustrate some lines of social development in an estate of an unusual type.

The best sources for early history are the custumals. Even if it is true to say that they represent the static rather than the dynamic aspect of the manor, two or three custumals of different dates show stages of development; and careful analysis of rents and services due may, by revealing primitive organization, allow a glimpse of earlier growth. Here, however, let the reader beware. When the first existing survey of the estates was made, most of the manors had been in the hands of the monks for periods varying from 80 to 150 years. It is not possible that the changing history of that period should be compressed within the four corners of the custumal. Further, it must be remembered that the survey of the southern and western manors exists in an early and a later form, whereas there is no indication of any early survey of the other manors; therefore in all probability two separate inquisitions have become bound into one volume. Apparent differences may be due to the fact that two sets of inquisitors based their inquiries on different *capitula*; the juries may have been silent about a custom, not because it did not exist, but because they were not asked about it.

On the whole the structure of the extents of the various manors is very nearly as uniform as their widely differing organization would permit. Classification of tenants, to be accurate, would have imposed differences of form, but it was not employed; the usual method was to describe the rents and services due from any standard tenants, giving a list of the names of tenants holding on the same terms, and then describe one by one the miscellaneous land-holders whose duties were peculiar. The surveys of some East Anglian manors, where standard holdings were few, consist of a long list of tenants with a brief individual description of the rent and works owed by each. Only at Bledlow and Cottisford were the *libere tenentes* classed apart. There was no attempt to make distinctions found in many other custumals, as for instance between *molmen* and *operarii*, or between land *ad opus* and land *ad censum*.

Taking the customs on the whole, they appear less complicated than on many monastic estates. Rents in kind were not numerous; poultry at Martinmas for churchset and eggs at Easter, due as a rule from the smaller tenants and sometimes from the virgaters as well, make up almost the whole list, though one must add an occasional pig instead of a money payment for pannage, and a lamb for the right of a private fold[1] and the nails and horseshoes from some smiths' tenements.[2] If food rents, which were common in primitive societies, had been owed during the Saxon period, they became unnecessary after the formation of the estate, for money was more valuable to a non-resident lord. As for the money rents, it is well known that the 'assized rents' of thirteenth-century custumals and account rolls often conceal complicated development, and may include, as well as ancient money payments, commuted labour services and commuted rents in kind.[3] On the Bec estates it is very likely that several elements were included in the money rent, particularly at Ruislip and on some East Anglian manors, where greatly varying rents were attached to standard tenements owing standard services. However, there were no separate categories to reveal the origin of each element; all were lumped together as *redditus assise* and paid at one or two, or at most four, terms of the year. Except at Combe and Ogbourne, where standard holdings owed *gabulum bosci*, the

[1] Blakenham (MS. Add. 24316, f. 41*v* [43*v*]). A lamb might also be given for pasturage, e.g. at Lessingham (ibid., f. 54 [55]).

[2] For instance at Lessingham (ibid., f. 55 [56]).

[3] See E. A. Kosminsky, 'Services and Money Rents in the Thirteenth Century', in *Economic History Review*, v (1935), 27–8.

inquisitors generally used *gabulum* as synonymous with *redditus*. Other common money payments whose origin is obvious were pannage and herbage for the pasturing of stock; and in addition small dues, such as $\frac{1}{2}$*d.* turbage at Lessingham and 1*d.* maltsilver at Blakenham, were owed here and there.[1]

It is from the balance between rents and services that we may learn most, and from the type of service required. Boon services at the rush periods of the year were almost universal, for whatever the size of the demesne the normal complement of ploughs and labourers was enough only for the ordinary daily work and could rarely meet emergencies like the short lenten ploughing or the harvest. On these occasions all tenants were usually expected to assist with any equipment they possessed; and this service, though often partly sold in practice, was in principle a constant factor as long as the framework of the manor endured. Less widespread was winter week-work—the predial labour which thirteenth-century judges, in an attempt to introduce novel distinctions between the free and unfree at law, sometimes adopted as a criterion of villeinage. It fell in some districts on the cottars only, but where the demesne was large half-virgaters and virgaters were likely to owe heavy week-works and comparatively light money rents, and these could fluctuate with the changes in the demesne. A third type of service was the duty of carrying produce or riding on the lord's business: this obviously was determined by the character of the manorial group and, though probably of very ancient origin,[2] was in its final details a later adaptation. As it raises less problems than any other type of labour service, it may be considered first.

Carrying and riding services occur on all the manors of Bec; since horses were necessary, they fell as a rule on the larger tenants, though occasionally a humbler tenant might have to fetch the lord's food on his back.[3] Most of the produce of the manors was sold, and carrying services to local markets have already been discussed. But the cheeses

[1] MS. Add. 24316, ff. 51 [52], 43*v* [44*v*].
[2] See N. S. B. Gras, *The Evolution of the English Corn Market*, p. 8.
[3] MS. Add. 24316, f. 41*v* [43*v*] (Blakenham).

sent to Bec were carried to Southampton by the tenants of Combe, Monxton, Quarley, and Brixton-Deverill, who were responsible for handing them over in good condition and were paid for their service.[1] It was necessary too for tenants to ride with the lord abbot and the proctor on their several progresses round the estates, and to carry the lord's revenue wherever it might be required. Both these services at times, like the service of fetching the lord's food whenever he visited the manor, fell upon the tenants of standard holdings;[2] occasionally, however, they were incumbent upon particular tenements, which were otherwise lightly burdened.[3] The service may have been falling into desuetude in the thirteenth century; certainly one tenure by this type of serjeanty at Quarley came to an end between the dates of the two custumals.[4] Where riding and carrying services were demanded they were generally regarded as a grace, and were rewarded either by the relaxation of other works or by a gift of food; and the long and responsible journey to Southampton with the cheeses was paid. On some manors, of which Lessingham was one, a fine was levied when the service was not performed.[5]

But apart from this obviously later adaptation the adjustment of customs to meet the abbot's needs can be discovered only by a detailed regional study of the manors. The East Anglian manors—Lessingham, Wretham, and Blakenham—with their clearly defined local peculiarities, are in strong contrast to the more 'classical' and rigidly organized manors of Wiltshire; and comparison of the two types is the first vital stage in the inquiry.

[1] King's College, Dd 33, mm. 3, 4, 7, 9. A service of carrying cheeses was also owed by tenants of Steventon, but these cheeses may have gone to Le Pré (Westminster, Dean and Chapter Muniments, no. 7301).

[2] MS. Add. 24316, ff. 28 [29] (Ogbourne St. George), 57*v*–58 [58*v*–59] (Wretham), 1*v* (Ruislip).

[3] Ibid., f. 59 [60] (Duties of Norman Franklyn of Wretham).

[4] King's College, Dd 33, m. 7. The following entry is deleted in the roll: 'Thebaldus filius Adhelardi tenet j virgatam terre pro iiij *s*. annuis ad predictum terminum Sancti Michaelis pro omnibus serviciis et consuetudinibus, excepto quod debet equitare cum dominis per universam Angliam vice armigeri, prima die ad expensas proprias et per dies sequentes ad expensas dominorum.'

[5] MS. Add. 24316, f. 51 [52]. This payment resembles the *horsgabulum* of some of the Battle abbey manors (*Custumals of Battle Abbey*, ed. S. R. Scargill Bird, pp. xxxi seqq.).

The study of East Anglian society made by Professor Douglas[1] has shown an underlying structure of peasant tenements, possibly pointing back to a primitive scheme of land-sharing, but modified by frequent exchanges in a remarkably free land-market. Superimposed, particularly on ecclesiastical estates, was a highly organized manorial régime with heavy services: six days' work a week were owed on the bishop of Ely's manors of Walpole and Walton, and three or four days were common elsewhere.[2] Conditions on lay manors differed greatly, and almost invariably the services were lighter. At Wykes, Bradcar, and Shropham rents and services were of a bewildering variety, but week-works scarcely ever occurred.[3] Forncett, a manor of the earl of Norfolk, contained many tenants rendering occasional labour services, and even free tenants had to plough at the boons; but the customary tenants owed no more than one or two days' work each week throughout the winter, and a few extra days in August and September.[4] Similar conditions existed on a few ecclesiastical manors, notable at Martham—the one manor of Norwich cathedral priory that was specially favoured with light services and has been shown to have preserved clear traces of its early organization.[5]

The East Anglian manors of Bec approximate more to this type than to the characteristic ecclesiastical manors. Boon works and occasional works might be common; most of the smaller tenants shared in the common works of harvesting, weeding, ditching, spreading manure, washing sheep, and, at Blakenham, preparing flax;[6] and some of the wealthiest free tenants joined them in the boon ploughings. But there was no week-work at all at Wretham, and at

1 *The Social Structure of Medieval East Anglia.*

2 Ibid., pp. 80 seqq.

3 W. Hudson, 'Three Manorial Extents of the Thirteenth Century', in *Norfolk Archaeology*, xiv (1901), 1–56.

4 F. G. Davenport, *The Economic Development of a Norfolk Manor*, pp. 62 seqq.

5 W. Hudson, 'Traces of Primitive Agricultural Organisation as suggested by a Survey of the Manor of Martham, Norfolk' (*T.R.H.S.*, 4th Series, i (1918), 28–59); and 'Status of "Villani" and other Tenants in Danish East Anglia in pre-Conquest times' (*T.R.H.S.*, 4th Series, iv (1921), 23–48).

6 MS. Add. 24316, ff. 41*v*–42 [43*v*–44]: 'Et sciendum quod omnes supradicti terras tenentes . . . debent . . . linerium domini parare, scilicet terram fodere, seminare, linum sarclare, a terra extirpare, per manipulos colligere, in aquam ponere, et ab ea extrahere.'

Blakenham ten tenements only were burdened with services varying from seven works a month to one a week. Seventeen tenements at Lessingham owed half a day's threshing each week from Christmas to Whitsuntide, together with threshing on the vigils of festivals; this was heavier than the threshing on the nearby manor of Martham, but in other ways the services of the standard holding were strikingly similar: on both manors, for instance, sixteen days' harvesting and ten days' weeding were required. Altogether Lessingham has much more in common with Martham than with the typical manors of Norwich cathedral priory.

At first sight it seems that the lord's requirements weighed very lightly on these manors, and this conclusion is borne out by examining the incidence of the services. Week-works fell upon the old holdings. At Lessingham tenements owing them mostly contained 6, 4, or 3 acres described as *de antiqua feodatura*, to which sometimes an acre or two *de nova feodatura* had been added. No such clear statement was made at Blakenham; but the tenements owing week-work were mostly fractions of 10 acres, which was the size of the most heavily burdened tenements at Forncett.[1] In East Anglia small free holdings of irregular sizes were very common,[2] and the standard ploughland, when it occurred, was usually 10 or 12 acres; it seems likely therefore that thirteenth-century holdings still traceable to a division of 10 acres are the original servile holdings, particularly when only a few of them occur in a manor amongst holdings of bewilderingly different sizes. It is not easy to draw any significant parallels with Domesday figures, but it may not be entirely coincidence that the number of villeins in Lessingham at the time of Domesday was 15,[3] and the number of servile tenements in the thirteenth century 17. For on the whole the surviving week-works stand out as relics of an earlier attempt to impose manorial organization on a recalcitrant society, and there had never been any real inducement for the lord to renew the attempt. Mid-thirteenth-century figures for the demesne at Lessingham[4] show that it was small and could probably be cultivated by

[1] Davenport, op. cit., pp. 60, 63.

[2] *V.C.H. Suffolk*, i. 365.

[3] *D.B.* ii. 133*b*–4; *V.C.H. Norfolk*, ii. 61.

[4] *Supra*, p. 44, n. 2.

the lord's two ploughs, without the boon works of the tenants. So although arrangements existed for marketing some corn at Norwich and Yarmouth, the manor shows no signs of having felt the thirteenth-century impulse towards increased production. Moreover, had the abbot needed extra labour in this period, he could easily have drawn upon the surplus population of undersettlers, which existed at the time of making the custumal,[1] without imposing new burdens on his customary tenants; and the economic structure of the manor may well have changed very little since the time it came into the hands of the abbot of Bec.

If conditions on some of the Wiltshire manors are examined, they show a contrast that is deeper and more significant than the obvious contrast between 'free' East Anglia and 'manorialized' Wiltshire. The large demesne manors there were Ogbourne St. George and Brixton-Deverill; Ogbourne St. Andrew had demesne lands of 352 acres only, but since there were fewer tenants the burden on individuals was also very heavy.[2] In all three manors week-works were owed by the virgaters as well as by the smaller tenants, and the services of the standard virgater on all three Wiltshire manors are strikingly similar.[3] The tenants were obliged to work three days a week from Michaelmas to 1 August, and afterwards every working day except Saturday. If corn was still standing in the fields after Michaelmas they were to continue until it was all harvested. They owed the usual ploughing boons and extra ploughing for herbage according to the number of beasts they possessed; and in addition had to plough, sow, and harrow from 1½ to 3 acres at Martinmas. All tenants in common worked at sheep-shearing and hay-making as long as necessary, receiving the customary rewards of a wether and a fleece. For threshing for malt at Christmas and Easter, and for carrying-services—which varied a little at Deverill and the

[1] *Infra*, pp. 92–3.

[2] Deverill was in the worst position. The figures, using the 1294 royal extents and the latest custumals, are as follows:

Deverill: 717 arable acres, 1,143 sheep, 30 working tenements.
Ogbourne St. George: 871 arable acres, 1,450 sheep, 64 working tenements.
Ogbourne St. Andrew: 352 arable acres, 969 sheep, 24 working tenements.

[3] MS. Add. 24316, ff. 28 [29]; King's College, Dd 33, mm. 2, 9.

two Ogbournes[1]—other works were relaxed. Half-virgaters owed half these services and received half the rewards. Only small money payments were demanded: from virgaters 10*d.* at Ogbourne St. Andrew and Deverill, and 15*d.* at Ogbourne St. George, where the payment is described as *gabulum bosci*,[2] and from half-virgaters half that amount. These resemblances are even more striking when the services are compared with those on the Glastonbury manors of Longbridge and Monkton Deverill, between which Brixton-Deverill lies; and Winterbourne and Badbury, which are only a few miles from the Ogbournes.[3] Naturally these were similar in type; one reason for the heavy services of all kinds was that the district combined valleys suitable for extensive arable farming with downlands where large flocks of sheep could be reared. But the incidence was different; at very nearly the same date the large tenants of Glastonbury on these manors paid much higher rents and owed boon works, common works, daily reapings in autumn, and carrying-services. Winter week-work fell upon the tenants of a few acres.

Even allowing for an illusory similarity produced by the fact that the same questions were probably asked on all three of the Bec manors, it seems that here at least a process of depression had been going on after the manors came under the management of the abbots. Certain changes in the customs of three tenants in the custumal of Ogbourne St.

1 Ogbourne St. George (MS. Add. 24316, f. 28*v* [29*v*]): 'Et sciendum quod si faciat summagium vel averagium pro quindecim leucis allocabitur ei unum opus, et pro xxx leucis duo opera, et ad summagium debet portare septem bussellos bladi cuiuscumque generis sit.' Deverill (King's College, Dd 33, m. 9): 'Item debet cum communa quando ad hoc summonitus fuerit cum duabus quadrigis salvo cariare caseum usque Suhampton' et per numerum recipere et ita liberare et deperdita vel fracta restaurare et recipere debet quelibet quadriga j *d.* et j panem, et ob hoc quietus erit de tribus operibus. Item cariare debet lanam usque ad Ockeborn' et quietus esse de tribus operibus. Et quando avrat Saftesbir' quietus esse debet de duobus operibus. Et quando ad propinquiora loca quietus de j opere. Et sciendum quod quando avrat bladum portare debet dimidium quarterium.'

2 At Combe, the only other manor where a payment called *gabulum bosci* was demanded, the amount was 10*d.* or 5*d.* and it was due from the half-virgaters even when the remainder of their rent had been relaxed in return for week-works (King's College, Dd 33, m. 3, and Combe Account Rolls, *passim*).

3 *Rentalia et Custumaria Michelis de Ambresbury et Rogeri de Ford, abbatum monasterii Beate Marie Glastonie*, ed. C. J. Elton (Somerset Record Society, 1891), pp. 59, 61–4, 133–47.

Andrew may even be the last stage in this process; in the first version each held a virgate for rents and lighter services excluding, in one case, winter week-works: in the second they held in the same way as all the rest.[1] If services were growing heavier, then the demesne was being either made larger or more intensively cultivated; and there are two signs of recent small increases in size. Brother William de Guineville bought back one piece of charter land; Geoffrey Marshall, one of the few tenants holding by charter in the first custumal,[2] granted the abbot of Bec a messuage and a virgate in return for 20*s*., a robe of russet, and a cloak for his wife;[3] and since this tenement cannot be traced in the second custumal it presumably went into the demesne. And part of the pension owed by the vicar of Ogbourne was relaxed in the second custumal as compensation for tithes lost to him because the tenements that owed them had been drawn into the demesne.[4]

It is impossible to tell with any certainty whether this was a temporary fluctuation in the size of the demesne, which was a fairly common event, or the last stage of a clearly defined

[1] King's College, Dd 33, m. 2: 'Item [ ] Saloman tenet unam virgatam terre pro iij solidis solvendis ad terminum Sancti Michaelis, et in omnibus tenetur eadem opera et iura et consuetudines eodem modo facere quam Robertus Siward, exceptis triturationibus, messuris cotidianis in autumpno, sed precarias binas vel plures eodem modo quam alii facere debet; et exceptis averagiis et fugacionibus, sed equitaturas ad opus dominorum facere debet, prima die ad custum proprium, et aliis ad custum dominorum, et etiam brevia portare. Item non potest filiam suam sine licencia maritare. . . . Item invenire debet j hominem ad comitatum et coram iusticiis ad custum suum', deleted and changed to 'Walterus Saloman tenet unam virgatam terre omni eodem modo sicut alii virgatarii.'

'Item Robertus Wilde tenet unam virgatam terre in omnibus eodem modo quam Saloman', changed to 'Item Robertus Wilde tenet unam virgatam terre omni eodem modo.'

'Item Ricardus Elaf tenet unam virgatam terre pro x solidis annuis ad predictum terminum solvendis, et debet arare omnes communes aruras et herciaturas, et pannagiare debet tam boves quam porcos eodem modo quam Robertus, oves lavare et tondere, prata falcare, levare, cariare, tassare, sarclare si precatus fuerit, et ad autumpnales precarias metere sicut alii, cariare si precatus fuerit. Item de filiis et equis et bobus nichil aliud potest facere quam alii', changed to 'Item Ricardus Elaf tenet unam virgatam terre omni eodem modo sicut Walterus Saloman.'

[2] King's College, Dd 33, m. 1.

[3] King's College, Dd 26.

[4] MS. Add. 24316, f. 31 [32]: 'Et sciendum quod relaxantur ei de dicta dimidia marca quatuor solidi et octo denarii, in recompensacionem minutarum decimarum quas consuevit percipere de terris que fuerunt Radulfi de Bosco, Rogeri de Bosco, Maghtildis de Bosco et Matill' que fuit mater Walteri de Wicha, quas terras omnes redegit dominus de Ockeburn' in dominicum suum.'

movement; but the balance of the evidence—the similarity of customs on manors about twenty miles apart subject to the same lord, and their difference from customs on the contiguous or neighbouring manors, the increase of labour services on some tenements, and the increase in the size of the demesne—is in favour of direct influence on manorial development and depression of the condition of the tenants by the lords of Bec. Ogbourne itself was one of the central manors, not infrequently a residence of the prior himself, and so supervision of the property there and at Deverill would have been comparatively easy. Good soil and a promising market, combined with the convenient situation of the manors, may have induced the lord and his steward to increase the area under direct cultivation at the period most favourable to demesne farming, and to do so at the cost of the customary tenants. Certainly there were at the time seven carucates of land in the demesne of Ogbourne St. George;[1] and as there seems to have been no large body of landless men in the manor, who might have provided a supply of hired labourers, the main burden of cultivation must have fallen on the customary tenants.[2]

The mid-thirteenth century was a period when the abbot was actively engaged in buying land, and this activity was not confined to any one part of the country. He bought pasture in Deverill worth 40*s*. in 1227,[3] later paying a further 40*s*. for the abbot of Glastonbury's claim in it;[4] and at the same period he acquired a virgate of land in Chisenbury and let it out at once to the former holder for 3*s*. annual rent.[5] Next year he added to his purchases a hide of land in Deverill for 100*s*.[6] There were other transactions at Cottisford in Oxfordshire, which brought to the abbot as his unquestioned right first 12 acres and half a hide, then 100 acres.[7] And in East Anglia he acquired 60 acres of land from Reginald of Wretham in 1240,[8] and in the custumal

1 MS. Add. 24316, f. 31 [32].

2 See *infra*, pp. 87 seqq., for a discussion of the place of wage labour in the manorial economy.

3 Feet of Fines, Wilts., case 250, 6/171.

4 Ibid., case 250, 8/50 (136).

5 Ibid., case 250, 70/195.

6 Ibid., case 250, 8/46 (124).

7 *Feet of Fines (1195–1291) Oxfordshire* (Oxfordshire Record Society, 1930), pp. 72, 76.

8 Feet of Fines, Norfolk, case 156, 67/842.

the donor was holding it from the abbey for an annual rent of 6*s*. 4*d*., boon-ploughings, and suit of court.[1] In 1255 he bought from Benedict of Blakenham a messuage and carucate of land in north Blakenham for the almost incredible sum of £300, and twenty-five years later he spent a further 50 marks to free it from homage and suit of court to the lord of the fee.[2] There were probably other transactions of which we have no record. It is not always possible to tell what use he made of the land. In two cases certainly the original tenant became the tenant of the abbey for an annual rent. In one case mentioned in the custumal, where Geoffrey Dubbel sold by charter all that he had in Bledlow to the abbot of Bec, his tenants remained the tenants of the abbey,[3] and so it is certain that the land was not drawn into the demesne. The abbot would in any case have been inclined to invest his profits in new purchases to consolidate his property; it is significant that he should still have considered purchases in England a wise investment.

This general and widespread buying up of lands and rents may not have affected the relation of the outlying manors, such as the East Anglian manors, to the group of which they formed a part. It is impossible to know what became of the substantial tenement bought from Benedict of Blakenham; possibly the expanding markets of the thirteenth century and the flourishing corn trade of East Anglia encouraged the prior of Ogbourne to increase the acreage of land under his own cultivation; possibly the former tillers of the soil merely transferred their rents and services from Benedict to the prior. In any case it appears that up to the time of making the custumal the prior of

[1] MS. Add. 24316, f. 59 [60]. This may be a disguised credit transaction.

[2] Feet of Fines, Suffolk, case 214, 24/13; case 215, 34/19.

[3] MS. Add. 24316, f. 67 [68]: 'Item sciendum quod Galfridus Dubbel vendidit per cartam suam ecclesie Beccensi quicquid habuit vel habere potuit in Bledel', exceptis dimidia acra terre cum quodam mesuagio, scilicet de Johanne Sparleng iij sol' redditus pro xij acris;

Item de Waltero Iuvene pro iij acris et dimidia terre xij den';

Item de Alano de Standene vj den' pro j mesuagio cum duabus acris terre et dimidia;

Item de Henrico Frith j den' pro parva grava;

Ita quod isti tenentes de cetero respondebunt abbati de Becco immediate et abbas respondebit capitalibus dominis de redditu ad eos pertinente unde omnes eschaete que poterunt evenire super illud feodum erunt dicti abbatis.'

Ogbourne had been interested in the East Anglian manors principally as a source of rent, and consequently his influence there, in contrast to his influence on the Wiltshire manors, showed itself most plainly in the very strong influence of local custom. Adequate knowledge of social conditions on each manor before it became a part of the Bec estates would help to explain local peculiarities of tenure.

Information about the other manors is too fragmentary to permit generalization about conditions. Ruislip, the manor which, like Ogbourne, was an important administrative centre, resembled Ogbourne in having a large demesne, and there too the custumal mentions four tenements drawn back into the demesne.[1] Also a later hand has added in the margin the names of tenants who had succeeded to holdings, and six times the entry is *dominus*.[2] There is only one version of the custumal, and consequently nothing can be known about changes in labour services; as they stand, however, they are potentially quite heavy. Half-hides and virgates owed 3 days week-work during the winter, and half-virgates 1½ days, but the lord could, if he preferred, take money rents; although there is no means of knowing which he habitually took, this would give him a reserve of about 5,600 winter works.

Of the smaller manors a large number were primarily pastoral. Combe, Quarley and Monxton (Hants), Chisenbury (Wilts.), Povington and Milburne (Dorset), Swyncombe (Oxon.), and Preston and Hooe (Sussex) all supported flocks of sheep, but some arable farming was practised in each. With the exception of Swyncombe, where labour services were almost as heavy as at Ogbourne,[3] most

1 MS. Add. 24316, ff. 4–4*v*: 'Terra Leonardi que solebat reddere xvij solidos vj denarios, et terra que fuit Arthuri capellani que solebat reddere x solidos, et terra Rogeri Malehere que solebat reddere iij solidos ix denarios, et terra Ricardi Brunman que solebat reddere tres solidos sunt in dominico in manu domini.'

2 Ibid., ff. 2*v*–3. There are two virgate and four half-virgate holdings.

3 Ibid., f. 13; *R.H.* ii. 757–8. The Hundred Rolls describe the tenants as *servi* holding each 8 acres, or two and a half virgates altogether; whereas the custumal calls them virgaters. Evidently the royal inquisitors were working with a standard virgate of 32 acres and the abbot with a unit of cultivation, whatever its size: at Swyncombe, where the wealth of the population was largely in sheep and each tenant might turn fifty sheep into the common pasture, it is not surprising to find the small pastoral virgate as the unit of measure. Cf. E. A. Kosminsky, 'The Hundred Rolls of 1279–80 as a Source for English Agrarian History', in *Economic History Review*, iii (1931–2), 33–5.

of these benefited from the lighter services characteristic of pastoral manors: at Preston only the virgaters owed week-work, while elsewhere cottars and sometimes half-virgaters owed from 1 to 3 days' winter week-work. It is clear that no simple formula will account for all local variations. Services on a pastoral manor might be heavy, as at Swyncombe; at Cottisford, Weedon Beck, Bledlow, and Atherstone we find primarily arable manors with very light labour services. At Weedon some of the cottars worked on Mondays throughout the winter; on the other manors there were no week-works at all. A small demesne and numerous tenants would in part account for this, but there was one other element in the manorial labour force that has to be taken into account on all the manors, though it is not always clearly separable from customary labour: the permanent manorial servants or *famuli*.

There are some essential agricultural tasks that demand constant, skilled, labour. Obviously large flocks and herds of every type must each have their own particular attendant, and shepherds especially have been permanent servants since long before the time of David. But ploughing is the backbone of agriculture, and it also is skilled work. It is no coincidence that Langland chose as his typical peasant Piers Plowman, and that Chaucer's 'trewe swynkere' was a ploughman too. Apart from the times of crisis in the agricultural year—hay and corn harvest and sheep-shearing—when the boon services of all customary tenants were demanded; apart from the special task of tending the demesne stock, two services were required continuously for many weeks at a time: ploughing and threshing. Threshing involved more risk to the persons of unskilled workmen than to the lord's property, and could be accomplished by the casual accumulation of labour services from a large body of tenants, or by the employment of bands of itinerant task labourers; ploughing demanded, in addition to the assistance of all the tenants at rush periods such as the short Lenten ploughing, the constant labour of a small body of experienced workmen. There can have been few manors that did not have their little core of demesne ploughs in the thirteenth century.

Shepherds, ploughmen, and other *famuli* were recruited in the main from two types of labour, customary and hired. Writers on manorial history have treated the *famuli* as landless men or customary tenants according to the area they were describing and the period under consideration. Thorold Rogers wrote of the farm-servants on Merton's manor of Cuxham (Oxon.) that they all had land and stock of their own;[1] Miss Page, on the other hand, believed the servants of Crowland abbey to be landless men; and certainly in the account rolls they received stipends, not acquittances of rent.[2] Vinogradoff has shown in passing the existence of both types in different places: the *carucarii* or *akermanni* of the Ramsey manors,[3] holding their land in return for the service of following the lord's plough; and the hired labourers whom he equates with the *anelipemen* of some Ely manors.[4] Sometimes both types of labour appear on one manor; at Crawley in Hampshire in 1257–8 six customary ploughmen received acquittances and two hired ploughmen wages.[5] The distinction was clearly recognized by the administrative officials: the Ramsey custumal for Shillington in Bedfordshire explicitly states that, although no one in the vill is obliged to go to the lord's plough to defend his land, any virgater or other who wishes on account of poverty to do so may drive the plough and receive wages like a hireling; but he must still defend his own land with work or rent in the usual way.[6]

If the work performed by these two types of servants was similar, their conditions were very different. On the one hand were hired labourers, men who could not support themselves on their own land and lived either in the *curia* of the manor or, more commonly, in cottages of their own or homes of villein tenants. In any case they were either fed

[1] *A History of Agriculture and Prices in England*, i. 18.

[2] *The Estates of Crowland Abbey*, pp. 104–5; Appendix, pp. 240, 255, and *passim*.

[3] *Villainage in England*, p. 147. The example drawn from Kent is doubtful, since it refers to *avermanni*, not *akermanni*. For Ramsey see also N. Neilson, *Economic Conditions on the Manors of Ramsey Abbey*, p. 32. Not all the Ramsey manors had customary ploughmen; there were none at Brancaster (Norfolk), though they existed at the other Norfolk manor of Ringstead. *Cartularium*, i. 408, 409.

[4] *Villainage in England*, pp. 213–14.

[5] Gras, *The Economic and Social History of an English Village*, pp. 222, 225.

[6] *Cartularium*, i. 473–4.

at the lord's table or given allowances of corn. On the other hand were customary tenants holding land of their own, who served the lord in return for a relaxation of rent and services, and whose land was sometimes ploughed by the lord's ploughs and weeded, like the demesne, by the service of the other customary tenants;[1] moreover, they owed the service as a condition of their tenure. An adequate study of the development and distribution of these two types of labour has yet to be made. It would begin with the varying sources of labour in the obscure pre-Conquest period,[2] consider the disappearance of the serf proper, so often attached to the manorial plough-team,[3] and then survey the factors determining the labour force of the twelfth and thirteenth centuries. Of these the three most important in any manor must have been the size of the demesne in the period when labour services were hardening; the function of the manor in providing cash or corn for the central household; and, perhaps most important of all, the existence or absence of an abundant supply of labour. If generalization at present would be tendentious, we may at least examine the influence of these three factors on conditions in the manors of Bec.

Analysis of the custumals shows the following customary servants on the manors:[4]

Ploughmen

Ogbourne St. George	Cottars holding 4 acres
Chisenbury	Cottars holding 5 acres
Combe	Half-virgaters
Monxton	Cottars or half-virgaters
Povington	Half-virgaters
Milburne	Virgaters or half-virgaters
Hungerford	Cottars
Brixton-Deverill	Half-virgaters
Bledlow	Half-virgaters of a special tenure

[1] Cf. King's College, Dd 33, m. 9 (Deverill), '. . . et debet . . . sarclare bladum domini et familie sue'.

[2] Cf. *Rectitudines Singularum Personarum*, in Liebermann, *Gesetze der Angelsachsen*, i. 448 seq.

[3] *V.C.H. Essex*, i. 361–3; Maitland, *Domesday Book and Beyond*, pp. 35–6.

[4] Smiths and millers are not included here. Their services were so closely bound up with their tenements—the forge or mill which they held of the lord—that their duties were governed by different principles.

Swineherds	
Ogbourne St. George	Cottar
Combe	Half-virgater
Shepherds	
Ogbourne St. George	Half-virgater
Chisenbury	Cottar
Quarley	Half-virgater
Monxton	Cottar
Combe	Half-virgater
Povington	Half-virgater
Milburne	Virgater or half-virgater
Hungerford	Cottar
Brixton-Deverill	Half-virgater
Swyncombe	Virgater
Preston	Virgater
Bledlow	Half-virgater of a special tenure
Cowherd	
Ogbourne St. George	One specified virgater
Foresters	
Ogbourne St. George	One specified half-virgater
Hungerford	Half-virgater or cottar
Bledlow	One specified half-virgater

One danger in dealing with these figures is immediately apparent: the line between the customary and other servants almost coincides with the line between the two custumals. It is possible that the questions were framed in such a way in the second inquisition that services of this kind were not mentioned by the presenters of customs. But against this must be weighed the facts that Swyncombe and Preston, which are not on the King's College rolls, had customary shepherds; Bledlow had a full complement of servants; and since the jurors of Lessingham described the duties of reeve and hayward, they would presumably have added the duties of any other manorial servants drawn from the customary tenants. On the other hand, there are no details of servants at Wantage and Ogbourne St. Andrew, which are in the western group.

The causes of the difference, then, cannot be explained so easily. Nor can they be explained by the hypothesis that the lord dispensed with the services of permanent *famuli* and relied on customary works; at Atherstone and Cottisford, and probably also at Weedon and Ruislip, the customary services were inadequate for the size of the demesne. And the lord's ploughs are mentioned incidentally in the customs of Lessingham and Ruislip.[1] The pipe roll shows that every manor enrolled had its staff of *famuli*;[2] furthermore, there are extensive lists of servants at Weedon, Ruislip, Cottisford, Blakenham, and Wretham at a later date. The royal inquest at Ruislip in 1294 mentions in the midst of household and administrative officials—doorkeeper, cook, baker, porter, carpenter, hayward, reeve and reeve of Northwood—a few agricultural servants: forester, gardener, cowherd, and swineherd.[3] And a list of the wages of servants for 1300–1 is copied into the custumal; although the first half has been obliterated by damp the legible section includes 8 ploughmen, 8 *fugatores*, 1 cowherd, 1 swineherd, and 2 shepherds; and the wage bill for regular servants amounted to £9. 10*s*. 8*d*. annually. Casual labour was additional; the autumn works required 2 pitchers, 2 collectors of tithe, and 2 stack-makers; and these, together with a boy to look after the goats, cost 14*s*. 2*d*.[4] There were less servants in the smaller manors, but at Weedon, for example, in 1324 the prior of Ogbourne employed annually a bailiff, 6 ploughmen (3 *tenatores* and 3 *fugatores*), 2 carters, a woodward and a hayward, a shepherd, a dairymaid, a cowherd, and a swineherd; and in the autumn a stack-maker, 2 pitchers, and 2 collectors of tithe. They required annually £4. 15*s*. 6*d*. in cash and 61 quarters 6 bushels of corn; and since the labour services of the customary tenants were extremely light they must have borne almost the whole weight of the agricultural labour.[5] Wages of *famuli* at Wretham, Blakenham, and Cottisford were regularly entered in the account rolls.[6]

1 MS. Add. 24316, f. 1*v* (Ruislip): 'Item herciare debet quotienscumque ei preceptum fuerit, ita quod quando caruce domini arare incipiunt herciare debet usque ad horam qua desinunt.' *Supra*, p. 44, n. 2, for Lessingham.

2 Eton, C 14. Liveries to the *famuli* occur in all the grange accounts except that of Blakenham, where the amount of corn used *in potagio domus* proves that a staff of farm servants was fed on the premises.

3 Exch. K.R., E. 106 2/1.

4 MS. Add. 24316, f. 6.

5 Exch. K.R., E. 106, 7/21.

6 *Infra*, pp. 97 seqq. for details.

The different methods of recruiting manorial servants must be explained, then, by different local conditions. It is not possible to divide the manors functionally; and with the reservation that some had to feed the prior of Ogbourne and his household, and that presumably Ogbourne and Ruislip where he most commonly resided bore the main burden, all were essentially cash manors. As regards size of the demesne certainly some manors where customary services were rigidly organized for large-scale cultivation had a staff of customary servants; Ogbourne and Brixton-Deverill are notable examples. The absence of servants of this type at Ogbourne St. Andrew may be explained by co-operation with the other Ogbourne; certainly one smith repaired the ploughs of both manors.[1] Their absence at Wantage is at present inexplicable: it was a small manor, but so were Hungerford and Milburne. In any case the size of the demesne in the twelfth century could not alone account for the variations; Ruislip, at one time a priory, was one of the most likely of all the manors to have been held in demesne, and its permanent servants were hired labourers. Here and elsewhere the local labour market seems to have been an influence of the highest importance;[2] in manors such as Ogbourne, where customary service was rigorously exacted, there must have been a labour shortage.

The superabundance of labour in East Anglia leaves no room for doubt. The surplus population, who already in the mid-thirteenth century went out to work for wages, may be glimpsed in the custumal. Landless men, like the *anelipemen* of the Ely manors, had settled in the cottages of the lord's tenants and, in common with the tenants' sons and daughters, were called out to work at the lord's boons as soon as they began to earn wages elsewhere, or sometimes as soon as they settled in the lord's fee.[3] This teeming

[1] King's College, Account Rolls of Ogbourne St. Andrew, *passim*.

[2] For the influence of local labour conditions on the demesne farming of St. Alban's abbey, cf. E. Miller, 'The Estates of the Abbey of St. Alban', in *The Saint Albans and Hertfordshire Architectural and Archaeological Society Transactions*, 1938, pp. 288–9.

[3] MS. Add. 24316, f. 56 [57] (Lessingham): 'Dicit iurat' quod omnes nativi sive native vel extranei commorantes infra socnam dominorum terram nec tenementa habentes tenentur singulis annis quamdiu fuerint sine tenemento unde communia servicia oriri debeant in autumpno per unum diem metere, vel unum

population of undersettlers began to come into its own at the time of the great pestilence; for in the court roll of 1350, 44 tenements fell vacant, and at least 38 were at once taken up, not always by a son or daughter. Until, and in some cases after, that date, the undersettlers must have supported themselves as hired labourers.

There is no evidence of this type of labourer in Ruislip, but there too was a very large population of men and women who could have lived only by hiring themselves to the lord or his more prosperous tenants; and their presence in the manor must have reduced the need for permanent customary servants and hastened the day of the hired labourer. These were the crofters, who held a messuage or an acre or two in return for rent and boon services, and their presence in large numbers is explained by the geography of the manor.[1] The open fields lay mainly south-east of the village; on the north-west side was the wooded park of Ruislip and beyond that the common. Assarting took place, and the park became in time almost completely surrounded on the sides away from the open fields by a little fringe of crofts. The proximity of the London market would help to keep prices high (it was almost certainly pushing up rents);[2] but even so the inhabitants of these tiny crofts could not have supported themselves on their own land,[3] and they must

denarium solvere, sed quamdiu filii vel filie sub patrum tecto commorantur et stipendium ultra x denarios non capiunt, quieti erunt de ista consuetudine, et si semel egredierint ad stipend' capiend', licet alias redierint, facient quousque feffati fuerint dictum servicium.' Ibid., f. 57*v* [58*v*] (Wretham): 'Et sciendum quod si idem Eustachius habuerit filium vel filiam vel qualecumque sue [do]micilio suo proprio per an[ ] sinendum infra manerium domini [ ] facere debent domino tria opera autumpnalia qualiacumque serviens voluerit et habere corredium, vel pro illis tribus operibus solvent unum denarium quod erit in electione domini. Et si huiusmodi familie semel predicto modo servierint in qualicumque loco in autumpno dum tamen soli fuerint et sine tenemento, eodem modo annuatim operabuntur, vel denarium solvent, ut predictum est.' Ibid., f. 58*v* [59*v*]: 'Et si aliquis sue advocacionis infra autumpnum egressus fuerit domum suam ad serviendum ut supradictum est, eodem modo operabitur vel denarium dabit.'

[1] This is illustrated by the 'Exact Map of the Demesne Lands in the Manor of Ruislip. . . . Surveyed and Map'd by John Doharty of Worcester, 1750' (King's College, P 28).

[2] Ruislip is the only manor where *incrementa novi redditus* are common in the court rolls. Extra rent was imposed when a tenement changed hands, and varied from ½*d.* to as much as 12*d.* per acre.

[3] The assarts were not held by the prosperous tenants; in the custumal the

have provided a very considerable reserve of labour for the manor.

On the type of person who followed the lord's ploughs at Weedon, Swyncombe, and Cottisford it is best to suspend judgement, though all had a large cottar population, and nowhere on the Bec estates have we definite evidence of farm servants living in the *curia* of the manor. Atherstone, however, occupied such a peculiar place among the lord's manors that it deserves attention. Situated on the Watling Street with a weekly market and a fair, it was a potential trading centre. Even in the mid-thirteenth century there were 13½ burgage tenements,[1] and in 1289 the abbot carried out a large-scale redistribution of property with a view to increasing the prosperity of the vill. Eighteen tenants received plots of land behind their houses. Seven others gave up their land along the Watling Street and around the place where the market was held; and of this land twelve new burgages were made.[2] There may have been a slight influx of new tenants and a division of burgages; in 1294 there were thirty-six free tenants on the manor.[3] The tenants of Atherstone were granted one pavage in 1319 and another in 1343,[4] but the place failed to thrive as a trading centre, perhaps because, as one writ granting pavage states, it was 'a market town which lies low, and in the winter time and in wet weather is dirty, whereby merchants and others with goods and wares come only in small numbers at such times'. The *Nonarum Inquisitiones* record that all the inhabitants lived by agriculture;[5] and in the extent of 1379, although the number of free tenants was not stated, the revenue of £6. 0*s*. 9*d*. received from them remained exactly the same as in 1294.[6] The burgage tenants may have acquired land in the common fields or had some means

virgaters and half-virgaters and the crofters were named, and they were different people.

[1] MS. Add. 24316, f. 50*v* [51*v*].

[2] King's College, C 9.

[3] Exch. K.R., E. 106 2/5.

[4] *C.P.R. 1317–21*, p. 327; *C.P.R. 1343–5*, p. 3.

[5] *Nonarum Inquisitiones*, p. 442.

[6] Exch. K.R., E. 106 11/5. This new evidence about the early history of Atherstone seems definitely to place it in the class of vills that had burgage tenements but never became boroughs during the middle ages. For a discussion of the status of Atherstone see *British Borough Charters, 1216–1307*, ed. A. Ballard and J. Tait (Cambridge, 1923), pp. l–li.

of livelihood unknown to the 1343 inquisitors, but there were also a number of cottagers even in the mid-thirteenth century, and it is possible that this abortive urban community, only partly able to support itself by trade, provided the labour force for the cultivation of the lord's demesne. In any case the demesne was sublet at an early date; by 1379 it was all in the hands of the tenants.[1]

The study of the influence of manor and group on the conditions of tenants in some of the manors, and on the type of labour employed to cultivate the demesne, has shown that pride of place must be given to local custom.

> 'These dispersed estates', wrote Miss Lees of the English property of the Templars, 'were brought into relation with one another as members of a highly centralized international organization, and administrative unity must have done something to obliterate economic diversity. All the more striking is the vitality of local characteristics under an external uniformity of government. . . . Were there many changes, it may be asked, when the Templars took over the lands in Warwickshire, Lincolnshire and Yorkshire, which Roger Mowbray . . . granted to them? Or was it the lords of the soil who changed while the tillers of the soil remained to carry on the old tradition? The persistence of local custom is a strong and abiding economic and social force.'[2]

The same general statement might be applied to the estates of the abbey of Bec; the prior of Ogbourne worked through English stewards, 'men of good family, with local connexions and interests, who would naturally manage their estates after the ordinary fashion of their neighbours, feudatories of the same class, with the same social training as themselves';[3] and the lowest grades of his hierarchy of English servants consisted of men of the manors brought up in the custom of the manor. And widely separated manors were bound to show fundamental differences in agricultural practice. In addition, the presence in any place of numbers of landless men ready to work for wages must have had a loosening effect on the organization of labour services, so that local social conditions no less than obvious differences of geography and geology must have helped to develop each of the

[1] Exch. K.R., E. 106 11/5.
[2] *Records of the Templars in England in the Twelfth Century*, pp. xxxvi–xxxvii.
[3] Ibid., p. xxxvii.

manors in its own individual mould. Nevertheless the abbot and his representatives had power to affect the growth of their manors, and there is no doubt that they used it. The depression of tenants on the Wiltshire manors, and the levelling of customs there is one good example; the attempt to foster a trading community at Atherstone, with the freedom that it brought to some of the tenants, is another. Where the demesne was large we shall not necessarily find oppression; it was large at Ruislip, and the lord reserved the right of exacting heavy labour services, but the hired labour that came to his hand must have reduced his need for regular week-work from all his customary tenants. On many of the manors it is not possible, through lack of evidence, to assess the relative importance of local practice and general policy; but in the main it seems that the abbot, up to the end of the thirteenth century, had been directly responsible for the increase of services on some of the central manors, leaving the outlying ones more readily to the gentle moulding of local custom.

III

THE FOURTEENTH CENTURY

THE approach of the economic historian to the fourteenth century has changed in the last three decades. Interest was at one time concentrated on the consequences of the Black Death, and the conditions before it were too easily taken for granted. A succession of scholars from Vinogradoff to Kosminsky[1] has, however, attempted to replace the cataclysmic view of the plague by a more careful examination of conditions extending over the whole fourteenth century. Unquestionably a catastrophe which swept away a large fraction of the population must have had deep and lasting consequences for agrarian development, but the consequences cannot be estimated until conditions before the plague are known. It seems that in many parts of England changes once attributed to the plague were beginning before it swept over the country in successive waves: marginal land was going out of cultivation, the land-hunger of the once overcrowded peasantry was being satisfied by grants of demesne land, and a scramble for land was taking place in which, in addition to humble men, prosperous villeins and free tenants, rising yeomen and aspiring knights of the shire took part; again, there were peasants' revolts on individual manors over eighty years before the great revolt of 1381. What changes then, it may be asked, can be seen taking place on the manors of Bec in the early fourteenth century?

For the estate as a whole no generalizations can be made. Occasionally the abbot leased a small portion of the demesne lands[2] or released a tenement from services due;[3] occasionally the services with which a villein tenement was

[1] Cf. Vinogradoff in *E.H.R.* xv. 779: 'The plague . . . was certainly a great crisis, but the important thing is to see how far existing economic conditions prepared or disqualified people from meeting it'; and E. A. Kosminsky, 'Services and Money Rents' in *Economic History Review*, vol. v (1935).

[2] e.g. *Select Pleas*, p. 33; *Court Rolls of Tooting Beck*, p. 247.

[3] e.g. Weedon, 1365 rental (Eton, B 11); Edward Bernard pays 4*d.* for a piece of 'Mundayland'; land which formerly owed works every Monday and no rent.

burdened made the occupation of it undesirable, and tenants made fine to be exempted from holding it.[1] But we cannot trace any general movement behind these isolated actions. And the royal extents of 1294 and 1324 are abbreviated and do not show which of the works whose value they assess were actually performed and which were sold. If any value is to be attached to their figures, the rents of customary tenants at Bledlow had been increased during these thirty years, and their services reduced.[2] Consequently attention must be confined to the few individual manors for which account rolls, rentals, or other records survive.

Among the manors where winter week-works were light or altogether absent Cottisford, Wretham, and Blakenham have all left a series of account rolls. Compared with the custumal, some customary labour had been abandoned on all the manors, even if there was little further change during the early part of the fourteenth century. At Wretham[3] from 1303 to 1338 the customary tenants still performed all ploughing services due and most of the autumn works, though half-day boons were sometimes remitted through the cost of food. Some weeding services were remitted for the same reason, the number performed varying from 93 to 46, and some mowing works were sold. All works due from the tenement of Attegrene were sold regularly for 5*s.* 'year by year, at the lord's will'. Task-workers were employed for threshing and cutting peat; the remainder of the work was done by the permanent *famuli.* They included 6 ploughmen, 2 of whom spent part of the year in other work, 3 shepherds of the lord's flocks, and 1 shepherd of the fold of the vill. During the period, although the same number of permanent servants was employed, there was a slight decline in the amount of land cultivated. Between 1303 and 1307 the number of acres sown varied from 295½ to 276; in 1307–8 it

[1] Combe, 1289 (King's College, C 9): 'Ricardus Shuphurde electus per curiam ad accipiendum dimidiam virgatam terre secundum consuetudinem manerii dat . . domino ut ad hoc non compellatur iij solidos. Johannes filius Alfredi eodem modo electus ad aliam dimidiam virgatam terre dat domino ut non compellatur ad hoc iij solidos.'

[2] The 1294 extent (Exch. K.R., E. 106, 2/1) values the rents of customary tenants at £11. 15*s.* 11½*d.*, and their works at £4. 6*s.* 1*d.*; the 1324 extent (ibid. 6/2) values rents at £13. 0*s.* 10*d.* and works at £2. 6*s.* 1*d.*

[3] Eton, A 20, Account Rolls.

was 266, and by 1336–9 it had fallen to a figure between 232 and 242. Probably some of the land was leased, for assized rents rose from £7. 8*s*. 5½*d*. in 1303–7 to £7. 15*s*. 9½*d*. in 1336–9; but since the big decline was in acres sown with oats, it is possible that some of the marginal land was going out of cultivation or being fallowed more frequently.

Crops grown at Wretham, 1303–8, 1336–9

Year	*Yield*	*Sown*	*Acres sown*	*Sold*	*Acres sown (all 4 crops)*
			RYE		
1303–4	122 q. 7 b.	34½ q.	134	40½ q.	279½
1304–5	117 q. 5½ b.	34½ q.	138	33 q.	287½
1305–6	133 q. 3½ b.	32 q.	128	72 q. 4 b.	295½
1306–7	103 q. 5 b.	33 q. 2 b.	133	38 q. 7½ b.	276
1307–8	93 q. 6 b.	35 q. 1 b.	120½	26 q. 7 b.	266
1336–7	102½ q.	31 q. 5 b.	126½	32 q. 5½ b.	242½
1337–8	99 q. 2 b.	28 q.	112	30 q. 1 b.	232
1338–9	96 q. 3 b.	32 q. 2 b.	129	30½ q.	*c.* 239½
			BARLEY		
1303–4	94 q. 6½ b.	33 q.	66	1½ b.	
1304–5	110 q. 1 b.	36 q.	72	..	
1305–6	98 q. 7 b.	38 q. 2 b.	76½	8 q. 7½ b.	
1306–7	76 q.	36½ q.	73	18 q. 2½ b.	
1307–8	114 q. 6 b.	32½ q.	65	14 q. 1 b.	
1336–7	70 q. 1 b.	34 q.	68	13 q.	
1337–8	61 q. 6 b.	31 q.	62	2 q. 5 b.	
1338–9	111 q. 5½ b.	32 q.	64	45 q.	
			OATS		
1303–4	97 q. 7 b.	37½ q.	75	..	
1304–5	88½ q.	35 q. 3 b.	70½	..	
1305–6	92 q.	41 q. 6 b.	83½	..	
1306–7	77 q. 1 b.	31 q. 7 b.	62½	1 q.	
1307–8	98 q. 6 b.	35 q. 3 b.	71½	16 q. 5 b.	
1336–7	55 q. 5 b.	19 q. 3 b.	38	4½ q.	
1337–8	72½ q.	26 q. 2 b.	52½	4 q.	
1338–9	64 q. 1 b.	20 q. 2 b.	40½	3½ q.	
			PEAS		
1303–4	9 q. 6 b.	1 q. 1 b.	4½	7 q. 7 b.	
1304–5	5 q. 2 b.	1 q. 6 b.	7	3½ q.	
1305–6	6 q.	1 q. 7 b.	7½	4 q. 1 b.	
1306–7	4 q. 6½ b.	1 q. 7 b.	7½	2 q. 5 b.	
1307–8	7 q. 7½ b.	2 q. 2 b.	9	4 q. 7½ b.	
1336–7	4 q.	1 q. 2 b.	10 (*sic*)	2 q. 5 b.	
1337–8	1½ q.	1 q. 3 b.	5½	1 b.	
1338–9	3½ q.	1 q. 6 b.	..	1 q. 5 b.	

At Cottisford[1] the details of customary labour are less precise since the works account is either missing from the roll or is summed up in one terse sentence: 'Of the ploughings and works he says that all the ploughings were used in cultivating the lord's land. And the works were expended in the lord's service within the court and outside it, by tallies between the reeve and the customary tenants.' Customary tenants still performed some weeding and mowing in addition to ploughing and harvest boons; in 1344–5 they were responsible for about 21 per cent. of the harvest work. As at Wretham there had been no winter week-works in the thirteenth century, but casual labour was employed for washing and shearing the sheep and some mowing and weeding as well as threshing. The number of *famuli* varied, for during the reign of Edward II there was a slackening in the activity of the manor: instead of 5 or 6 ploughmen and 3 shepherds, 3 or 4 ploughmen and 1 or 2 shepherds were employed; but by 1340 the conditions prevailing in the 1292 account roll had returned. Possibly part of the manor was let out during the central period, but certainly in 1340 the breakdown of demesne farming had not yet definitely begun.

Payments for Task Labour at Blakenham

Year	*Mowing*	*Weeding*	*Threshing*	*Harvest*	*Total*
	s. d.	*s. d.*	*£ s. d.*	*£ s. d.*	*£ s. d.*
1297–8	7 5	..	19 4	2 7 8	3 14 5
1298–9	11 3	..	7 6	2 12 4	3 11 1
1299–1300	7 8	..	6 3	(lost)	..
1300–1	9 3	..	19 9½	2 19 5	4 8 5½
1301–2	..	..	16 7½	2 11 5	3 8 0½
1302–3	8 7½	..	16 6	2 2 9	3 7 10½
1331–2	15 8	5 0	17 6¼	4 8 6	6 6 8¼
1332–3	18 6¾	3 3	1 5 2¾	6 3 0	8 10 0½
1334–5	14 0½	3 6	1 4 9¾	4 10 0	6 12 9¾
1335–6	(£1. 10*s*. with weeding)		1 4 10¼	6 8 4½	9 3 2¾
1336–7	£1. 3*s*. 8*d*. with weeding)		1 3 0	6 16 9½	9 3 5½
1337–8	13 9	4 10	1 3 3¼	4 5 5½	6 7 3¾
1338–9	16 5	5 8	1 14 9¼	3 18 1¼	6 14 11½
1347–8	8 1½	3 0	1 1 9¼	3 14 10½	5 7 8¾

[1] Eton, C 14, Account Rolls.

Blakenham shows the most interesting history.[1] There are two series of accounts, 1297–1303 and 1331–9; and one odd roll for 1347–8. The earlier series has no works account, but throughout the period the wages paid for labour are recorded.

Value of Works sold at Blakenham

Year	*Ploughing*	*Winter*	*Autumn*	*Carrying*
	s. d.	*s. d.*	*s. d.*	*s. d.*
1298–9	2 7	..	..	..
1299–1300	2 1	..	..	..
1300–1	..	3 0	..	1 3
1301–2	4 7	..	..	1 0
1302–3	4 4	3 10	18 0	5
1331–2	10 6	3 0	1 6	2
1332–3	10 6	4 6	..	2
1334–5	10 6	9 3	11 4	..
1335–6	6 6	4 0	2 5	..
1336–7	..	2 0	4 5	1 0
1337–8	6 0	15 0	5 0	..
1338–9	9 0	15 0	5 8	..
1347–8	No details given			

Rents and Farms at Blakenham

Year	*Assized rents*	*Farms*
	£ s. d.	*£ s. d.*
1297–8	7 11 1¾	..
1298–9	7 12 8¾	..
1299–1300	7 16 4¼	..
1300–1	7 13 3¼	..
1301–2	7 11 9¾	..
1302–3	7 12 3¼	..
1331–2	6 12 6¼	2 12 10½[2]
1332–3	6 8 7¼	3 9 4½
1334–5	6 9 3¾	4 1 8½
1335–6	6 9 3¾	4 4 4½
1336–7	6 9 3¾	4 4 4½
1337–8	6 9 2¾	4 4 4½
1338–9	6 9 2¾	4 1 8½
1347–8	4 14 2	4 0 10

[1] Eton, D 5, 8.

[2] The farm of the fulling mill is transferred from assized rents to farms in 1331–2.

Crops grown at Blakenham

Year	*Yield*	*Sown*	*Acres sown*	*Sold*
		WHEAT		
1294–5	51 q.	20 q.	..	25 q. 5 b.
1297–8	73 q. 4 b.	17 q. 1 b.	..	1 q. 3 b.
1298–9	39 q. 6 b.	13 q. 4 b.	..	20 q.
1299–1300	54 q. 3 b.	18 q. 5 b.	..	26 q. 4 b.
1300–1	57 q. 7 b.	18 q.	..	30 q. 3 b.
1301–2	45 q. 2 b.	14 q. 2 b.	..	25 q.
1302–3	49 q. 6 b.	18 q. 2 b.	..	26 q. 1 b.
1331–2	17 q. 5 b.	10 q.	40	..
1332–3	23 q. 6 b.	15 q. 1 b.	60½	1 q. 2 b.
1334–5	30 q. 5 b.	12 q. 2 b.	49	4 q. 4 b.
1335–6	30 q. 2 b.	18½ q.	74	10 q. 7 b.
1336–7	30½ q.	14 q. 7 b.	60	14 q. 5 b.
1337–8	38 q. 6 b.	15 q. 7 b.	64	21 q. 7 b.
1338–9	57 q. 1 b.	17½ q.	70	37 q. 2 b.
		RYE		
1294–5	62 q. 7 b.	16 q.	..	6½ q.
1297–8	47 q. 4 b.	15 q.	..	..
1298–9	52 q. 5 b.	15 q. 6 b.	..	..
1299–1300	49 q. 4 b.	16 q.	..	..
1300–1	50 q.	13½ q.	..	1 q. 6 b.
1301–2	48 q. 5 b.	13 q.	..	..
1302–3	47 q. 7½ b.	13 q. 7 b.	..	..
1331–2	33 q. 6 b.	12 q. 1 b.	48½	6½ q.
1332–3	34½ q.	10½ q.	42	10 q. 4½ b.
1334–5	35 q. 2 b.	12 q. 3 b.	49½	8 q. 1 b.
1335–6	33 q. 3 b.	17 q. 2 b.	69	4 q.
1336–7	29 q. 2 b.	8 q. 7½ b.	35½	3 q. 3½ b.
1337–8	30 q. 6½ b.	7½ q.	47½	2 q.
1338–9	35 q. 4½ b.	12 q. 7 b.	51	3½ q.
		BARLEY		
1294–5	63 q. 3 b.	17 q. 5 b.	..	45 q. 4 b.
1297–8	47 q.	18 q. 4 b.	..	29 q.
1298–9	53 q. 2 b.	23 q. 2 b.	..	30 q.
1299–1300	61 q. 3 b.	20 q. 3 b.	..	41 q.
1300–1	42 q. 2 b.	19½ q.	..	22 q. 6 b.
1301–2	56 q. 2 b.	22 q.	..	34 q. 2 b.
1302–3	63 q. 7 b.	22 q. 6 b.	..	41 q. 1 b.
1331–2	27 q.	20 q.	41	..
1332–3	55 q. 5 b.	20 q. 7 b.	42	..
1334–5	32 q. 6 b.	21 q. 1 b.	44½	11½ q.
1335–6	43 q. 6 b.	18 q. 1½ b.	37	25 q. 3½ b.
1336–7	36 q. 6 b.	19 q. 6 b.	39½	17 q.
1337–8	38 q. 1 b.	15 q. 6 b.	31½	22 q. 3 b.
1338–9	65 q. 2½ b.	19 q. ½ b.	38	46 q. 2 b.

Year	*Yield*	*Sown*	*Acres sown*	*Sold*	*Acres sown (all 5 crops)*
		OATS			
1294–5	44 q. 3 b.	21 q. 7 b.	..	1 q.	..
1297–8	40 q. 4 b.	34 q. 2 b.	..	..	..
1298–9	45 q. 1 b.	34 q. 5 b.	..	1½ q.	..
1299–1300	35 q. 4 b.	28 q. 4 b.	..	..	..
1300–1	57 q. 2 b.	34 q. 6 b.	..	..	c. 248[1]
1301–2	51 q. 2 b.	35 q.	..	9 q.	..
1302–3	37 q. 5 b.	28 q. 1 b.	..	..	..
1331–2	28 q. 1 b.	16 q.	37	..	171
1332–3	32 q. 4½ b.	20 q. 2 b.	46 1r.	..	163 1 r.
1334–5	32 q. 5 b.	21½ q.	47	..	187½
1335–6	42 q. 1 b.	22 q. 3 b.	49½	..	235½
1336–7	45 q.	28 q. 5 b.	68	2 q.	208
1337–8	40 q. 4½ b.	18 q. 7½ b.	41	5½ q.	190½
1338–9	37 q. 1½ b.	22 q.	50	..	214
		PEAS			
1294–5	8 q. 6 b.	1 q. 4 b.	..	5 q. 6 b.	
1297–8	..	..	..	..	
1298–9	1 q. 1 b.	1 q. 1 b.	..	..	
1299–1300	5 q. 3 b.	1 q. 7 b.	..	3 q. 4 b.	
1300–1	9 q. 7 b.	3 q. 3 b.	..	6 q. 4 b.	
1301–2	9 q. 4 b.	1½ q.	..	8 q.	
1302–3	4 q. 6 b.	3 q.	..	1 q. 6 b.	
1331–2	2 q.	1 q. 1 b.	4½	6 b.	
1332–3	1 q. 3 b.	1 q.	4	1 b.	
1334–5	6 q. 3 b.	1 q. 7 b.	7½	4½ q.	
1335–6	5 q. 4 b.	1½ q.	6	3 q. 7 b.	
1336–7	1½ q.	1 q. 2 b.	5	2 b.	
1337–8	4 q. 2 b.	1 q. 5 b.	6½	2 q. 5 b.	
1338–9	5 q. 5 b.	1 q. 2 b.	5	3 q. 5 b.	

Between 1303 and 1331 the wages paid rose sharply by very nearly 100 per cent., and the wages of the permanent farm-servants too were increased from about 14*s*. to 30*s*. If slightly higher wages were being paid, they would not account for so sudden a change. An increase in the number of works sold annually helps to bridge the gap, and certainly accounts for the appearance of weeding in the wage bill; but these works, including ploughing, were almost always less than £1. 10*s*. in value. The corn account shows

[1] Acres sown with each crop are not stated before 1331; but a note at the foot of the 1300–1 account gives an estimate of the number of acres sown that year.

that there was actually a decrease in the acreage under cultivation. On the whole the most convincing explanation is the disappearance of regular week-works. Ten tenements had owed them in the mid-thirteenth century; by 1331 the number had been reduced to 5 and afterwards to 4½, and 2 or 3 of these were always in the lord's hand. In one case the details of the change are clear. The works accounts regularly note the lapse of works 'in default of the tenement of J. Caudesce, because it is in the lord's hand'; and the 1334-5 receipts for *firme terre* include 13*s.* 4*d.* for this same tenement. Whereas assized rents remain roughly the same, *firme terre* is a new item beginning in 1331 and amounting to between 50*s.* and £3 (excluding the farm of the fulling-mill). Very probably, then, the tenements burdened with week-work had lapsed one by one into the lord's hand and been let out again—possibly to a member of the same family—for an increased money rent; and the process had taken place chiefly in the first quarter of the fourteenth century. As at Wretham there was a perceptible decline in the amount of demesne land under cultivation: it had been 248 acres in 1300–1, dropped to 163 acres in 1332–3, rose again to 235½ acres, and then declined to a figure in the neighbourhood of 210 acres: the various types of grain, however, were still sown in roughly the same proportions. Probably the item *firme terre* included some leases of demesne, as well as customary, land.

In all three manors two obvious changes were taking place. All could draw upon an abundant supply of both regular and task labour; their organization was independent of their customary tenants, and so the minor, supplementary source of customary labour was gradually drying up, though with varying speed on the different manors. Secondly the cultivation of the demesne was beginning to become less vigorous; the decline was steady and marked at Wretham and Blakenham, and at Cottisford alone a revival appears to have begun about 1340.

Of the manors principally dependent on customary labour, Combe alone has satisfactory accounts, for 1306–18, and these may be compared with the custumal. Here the half-virgaters had been the workmen, though the lord might, if he wished, take rent instead; and the same class provided the *famuli*. There were 16 according to the 1324 extent,[1] and most of them worked either as permanent servants or as *operarii*; apart from the reeve and smith, who were virgaters, 6 ploughmen, 1 shepherd of the wethers, and 1 swineherd were drawn from the half-virgaters.[2] In addition the lord employed as hired labourers a hayward, a carter, and a shepherd of the ewes at 5*s*. each; 2 keepers of the oxen and 1 daye at 4*s*. each; 1 swineherd at 3*s*. 6*d*.; and 1 cowherd and 1 bedel, each at 3*s*.; and these did not include the task workers hired for harvest, threshing, and some weeding. Consequently, not all the works of the *operarii* were required; apart from the boon-ploughing they performed no ploughing services at all; and between a third and a quarter of the works were sold every year.[3] The service of malting had certainly been commuted for a total sum of 14*d*. which appears annually under the exits of the manor. In general the conditions revealed in the custumal had not undergone any radical change; the manor was then, as before, cultivated principally by customary labour, but wage labour was making its appearance, and possibly this was responsible for the regular annual sale of some works.

The accounts of Ogbourne St. Andrew illustrate only abnormal conditions. In both Ogbournes continuous repression was punctuated by intermittent rebellion, and the tenants opposed the abbot by every legal device open to them and, law failing, by undisguised violence. We have

[1] Exch. K.R., E. 106, 8/9.

[2] The following entry occurs regularly under acquittances of rent: 'In acquietanc' redditus ipsius prepositi et j fabri qui sunt virgatarii, x *s*. In acquietanc' vj carucariorum, j custodis multonum et j porcarii qui sunt semi-virgatarii per annum xxxij *s*. cuiuslibet iiij *s*. Et in acquietanc' viij semivirgatariorum . . . operancium per annum xxxij *s*.' From 1314 to 1316, however, the services of the half-virgaters were not required, and in 1316–17 the number of ploughmen fell to five.

[3] Analysis of the works account in a typical year (1316–17) gives the following result: Works owed, 1,578. Performed in spreading manure 66, in collecting manure 26; in gathering thatch 30; in making hurdles 23; in making a large straw stack 102; in weeding 62 acres of bere, 80 acres of barley, and 64 acres of oats 200; in enclosing part of the wood and garden 50; in making hurdles 8; in treating sheep 112; in carting manure 32; in reaping 337. Sold 408; excused on feast days and other holidays 184.

seen that there was evidence of depression of tenants before the middle of the thirteenth century; we do not know if they accepted their new burdens without question or by what methods they may have resisted them. But the history of their opposition during the fourteenth century is worth recounting at length as an example of a thoroughly organized peasant revolt. The struggle began legally with a claim to ancient demesne, possibly encouraged by the success with which the tenants of Steventon had maintained their status as sokemen of the demesne in 1288.[1] Some time before 1309[2] four tenants of Ogbourne brought a writ against the abbot which he refused to answer because they were his villeins: in the Hilary term, 1312, two more writs were brought against him. Twenty-two tenants supported the first but did not follow it up; Walter Wyche, Richard White, William Chichely, and Henry Richard, the four men who had begun proceedings before, initiated the second writ and stated their grievances fully. They claimed that their ancestors had been sokemen of the ancient demesne and had held each virgate for *5s. 10d. wodegavel* at Hokeday and two suits of court; and that the abbot of Bec had depressed their condition and compelled them to perform all kinds of villein services, including winter work for three days a week.[3] The evidence of Domesday, however, proved that Ogbourne had belonged to Miles Crispin, not to the king, and the abbot showed his displeasure by confiscating the lands of one or two of the offending villeins.[4]

[1] *Abbreviatio Placitorum*, pp. 198, 200, 205; Westminster, Dean and Chapter Muniments, no. 7301.

[2] P.R.O. Plea Rolls, K.B. 27/207, rot. 82: 'Et predictus abbas dicit quod predicti Walterus et alii alias in curia domini regis coram Radulpho de Hengham et sociis suis iusticiariis de Banco anno etc. tulerunt consimile breve versus predictum abbatem. . . .' Hengham died in 1309.

[3] Ibid.: 'Quod idem abbas et predecessores sui iniuste induxit ipsos per suas graves districciones ad faciendum villana servicia, scilicet operari in septimana per tres dies a festo Sancti Michaelis usque ad festum Sancti Petri ad Vincula, et falcare pratum et metere cotidie tempore messionis unam acram bladi vel dare per diem tres denarios et obolum, et cariagia facere pro voluntate sua, arare unam acram terre ad semen yemale et unam acram ad semen quadragesimale, talliare ipsos alto et basso, et marchetum facere pro filiabus suis maritandis, et ad voluntatem suam prepositos facere, et ad multa alia villana servicia faciendum.'

[4] King's College, C 13 (26 June 1312): 'Robertus Bonde reddit in manus domini terras et tenementa sua ac bona sua et catalla omnia et singula in gracia domini, ut forisfacta causa placiti in curia domini regis contra dominum prosecuti.

The opportunity of the men of Ogbourne came in 1327. It was a year of political upheaval and civil strife, which saw the revolt of the men of St. Albans, St. Edmundsbury, and other towns. It happened that there was a break in the administration of the estates of Bec in England, for Gilbert of Saint-Étienne died on 24 August and the estates were taken into the king's hand; when Richard de Beauseville was given the custody of the temporalities his servants were impeded in the exercise of their duties by the tenants of Great and Little Ogbourne. The men of these vills then formed a conspiracy to aid in resisting, supported, it was alleged, by a common purse for which they collected large sums.[1] A petition by the abbot of Bec led to an inquisition which declared the men to be his villeins;[2] but the tenants continued to withhold rents and services and were supported, it seems, by Hildebrand of London, knight, and John Strympel of Hungerford: when a second commission was appointed to inquire into the conspiracy these two men 'assaulted some of the king's ministers while preparing jury panels for the session, and other ministers as well as the jurors set upon the panels, so that they dared not proceed in the matter'.[3] What causes led one of the lesser gentry to support a body of discontented villeins we do not know. The outcome was almost wholly to the disadvantage of the rebels; many were fined and left in gaol pending payment,[4] and the abbot's men, if the villeins are to be believed, took savage vengeance.[5] Concurrently with their violent resistance

Postea venit predictus Robertus et dat domino de fine pro predictis terris, bonis et catallis rehabendis xl solidos. . . . Et idem Robertus submittit se gracie domini de arreragiis reddituum et serviciorum a retro existent' per plevinam predictam.' 'Walterus Wylemot prepositus de magna Okeburn' seisitus est uno mesuagio et una dimidia virgata terre que tenuit Galfridus Turyg. Et dat domino de fine . . . lx *s*. Et faciet omnia servicia. . . .' Geoffrey Turyg was one of the tenants who had been concerned in the first suit, and this looks like the conveyance of confiscated territory to a loyal reeve.

[1] *C.P.R. 1330–4*, pp. 299, 347.

[2] *Cal. Misc. Inq.* ii, no. 1269; Ancient Petitions, S.C. 8, 164/8157.

[3] *C.P.R. 1330–4*, p. 501; Ancient Petitions, S.C. 8, 239/11950.

[4] *C.F.R.* iv. 383–4.

[5] Ancient Petitions, S.C. 8, 3133: 'A nostre seignur le Roy e a soun counsayll monstrent les poveres gentz de Okeburn' que le . . . abbe le Bekeherlewyn les travayle tortenousement en dyvers maneres, ceo est asaver par prisonnement en dyvers lues . . . e auxi quant les tenauntz de la dit vile ount este mortz il ad fait abater lour mesounes e seysi lour terre en sa mayn demayne issint q' lour heyres ne pount ioier

they brought, at Easter 1332, yet another suit against the abbot claiming ancient demesne;[1] and it seems to have been at their prompting that an investigation was made into the withdrawal of alms at Ogbourne.[2] Failure did not discourage them; in 1341 and again in 1416 they tried to claim ancient demesne, and the entry in Domesday Book had to be explained to them;[3] and they formed another confederacy in 1389.[4]

There was a period of upheaval in the economy of the manor, and the account rolls reflect it. We find the bailiff of Ogbourne St. Andrew paying in 1333–4 £4. 7*s*. 10½*d*. for threshing and winnowing and £12. 8*s*. 2*d*. for autumn works;[5] and in 1332–3 the value of the works 'sold' soared to £15. 4*s*. 3*d*.[6] From the time the rolls begin, however, he was able to levy money rents; it was the labour services that were lost through the imprisonment of so many of the tenants. Order was gradually restored, and by 1341 even the hardened rebels like William Hore seem to have settled down to their established tasks and to be carrying on once more the normal business of any villein tenant in the manorial courts.[7] During the period of upheaval the abbot had transplanted at least one tenant from another manor; there exists an indenture drawn up and sealed between the prior of Ogbourne and John Guylot of Ruislip, who received a messuage and a virgate in Ogbourne St. Andrew. The services were copied word for word from the custumal of a hundred years earlier, and the document

les ditz tenementz cum lour auncestres ount touziours fait du temps dount memoyr ne court, et il ad fait occire Walter le Vynour de mesme la vile e plusours altres gentz malement naffrer, e pus lour endita de conspiracy e de counfederacy, pur quoi il furunt amercyez devaunt jousticy nostre seignur le Roy. . . .' Their complaints led to the establishment of a royal commission in July 1334 (*C.P.R. 1330–4*, p. 583).

[1] P.R.O. Plea Rolls, K.B. 27/288, rot. 73.

[2] Ancient Petitions, S.C. 8, 3133: 'Le dit . . Abbe a detenue ces xxx auntz e plus les aumouns qe furent dones pur notre seignur le Roy e pur ses auncestors, chescun semayn iiij iours payn et troys iours blee a ceaux qe vodrait venyr le aumoigne ressayver, cum ad este trove par leur enquest devant Robert Selman e ses cumpaignouns.' See also *Rot. Parl.* ii. 76 *b*.

[3] *C.P.R. 1340–3*, p. 231; *C.P.R. 1416–22*, p. 50.

[4] *C.P.R. 1388–92*, p. 53.

[5] King's College, Account Rolls, m. 2.

[6] Ibid., m. 1. Unfortunately the rolls cannot be taken as a guide to normal conditions.

[7] King's College, C 20.

ended with a recognition that if any of the services were withheld the prior might take into his hands the tenement and any chattels found upon it.[1] It may have been an attempt to establish the ancient services on a more reliable basis, rather a general declaration of right than an exact guide to the services habitually required at that date; but if any reliance can be placed on the statements at law of the tenants of Ogbourne, the abbot was in fact trying to exact all the traditional services recorded in the custumal. John Guylot took root at Ogbourne, and in 1349 he came into another half-virgate after the death of the former occupant.[2]

This was not the only rebellion on the Bec manors. At Weedon and Hooe in 1297 there had been resistance to the abbot's servants, and again the rebels seem to have had the support of influential neighbours.[3] The rebellion at Weedon is explained more satisfactorily by the court rolls than the custumal. The virgaters and half-virgaters who supported it defended their tenements mainly by rents and performed only occasional light services, but the entry fines charged for taking up tenements were frequently extortionate[4] and could be made an instrument of real oppression. Probably a desire to escape from burdens of this kind made them put forward a claim to be free men[5] and refuse their services. The revolt evidently failed, for a rental drawn up shortly afterwards shows that the land of rebels had been confiscated and was gradually being redeemed for the payment

[1] King's College, Dd 30.

[2] King's College, C 22.

[3] Ancient Petitions, S.C. 8, E 959: 'A nostre seyngnur le Roy e a soun consayl monstre le priur de Okeburn' q' kant ce terres e ce tenementz furent prins en la mayn le Roy a comencement de la guerre entre ly e le roy de Franc, cez tenanz de son maner de Ho en le conte de Sussex, et de son maner de Wedon en le conte de Norhampton' ky de luy tyndreynt en vilenage e paysiblement aveent fet a ly e a ce predecessors dount memorie ne court custumes vilaynes e services ieqes a tant q' nostre seingnur le Roy bailla les avant diz maners ensemblement ove ces autre terres a lavauntdit priur, rendant par an certene estente, e dount il ad rendu toteners pus lees estente dez avant dit maners aucy byen come de ces autre terres, lez avant dit tenanz toiors pus ount retenu et dedit lour custumes e lour services e ne sustreent estre iusticez par ades q' eus unt de genz de pors e de autrez dont cez bailiffs ne sunt si ardy de eus destrendre ne court ilekey teneyr, dount il prie remedie e ayde . . . de ceste choses.'

[4] £2. 13*s*. 4*d*. was a common fine for entry to half a virgate, and fines were sometimes much higher (King's College, Court Rolls, *passim*). In 1288–9 the profits of the court amounted to £55. 14*s*. 7*d*. (*supra*, p. 45).

[5] *C.P.R. 1292–1301*, pp. 462–4.

of a higher rent or let to others.[1] One tenant only, John Brockhall, achieved a small success. He had refused services and removed his goods and chattels out of the lord's fee, claiming to be a free man; and though he was found by a jury to be the abbot's villein, the court awarded him 40*s.* damages because the abbot's bailiffs had thrashed him grievously, 'against the King's peace'.[2]

John Brockhall himself is typical of a class of prosperous peasantry that was gradually building up a small property within the manorial framework, often at the expense of their weaker neighbours rather than of the lord himself. Their history can be traced through the custumal and rentals of Weedon.[3] Outwardly the rent-collector would have noticed comparatively little change between the mid-thirteenth and mid-fourteenth centuries apart from one initial rise: £16. 12*s.* 10*d.* was due in the 1240's; in 1288–9 £17. 6*s.* 10*d.* was collected; by 1304–5 there had been an abrupt rise over the period of the rebellion to £19. 6*s.* 5*d.*, but from that time there was very little change up to 1365; some rents fell, but more land was leased. Actually, however, a very considerable change in the distribution of property and wealth had taken place. When the custumal was made most of the tenants held virgates or half-virgates, and there was also a small cottar class; by the beginning of the fourteenth century the population had risen from 81 to 110 with the result that holdings were being divided, and though a few families were accumulating fractions of tenements, far more held half or quarter virgates. By 1365, when the next rental

[1] Eton, B 11, undated rental: 'Petrus Leytard tenet dimidiam virgatam terre et unum mesuagium, et reddit domino ij *s.* vj *d.* In manu domini quia implacitavit dominum priorem.' 'Nicholas Nouweys tenuit mesuagium et dimidiam virgatam terre, et reddidit domino ij *s.* vj *d.* et est in manu domini quia implacitavit dominum priorem, et postea venit Emma que fuit uxor predicti Nicholai et finem fecit cum domino tenend' dictam dimidiam virgatam terre ad terminum vite sue, reddendo per annum v *s.* et faciendo inde servicia et consuetudines que facere prius consuevit, quia ballivus locavit dictam pro v *s.*' 'Johannes Caretarius tenet dimidiam virgatam et reddit domino ij *s.* vj *d.* que est in manu domini quia dictus Johannes implacitavit dominum. Item Emma relicta Willelmi Carectarii tenet dimidiam virgatam terre in dotem et reddit domino ij *s.* vj *d.* de dicta dimidia virgata, et est in manu domini quia prosecuta est dominum, et postea dicta terra vend' per dominum Johanni Donekan pro v marcis.'

[2] P.R.O. Plea Rolls, K.B. 27/169, rot. 13 *v.*

[3] Eton, B 11 includes two rentals, one of *c.* 1300 and the other of 1365.

was made, more tenant land was under cultivation; though the number of virgates—often considerably subdivided—was about the same, there were far more small crofts of a few acres. Probably the demesne was being leased; assarting would scarcely have taken place whilst the population was declining, and the number of tenants had fallen to 73. This meant, however, instead of more abundant land all round that some families had acquired considerable property, and the proportion of small cottars—a kind of rural proletariat—was slightly greater than before.

Rents paid at Weedon Beck

	c. 1248		*c. 1300*		*1365*	
Rent Paid	*No. of tenants*	*Per cent.*	*No. of tenants*	*Per cent.*	*No. of tenants*	*Per cent.*
Over £1	..	..	..	..	2	2·7
15*s.* to £1	..	..	..	..	1	1·4
10*s.* to 14*s.* 11*d.*	3	3·7	4	3·6	7	9·6
5*s.* to 9*s.* 11*d.*	46	56·8	33	30·0	26	35·6
2*s.* 6*d.* to 4*s.* 11*d.*	15	18·5	26	23·6	8	10·95
1*s.* to 2*s.* 5*d.*	7	8·6	18	16·4	8	10·95
Under 1*s.*	1	1·2	19	17·3	18	24·65
Works only	9	11·1	7	6·4	3	4·1
Hens	..	..	3	2·7	..	..
TOTAL	81	..	110	..	73	..

Not all these people were old tenants. Out of 61 families only 27 can definitely be traced back, 11 to the beginning of the century only and 16 to the earliest custumal. Even if some surnames had changed there must have been a considerable influx to account for the 34 new names: were they, it may be asked, once landless men beginning to establish themselves in a partly depopulated village, or tenants of lords in neighbouring villages extending their property, or entirely new settlers? and the question must, for the present, be left unanswered. They represent almost every class of the peasantry, from cottars paying a few pence to tenants of several virgates or large crofts. Extremes of wealth and poverty were apparent amongst the old tenants too; a few small-holders plodded on in the same humble way as before, and one or two once prosperous families were represented by a single cottar, possibly of the 'povre wydwe' type: the majority, however, accumulated more land. Of the 27 old families 19 definitely enlarged their holdings during the period, and the 3 tenants who held most land and paid the highest rents in 1365 were all descended from virgaters of the mid-thirteenth century. One of them bore the name of Brockhall.

Peasant Families in Weedon Beck

Name	*Holding c. 1248*	*Holding c. 1300*	*Holding c. 1365*
Godfrey	1 virgate (rent 5*s.*)	1 virgate, 1 curtilage, 1 cotland (rent 5*s.* 9*d.*)	3½ virgates, 3½ acres, ½ rood and meadow (rent 18*s.* 10½*d.*)
Bernard	1 virgate (rent 5*s.*)	2 virgates, 1 virgate less a messuage and 3 acres (rent 13*s.*)	3½ virgates, 2 quarter virgates, 1½ acres, ¼ cotland alone; 1½ virgates 1 cotland conjointly (rent £1. 2*s.* 4*d.*)
Brockhall	2 virgates (rent 10*s.*)	2½ virgates, 1 placea, 1 acre (rent 13*s.* 7*d.*)	3½ virgates, 2½ acres, 1 quarter-virgate, 1 cotland and meadow (rent £1. 2*s.* 2*d.*)

A fourth family, named Brother, was establishing itself. One member had held a virgate *c.* 1248, and in 1365 there were three members all holding at least a virgate; by 1439 John Brother was farmer of the demesne land of the manor for £45 annually,[1] and in 1447–8, after it had passed into the hands of the provost and fellows of Eton, William and Richard Brother farmed the demesne for £40.[2]

In many ways it is impossible to pronounce definitely upon social changes on the estates of Bec during the fourteenth century. The manors were not built on any one pattern during the thirteenth century, and later each developed after its own individual fashion. But existing records for a few manors show here and there land going out of cultivation, the population declining, customary services dwindling on manors where they had never been very strong and showing more tenacity where they had long been an integral part of the manorial economy, peasants organizing conspiracy and rebellion on widely different manors. And all these changes were in progress before the first outbreak of the Black Death; indeed most of the record sources dry up

[1] Ministers' Accounts, S.C. 6, 949/14.
[2] Eton, B 11, 1447–8 Account Roll.

after the middle of the century, and a single account roll for Cottisford in 1360 begins with the statement that no accounts have been kept for many years.[1] It is impossible to gauge even roughly the effects of the plague But from the redistribution of land in the earlier period one fact is clear: the manors were producing a class of men ready to take over the farming of the demesne land or the whole manor when the lord should abandon it to them. Sometimes, as we shall see later, they became administrative servants of the abbot, and their twofold training—by their upbringing as cultivators of the soil, and by their employment as manorial administrators—fitted them to undertake on their own behalf the farming of the manor where they lived and held their land. Further, the stock and land lease provided the enterprising tenant with a means of farming without an outlay of capital beyond his resources.

Administrative changes too can be clearly discerned: demesne farming was gradually giving way to the leasing out of manors and the collection of rents. On the estates of Bec, as was normal, the primarily cash manors with small demesne lands went first;[2] the movement had begun in 1323 and during the century stock and land leases, interspersed with occasional long-term leases, rapidly succeeded one another on an increasing number of manors. Although some of the manors, including Ruislip, were held in demesne until the end of the century, we have record of the following leases:

Manor	*Date*	*Lessee*	*Rent*	*Term*
Dunton	1322	Thomas of Bardfield	£20	6 years[3]
"	1341	Simon of Barking, goldsmith	£22	6 years[4]
"	1351	John Tyrel	£18	9 years[5]
"	1361	Thomas and Alice Tyrel	..	Life[6]
"	1393	John and Elizabeth Pykenham	..	Life[7]

1 Eton, C 14.

2 Cf. J. Thorold Rogers, *A History of Agriculture and Prices*, p. 25.

3 Exch. K.R., E 106, 7/3.

4 *C.P.R. 1340–3*, p. 234

5 King's College, M 2, M 3.

6 King's College, M 7; *C.Cl.R. 1392–6*, p. 481.

7 The reversion of the manor after the death of Alice Tyrel was granted in 1379 (ibid.), and John Pykenham held his first court in 1393 (King's College, M 8).

Manor	*Date*	*Lessee*	*Rent*	*Term*
Bledlow	1323	James Freysel	£80	4 years[1]
"	1326	" "	£60	7 years[2]
"	1336	" "	£60	6 years[3]
Tooting	1323	William Roce	20 marks	9 years[4]
"	*ante* 1347	Henry Ingleby	..	10 years[5]
"	*ante* 1359	Sir David Wollore	..	..[6]
"	1394	The prior of Merton	..	..[7]
Lessingham	1332	Edmund and Roger of Lessingham	..	..[8]
"	1368	Robert Crispin of Hapesbourgh	53 marks	7 years[9]
"	1387	Edward and Margaret Metteleye	£20	Life[10]
Blakenham	1343	John Broughton	£20	6 years[11]
"	1356	John Mabbe of Tilbury	..	7 years[12]
Atherstone	1344	Abbot of Merevale	..	..[13]
Weedon	1353	William Combe of Chyselden	£50 first, £60 later years	6 years[14]
"	1356	John Chesterton and John Bodecote	..	..[15]
"	1369	John Newenham, dean of Wolverhampton, Thomas West, parson of Sketon and John Leyre, parson of Doddington	£45	9 years[16]
Preston and Glynde rectory	1374	Robert Gosselyn and Robert Gardiner	£58	9 years[17]
Povington and Milburne	1380	William Chyke and Matthew Raulyn of Wareham	£22	40 years[18]
Cottisford	1391	Edward Metteleye	£10	9 years[19]

1 Exch. K.R., E. 106, 6/2.
2 Eton, C 5, Bledlow charters.
3 Ibid.
4 Exch. K.R., E. 106, 8/16.
5 *C.P.R. 1345–8*, p. 228.
6 *C.Cl.R. 1354–60*, pp. 625–6.
7 *Court Rolls of Tooting Beck*, p. vi.
8 *H.M.C., Rep. IX*, i, p. 351.
9 Windsor, XI G 67.
10 *C.P.R. 1385–9*, p. 329.
11 Eton, D 5/5, Blakenham charters.
12 Eton, D 5/4, Blakenham charters.
13 *C.P.R. 1343–5*, p. 197.
14 Eton, B 11, Weedon charters.
15 Ibid. 16 Ibid.
17 Windsor, XI G 69.
18 *C.P.R. 1377–81*, pp. 626–7.
19 Eton, C 14, Cottisford charters.

Large tenements leased:

Tenement	*Date*	*Lessee*	*Rent*	*Term*
Northwood in Ruislip	*ante* 1384	Roger Reding	..	..[1]
" "	1384	John St. George and his wife	5 marks	Life[2]
" "	1392	Richard Randulf	5 marks	27 years[3]
Barstenement in Cottisford	1375	Edward Metteleye	1 mark	8 years[4]
" "	1400	Edward and Margaret Metteleye	Red rose	Life[5]

It is very probable that this list is incomplete; leases recorded in the close and patent rolls were almost always long-term leases. Evidently royal permission was not necessary for leases of a few years only, and many may have perished among the manorial records after their dispersal. They had no value as title-deeds after their expiry; significantly two of the Weedon leases at Eton have been endorsed in a later hand *Nichil valet*. But there are enough to show that some of the manors, notably Dunton and Tooting, were almost continuously leased from about 1322, and that leases were common on other manors long before 1379, when the abbot and convent of Bec resolved upon a policy of letting out their English manors whenever a lessee could be found to take them.[6] The absence of leases for the Wiltshire and Hampshire manors may be pure chance, but it is possible that since they formed a convenient central group naturally suited to sheep-farming, the prior of Ogbourne chose to keep them in his hand longer than the manors on the fringes of his estate.

There are several examples of local men, some of them tenants or servants of the abbey, among the lessees. One of these was James Freysel of Bledlow, who settled an estate in the manor of Bledlow on his sons in 1316–17,[7] and who at the same period was one of the estate officials of the prior of Ogbourne.[8] His antecedents are obscure; his father, Robert Freysel, had been of sufficient substance to

[1] King's College, Q 8. [2] Ibid. [3] King's College, Q 45.
[4] Eton, C 14, Cottisford charters. [5] Ibid.
[6] See *infra*, p. 124, for the causes of this decision.
[7] *V.C.H. Bucks.* ii. 249. [8] *Supra*, p. 55

appear on a jury giving information about fees in the hundred of Risborough,[1] and had on one occasion appeared in the manor court of the abbot as a pledge for Hugh Pinel.[2] We do not know if he was actually a tenant of the abbot and had received part of his property from him, but his connexion with the abbey was very close. In 1319 he was among the men and servants who accompanied the prior of Ogbourne overseas to the mother abbey,[3] and in 1324 he was one of the mainpernors of the prior of Ogbourne that he would conduct himself well and faithfully towards the king.[4] In the same year he was holding the manor of Bledlow on a stock and land lease for a term of four years, and his lease was periodically renewed until his death.[5] He was a knight of the shire in 1329[6] and died a wealthy man on 16 August 1341, leaving substantial benefactions to the abbot of Bec and the prior of Ogbourne,[7] as well as to the church of St. Paul, London, where his obit was celebrated afterwards.[8]

Another is William Roce or Rouce of Tooting. The family of Rouce were tenants of the abbey,[9] and included one or two enterprising men who appear to have been improving their status. Richard Rouce was for a time a lesser administrative official, being bailiff of Preston in 1308,[10] and later bailiff of Tooting.[11] In 1312–14 he was wealthy enough to take on the lease of 10 acres of demesne land and 2 acres of demesne pasture.[12] His son William Roce of Tooting had had some business dealings with the abbot as early as 1321,[13] and is described in some records as bailiff or farmer of Tooting.[14] In 1323 he received the whole manor of Tooting on a stock and land lease for 9 years, paying 20 marks a year. Like James Freysel, he became a knight of the shire and was elected for Surrey in 1339;[15]

1 *Feudal Aids*, i. 97 (1302–3).
2 *Select Pleas*, p. 30.
3 *C.P.R. 1317–21*, p. 326.
4 *C.Cl.R. 1323–7*, p. 209.
5 *Supra*, p. 114.
6 *C.Cl.R. 1327–30*, p. 528.
7 *H.M.C.*, *Rep. IX*, App. I, 47 *a*.
8 *Documents illustrating the History of St. Paul's Cathedral*, ed. W. Sparrow-Simpson (Camden Society, 1880), pp. 69, 91. The date of his death is given, erroneously, as 1323. Ibid., p. 197.
9 *Court Rolls of Tooting Beck*, pp. 238–40, 243, and *passim*.
10 *Supra*, p. 66.
11 Windsor, White Book, f. 135.
12 *Court Rolls of Tooting Beck*, pp. 247–9.
13 *C.Cl.R. 1318–23*, p. 484.
14 Windsor, White Book, ff. 128, 135.
15 *V.C.H. Surrey*, i. 433.

he died not later than 1343.[1] It is not certain that these men were descended from the humbler tenants of the abbey, though either of them, and particularly William Roce, may have been.

Another type of lessee was the manorial official, not necessarily a native of the manor let to him. John Mabbe of Tilbury was actually a tenant of the abbot for land in west Tilbury appendent to the manor of Dunton,[2] but the manor that he leased in 1356 was Blakenham, where for a time he had been bailiff.[3] And John Broughton, chief steward of the estates, who had held the same manor shortly before him, was not a native of Suffolk. Other types too were represented: Simon of Barking, goldsmith, seems to have been a rich citizen of London investing in the land. And Edward Metteleye, who half a century later held both Lessingham in Norfolk and Cottisford in Oxfordshire, was a small country gentleman, as far as is known unconnected with the abbot's estates either by service or by tenure. His antecedents are unknown; when he first appeared in the records he held land in Honingham in Warwickshire, partly as a result of his marriage with an heiress, Margaret widow of William Cotes.[4] His son was a lawyer;[5] we cannot tell if he was one himself. Certainly his relations with the abbot of Bec show him to have been something of a speculator in land.

By the end of the century the abbots of Bec had lost contact with their English estates. They no longer farmed so extensively on their own account, but were becoming rentiers who both leased out whole manors and divided the demesne lands among their tenants. By 1439 certainly all

[1] *C.R.P. 1343–5*, p. 38.

[2] The Dunton rental (King's College, M 19) under forinsec tenants in West Tilbury contains the entry: 'De tenentibus parcell' dicti tenementi que quondam fuit Johannis Mabbe, xvj *d*.' 'De tenentibus unius pecie prati nuper Johannis Mabbe in West Tilbery, iij *d*. *ob*.'

[3] Cf. the terms of the lease, Eton, D 5/4. The account roll of 1347–8 for Blakenham contains under the steward's expenses the entry: 'De quibus in allocat' pro expensis Johannis Mabbe, vj *d*.'

[4] Dugdale, *Warwickshire*, pp. 250–1. His bailiff is mentioned as early as 1385 in the *Rolls of the Warwickshire and Coventry Sessions of the Peace, 1377–97* (Dugdale Society), ed. E. G. Kimball, p. 165.

[5] Dugdale, *Warwickshire*, p. 25.

the demesne lands of Atherstone and Lessingham, the arable of Tooting, and much of the arable of Ruislip were in the hands of the tenants.[1] But social disruption and economic change were not the only causes of the change in estate management; war with France, which cut off the abbots of Bec from their English estates and poured the profits into the royal coffers, contributed to the gradual drying up of enterprise and initiative during the fourteenth century, and finally to the policy of indiscriminate leasing adopted in 1379.

1 Ministers' Accounts, S.C. 6, 937/19, 949/13, 1015/6, 917/26, 917/27. The demesne—or part of it—was still intact at Wretham and Weedon. Ibid. 937/19, 949/14.

PART III
THE SUPPRESSION

FROM the middle of the twelfth century the history of the order of Bec had been 'une histoire intime, celle des abbés du Bec et de ses religieux',[1] and, one might add, of its manors and tenants as well; it no longer sent out a succession of great abbots and ecclesiastical statesmen, and through them helped to mould the thought and institutions of the Anglo-Norman world.[2] When in the late thirteenth century the history of its English cells became once more inseparably bound up with the history of other religious houses and the royal policy, it was in a different, more ignominious, and wholly passive way. As priories dependent on French superiors during almost continuous wars with France they were frequently in the royal hands and entirely beyond the control of the abbot of Bec. For over a hundred years they were gradually slipping from him, and by the end of the fifteenth century two priories had become independent English houses and the remainder had been absorbed by English monasteries and colleges. They were no longer an integral part of an order, whose needs might be met by the legislation of the abbot and convent in chapter; their estates were no longer peaceably and steadily developed for the profit of mother house and dependent priories; their relations with patrons and diocesans were no longer governed by a judicious compound of canonical principle, precedent, and hard necessity. Hard necessity predominated: they existed as best they might. By the early years of the reign of Richard II they had, by a gradual process, been cut off from the abbey of Bec first financially and then spiritually; and though later a few slender ties were renewed for a time, the purpose of their existence had disappeared, and their days were numbered.

[1] Porée, i. 543.

[2] 'Bec in the days of its greatness—and its greatness endured for at least a century—had that rare fortune which comes now and again to a city or a university of attracting to itself, refining and handing on to the world around it all that is best and most characteristic of an age' (Dom Knowles, *The Monastic Order in England*, pp. 88–9).

It would be a mistake to see the gathering clouds of confiscation at too early a date. Uncertainty about the possibility of collecting revenue from England might arise naturally, even before the loss of Normandy, through the distance and danger of civil strife. When in 1130 the religious of Conches granted their half of the manor of Wretham to the religious of Bec in return for some Norman property, it was on the understanding that the agreement should be suspended if the revenue of the manor could not be collected;[1] and it was in fact suspended in 1244 on account of the wars between David of Wales and Henry III.[2] When Normandy was lost King John seized some of the alien priories, and the prior of Ogbourne paid £100 to hold in his custody all lands and possessions of the monks of Bec in England, promising to send none of the issues abroad.[3] All abbeys, however, were used to the process of confiscation and redemption of their English estates on the death of each abbot, and John's seizures of church lands were too widespread to cause special alarm among the French abbots. Communication with Normandy probably became more difficult during the thirteenth century, and some monasteries—especially those with only a few manors in England, who were least able to organize the administration of their estates—began to have difficulty in collecting their revenue from England.[4] Nevertheless the expansion and orderly administration of the estates of Bec during the century is a clear proof that their security was not seriously disturbed,[5] and this steady administration continued well into the fourteenth century even after the brief seizures of the alien priories by Edward I and Edward II.

Had the action of Edward I, it may be asked, any imme-

[1] MS. Lat. 12884, f. 174 *v*.

[2] Ibid., f. 344.

[3] *Rot. de Oblatis et Finibus, 1199–1216*, p. 314.

[4] See Rigaud, *Reg. Visit.*, pp. 192, 224, 301, 351, 458, 499, 544, 583, 597, 626. Delisle considered the diminution of English revenues an important cause of the debts with which most Norman houses were burdened at this period ('Le Clergé normand au treizième siècle', in *Bibl. Éc. Chartes*, Series ii, vol. iii (1846), p. 488).

[5] Many French houses continued to draw some revenues from England. There are examples in *Reg. Visit.* 67, 77, 94, 231, 236, 318, 326, 497. The abbey of St. Denis received 80 marks from England in 1284–5 (G. Lebel, *Histoire administrative, économique et financière de l'abbaye de Saint-Denis*, Paris, 1935, p. 323).

diate effect on the English priories of Bec?[1] There was certainly a brief dislocation of religious life, whilst the monks whose houses were near the sea or a navigable river were moved to inland manors or priories, and secular guardians occupied all the property;[2] but two or three months later all the property was restored for the payment of an annual farm and the monks returned.[3] The farms were assessed as follows:

Priory	*Estimated revenue 1294*[4]			*Farm 1295*[5]			*Farm 1324*[6]			*Farm 1337*[7]		
	£	*s.*	*d.*	£	*s.*	*d.*	£	*s.*	*d.*	£	*s.*	*d.*
Ogbourne	Not known			500	0	0	520	0	0	520	0	0
Stoke-by-Clare	300	12	1	200	0	0	200	0	0	200	0	0
St. Neot's	206	12	6	150	0	0	160	0	0	160	0	0
Goldcliff	Not known			100	0	0	66	13	4[8]	10	0	0[9]
Cowick	53	18	8	38	13	4	40	0	0	40	0	0
Steventon	50	2	3½	45	0	0	60	0	0	60	0	0
Wilsford	46	10	0	40	0	0	45	0	0	45	0	0

If the assessments of annual income made at the time were fairly accurate, the farms during this and succeeding confiscations were unreasonably high. When investigations were made into the condition of all houses with convents[10] five of the priors of Bec showed that the following obligations were incumbent on their houses:

Stoke-by-Clare[11]

£81 for the maintenance of the prior and seventeen monks.

£65. 3*s.* 4*d.* for salaries and pensions granted by charter before the war.

£28. 1*s.* 6*d.* for various alms established by the founders.

[1] For an outline of the general history of the alien priories in England after the first confiscation of 1295 see 'The Suppression of the Alien Priories', in *History*, xxvi. 204–12.

[2] *C.F.R.* i. 362–4. Monks from Wilsford were sent to Stoke-by-Clare and from St. Neot's to the manor of Turvey; the monks of Goldcliff must also have been moved (Exch. K.R., E. 106, 3/19).

[3] Bartholomew Cotton, p. 302.

[4] Exch. K.R., E. 106, 4/18, 16.

[5] Ibid. 3/19.

[6] Ibid. 5/2.

[7] *C.F.R.* v. 28 seq.

[8] Reduced on account of floods (Exch. K.R., E. 106, 5/2).

[9] Reduced on account of the dissipation of the property by William Martel (*C.F.R.* v. 49).

[10] These investigations were the result of a petition presented in the Lincoln parliament of 1301 by the prior of Tickford, a dependency of Marmoutier (Exch. K.R., E. 106, 4/15).

[11] Ibid. 4/16.

St. Neot's[1]

£85. 10*s.* for the prior and eighteen monks.
£42. 6*s.* 8*d.* for salaries and pensions.

Cowick[1]

£27 for the prior and five monks.
20 marks for the fees and robes of a steward and an advocate, and others.

Steventon[1]

£9 for the prior and one monk.
6 marks granted to Robert Gunneys.
1 mark for the robe of Robert Gunneys.
5 marks for the robe and fee of Henry of Aunwick, steward.

Wilsford[1]

£9 for the prior and one monk.
£2 to two proctors.
£2 to a bailiff looking after the temporalities.
£4 in pensions, &c., to others.

The record for Goldcliff is lost, and probably no investigation was made at Ogbourne; but plainly in every case the farm was exorbitant and could have been paid in full only if the priors and convents had chosen to live on their capital. Actually, after the first year it was not paid in full. The arrears mounted—at Stoke to just under £500—and all were finally pardoned; the king, having drawn over £5,000 from the order of Bec alone, exacted no more. In the next confiscation exactly the same procedure was adopted.[2] Consequently the priors were not obliged to exhaust their capital to pay their debts, and the first two confiscations were a warning and a temporary loss, not an economic disaster.

To restrictions during the wars, however, was added the veto imposed on the export of apports and tallages by the 1307 parliament of Carlisle.[3] There were leakages, no doubt, for no medieval government had the ruthless efficiency of a twentieth-century totalitarian state. From 1284 to 1303, including all the years of Edward I's confiscation, sums of money were regularly sent from the English priories to Bec, as contributions towards the rebuilding of the abbey church after the central tower had fallen.[4] On

[1] Exch. K.R., E. 106, 4/18.
[2] Ibid. 5/4.
[3] *Rot. Parl.* i. 217.
[4] Porée, ii. 3, n. 3.

30 November 1310, after the Statute of Carlisle, the prior of Ogbourne sold wood at Bledlow to the value of £450 for the building of the church of Bec, evidently in the hope of sending the money to France.[1] Nevertheless the barrier was sufficiently effective for the pope to grant two French priories to the abbot and convent of Bec in 1312, the grounds of the grant being that so much of their property lay in England and, by reason of the wars between the two realms, was of little use to them.[2]

There was no sudden breakdown in the administration of the estates. Where account rolls exist up to 1340 they show stewards still going on their rounds, accounts being audited at Ruislip, the demesne being farmed with only slightly diminishing vigour. If there was some contraction, this was a period when one would not be surprised by contraction on any large estate. There was, however, one change which began in the early 1320's: the farming out of whole manors on stock and land leases; and it was sometimes directly attributed to the confiscations. Edward II ordered an investigation into the farming of alien manors, on the grounds that they had been let after 1324 and the leases antedated; in the charge the prior of Ogbourne was implicated by name, though nothing was proved against him.[3] On the whole the table of surviving leases shows that the movement was fairly steady between as well as during the periods of confiscation. By the reign of Richard II, however, the condition of alien priories was far more hopeless. Manors had sometimes been handed over, at the royal command, to lay farmers who had no interest in their welfare.[4] Debts, due to the regular demand for a very heavy farm in bad no less than good years, had accumulated; and sometimes the priors

[1] Eton, C 5, Bledlow charters: 'Die lune in festo Sancti Andree apostoli anno regni regis Edwardi filii regis Edwardi quarto convenit inter fratrem Willelmum de Ponte Episcopi dictum priorem de Okeburn' ex parte una et Johannem Romayn et Osbertum Romayn ex altera, ita videlicet quod predictus frater Willelmus vendidit predictis Johanni et Oseberto tria milia fagorum in bosco suo de Bledelawe certo signo signatorum, videlicet quamlibet centenam predictorum fagorum pro quindecim libris sterlingorum penitus convertendis in fabricam ecclesie Beccensis.'

[2] *C.P.L.* ii. 103.

[3] Exch. K.R., E. 106, 5/2.

[4] The earliest examples of the farms of manors belonging to Bec being granted to persons other than the priors are *C.F.R.* v. 49, 100, 367.

were compelled to part with fragments of their property. In 1352 the prior of Ogbourne was obliged to sell his London house to the Dominican friars in Castle Baynard Ward, who coveted it for the enlargement of their friary and paid 80 marks in return.[1] So black was the future prospect after the peace of Brétigny that the abbot of Bec attempted to sell some of his English property during the period that he had the administration of it, apparently without success.[2] After 1377 the alien priories were treated much more strictly, and many of the monks returned to France,[3] where the abbey was already suffering a financial crisis for other reasons.[4] In 1379 the abbot and convent of Bec assembled in chapter for several days 'to deliberate concerning the estate of the monastery; that they were burdened with debts to urgent creditors in the court of Rome and elsewhere, that they must needs incur great costs in prosecution and defence of many causes against noble and powerful persons in the king's parliament, the exchequer of Normandy, and elsewhere, that the number of monks had increased because those in England had returned to the monastery and had been admitted out of compassion; that their rents and revenues were not coming in as well as heretofore owing to the wars, pestilences, and the hardness of the times, that for fifteen years they had received nought from England where great part of their property was, and whence they used to obtain great aid, and that these debts and costs could only be borne by taking money beforehand for leases of their property', and resolved 'to grant such leases of property in England, if any could be found to take it'.[5]

Thenceforward they not only leased their English manors for longer terms, but sold freely, whenever the royal permission could be obtained. Steventon and Wilsford were sold before the end of the century. Steventon was granted at farm to Hugh de Calvyley in March 1379,[6] having just been leased to him by the prior and convent of St. Mary du

[1] King's College, T 3; *C.P.R. 1350–4*, p. 323. [2] *C.P.L.* iv. 80.

[3] *Rot. Parl.* iii. 22–3.

[4] The abbey was fortified and occupied by the troops of Louis d'Harcourt, who lived on its revenues; and its wealth was further dissipated by its abbot, Estout d'Estouteville, a papal nominee (Porée, ii. 131–46).

[5] *C.Cl.R. 1392–6*, p. 482. [6] *C.P.R. 1377–81*, pp. 494–5.

Pré, with the assent of the abbot of Bec. The lease was for fifty years, for an annual payment of 50 marks in time of peace; and Hugh de Calvyley was obliged to discharge all obligations to the king whilst the war lasted and keep a monk in the manor to perform divine service at his own expense.[1] In 1380, however, the king exempted him from the farm of £60 yearly,[2] and in 1389 the prior and convent of Le Pré obtained permission to alienate to him the manors of Steventon and Westbury, parcel of the possessions of their priory of Steventon.[3] After his death the priory was granted to Thomas Chalumley, John Briddesmer, and Richard Merser, who assigned it to Roger Walden, archbishop of Canterbury, and from him it passed to King Richard II.[4] Finally Richard II, in 1399, granted it to the abbot and convent of Westminster, and they, in spite of a claim put forward by the son of Hugh Calvyley, remained from that time in secure possession of it.[5]

Wilsford had passed from farmer to farmer and had suffered dilapidation in the process. William Bark, monk of St. Peter of Castres in Aquitaine, who had the administration about 1380, presented a petition in parliament complaining that the buildings and chapel were too dilapidated to be habitable without heavy expense, and that there was no longer any kind of chattel or beast, plough or cart, corn or any other thing left in the manor, and asking for the reduction of his farm.[6] An extent showed that the value of the priory did not exceed £12. 16*s.* 8*d.*, and in 1380 the farm of 12 marks, together with the clerical subsidy of 10 marks, was remitted for two years.[7] In 1387 another inquiry showed that William Bark no less than previous administrators had been driven to waste the property still further by cutting down trees, and that Richard of Cotington, who had the priory after him, had not even found a

[1] 'Et trovera un moigne de mesme la meson a faire les divines services en le dit manoir a cez coustages propres si ency soit q' le priour envoie nulle pur demorer la' (Westminster, Dean and Chapter Muniments, no. 7408). There is an inspeximus of these letters on the Patent Roll for 1384 (*C.P.R. 1381–5*, p. 490).

[2] *C.P.R. 1377–81*, pp. 494–5.

[3] *C.P.R. 1388–92*, p. 6; Westminster, Dean and Chapter Muniments, no. 7402.

[4] *C.P.R. 1399–1401*, pp. 319–20; Westminster, nos. 7396, 7397, 7398, 7401.

[5] *C.P.R. 1399–1401*, pp. 260–1; Westminster, no. 7579.

[6] Exch. K.R., E. 106, 11/16.

[7] *C.P.R. 1377–81*, p. 506.

chaplain to celebrate the holy office in the priory chapel.[1] At last in 1397 the patron, Thomas, earl of Kent, was licensed to acquire in fee the priory and all its appurtenances, and then grant it in mortmain to the abbot and convent of Bourne.[2] The abbot and convent of Bec, who were 'more desirous to alienate the priory to the abbot and convent of Bourne than to any secular person, as more conformable with law, because the priory was endowed with tithes and other spiritual possessions', were to receive 5 marks yearly.[3] Papal consent to the transaction was given in 1401.[4] Nevertheless the abbey of Bourne was not to enjoy undisturbed possession, for the commission appointed in 1440 to deal with the alien priories granted it to Ralph, Lord Cromwell, and Nicholas Dixon;[5] in 1444 the letters patent granting it to the abbot of Bourne were revoked,[6] and in 1462 it was granted to the master of the college of Fotheringay.[7] At the intercession of Lady Margaret Beaufort, however, it was finally restored to the abbot and convent of Bourne, and they held it from 1486 until the Dissolution.[8]

As far as the estates were held together at all during the last years of the century, it was largely due to the activities of a long-lived proctor-general. William of Saint-Vaast, who had been granetar of the abbey in 1363,[9] was nominated prior of Ogbourne and proctor-general in England in March 1364,[10] and two years later he was appointed to this office for life.[11] When the priory of St. Neot's fell vacant he became prior, and from 1377 until his death in the early years of the fifteenth century he held both offices and administered both groups of estates.[12] He bestrode the period when the English priories were not only weathering financial difficulties but were cut off from the discipline of

[1] Exch. K.R., E. 106, 11/11.
[2] *C.P.R. 1396–9*, p. 144.
[3] Ibid., p. 374.
[4] *C.P.L.* v. 432.
[5] *C.P.R. 1436–41*, p. 435.
[6] *C.P.R. 1441–6*, pp. 269–70.
[7] *C.P.R. 1461–7*, p. 216.
[8] *C.P.R. 1485–94*, p. 94.
[9] Porée, ii. 136.
[10] *C.P.R. 1361–4*, p. 471.
[11] *C.P.R. 1374–7*, p. 76 (confirmation of letters of 23 Oct. 1366).
[12] *C.P.R. 1377–81*, pp. 446–7. He was very infirm in 1402, but was still alive on 28 Oct. 1404 (Gorham, op. cit., pp. cxlv–cxlvi).

their mother house by the Great Schism.[1] From the first, whatever the attitude of the abbot of Bec may have been, priors presented by him to other houses in virtue of his powers as proctor-general were accepted by the diocesans.[2] And in 1391 the situation was improved by a papal privilege temporarily granting the English priories limited autonomy; the bishop of London and the priors of Ogbourne and Cowick were given power to convoke general chapters of the order in England, receive the professions of monks, and appoint priors.[3] They appointed Richard of Cotesford, an English monk, to be prior of Stoke in 1391,[4] and in 1398 the bishop of London and prior of Ogbourne presented John de Bourgeauville to the bishop of Exeter as prior of Cowick.[5] So as a result of William of St. Vaast's authority the estates, though heavily burdened by the annual farms, were spared the reckless dilapidations of lay farmers for a remarkably long time; and although the numbers of monks in each house must have fallen, and the granges of Wilsford and Steventon had been sold, Goldcliff, St. Neot's, and Cowick remained in the hands of administrators of the order of Bec until the early years of the fifteenth century. But the laboured existence of the priories of Bec in England could not be prolonged indefinitely.

Stoke-by-Clare was the first conventual priory to break away. It had already been farmed to the abbot of Westminster, and the buildings had suffered seriously from fire; in 1395 it obtained a charter of denization through the intercession of the patron, the earl of March. The charter was granted after payment of 1,000 marks, on the usual plea that it had suffered through the waste and bad governance of its French priors and monks.[6] It seems, however, that English monks were never established there, and the house declined after the recall of the French monks; in 1414

[1] The effect of the Great Schism on the Cluniac and other priories in England has been admirably treated by E. Perroy in *L'Angleterre et le Grand Schisme d'Occident*, pp. 76–95.

[2] In 1382 on the death of Robert de Glanville, brother William de Estrepeny was presented to the priory of Cowick, and the bishop of Exeter accepted the presentation (*Reg. Brantyngham*, p. 80).

[3] *C.P.L.* iv. 412.

[4] *C.P.R. 1388–92*, p. 514.

[5] Cowick Priory Documents, D 82, no. 11; *Reg. Stafford*, p. 159.

[6] Dugdale, *Monasticon*, vi. 1415–16; *C.P.R. 1391–6*, p. 640.

Edmund Mortimer, earl of March, pleaded that it had originally been founded as a college of secular canons, and obtained permission from king and pope to erect it once more into a college.[1] St. Neot's remained subject to Bec for some years longer, but in 1409 it too sought and obtained denization. The petition of the prior, Edward Salisbury, stated that the founders of St. Neot's

'ordained that its prior and monks should be Frenchmen; that the abbot and convent of Bek Herlewyn should appoint them, visit them as a dependent cell, and receive from them a yearly pension of 30*s.*; that during the French wars the pension had been paid to the king of England; that in course of time, on account of alienations by abbots of Bek Herlewyn and by priors and monks, by reason of the foreign rule of the said abbots, priors and monks, ignorant of the English language, the priory goods, formerly of no small value, had been so much wasted that they were utterly insufficient; that upon the death of William de Sancto Vedasto, monk of the said monastery, prior of the priory, a Frenchman, all the French monks except two had betaken themselves to France, since when the priory had been in the hands of prior Edward and a few English monks.'[2]

Consequently the convent was exempted from the abbot and convent of Bec, subjected to the bishop, and granted the right of electing its own prior. In fact, worn out by the long-continued *torture à petit feu* of the royal confiscations, most of the priories of Bec ceased to depend upon the mother house some years before the act of suppression. Just before William of St. Vaast died, in 1404, the extensive property in the bailiwick of Ogbourne was granted at farm to him and John, duke of Bedford, for life or as long as the war should last.[3] No new prior of Ogbourne was appointed after William's death. Consequently, except in the priories of Cowick and Goldcliff, no white monks of Bec remained in England when Henry V became king.

Since waste and dilapidation were declared to be the motives for almost every act of sale or denization, it may pertinently be inquired how far the possessions of Bec in England had suffered either temporary or permanent harm

[1] *C.P.R. 1413–16*, p. 291; *C.P.L.* vi. 456; Dugdale, *Monasticon*, vi. 1416 seq.
[2] *C.P.L.* vi. 250.
[3] Windsor, White Book, ff. 91–91*v*.

from the confiscations. Frequently farms were reduced in the late fourteenth century,[1] but the period was in any case one of declining prosperity for landlords, and this in itself may have compelled the Crown to ask for less. A rough estimate may be reached by comparing the extents of 1294 with late-fourteenth-century extents—when they exist—and the *Valor Ecclesiasticus*, with the reservation that by 1536 the tide had turned and agriculture was more lucrative for the large landlord than it had been in the reign of Richard II. There is a clear case of dilapidation at Wilsford; in 1294 the revenue of the priory was stated to be £46. 10*s.*;[2] by 1387 the extended value of the property, which normally would probably have been higher than the revenue, was £36. 4*s.* 1*d.*, of which the spiritualities were worth £20. 7*s.* 3*d.* The total value of the temporalities was only £15. 16*s.* 10*d.*, and five carucates of arable land were worth no more than 40*s.*, because more than two-thirds was sandy and lay uncultivated on account of its sterility and for lack of tenants. The depopulation may have been due to the pestilence, but the collapse of buildings—barns, sheep-folds, brew-house, and bakery—described at the same time must have been caused by neglect.[3] Nor did the value increase later; in 1536 rents from tenants and the farm of the demesne were together worth £13. 7*s.* 6*d.*[4] But this is the only priory where permanent deterioration can be proved. The figures for Steventon show that the extended value of the priory in 1536 was almost exactly the same as in 1294, whatever may have happened in the interval.[5] The returns for 1294 and 1324 are incomplete, but for St. Neot's, Stoke-by-Clare, and Cowick it is possible to compare the estimated annual

[1] The farm of the priory of Ogbourne, which had been 1,000 marks in 1341 (*C.P.R. 1340–3*, p. 270), had by 1377 been reduced to £420 plus tenths and other clerical levies; the farm of St. Neot's at the same date was £80, which was less than the amount demanded by Edward II and Edward III, but was the maximum that the prior had declared himself able to pay in 1302 (*C.P.R. 1377–81*, pp. 446–7).

[2] *Supra*, p. 121.

[3] Exch. K.R., E. 106, 11/11.

[4] *Valor Ecclesiasticus*, iv. 103.

[5] According to the extent of 1294 (Exch. K.R., E. 106, 2/2, 2/6), the assized rents and works owed by customary tenants were worth £47. 12*s.* 3*d.*, the demesne land £31. 19*s.* 6*d.*, and the rectory £20, making a total of £99. 11*s.* 9*d.*, plus £12. 7*s.* 3*d.* for the manor of Westbury. The *Valor* (i. 417) gives a total value of £96. 10*s.* 1¼*d.*, and £10. 10*s.* for Westbury.

incomes of 1294 and 1536,[1] and there is a slight rise for all three priories.

Priory	Estimated income, 1294			Estimated income, 1536		
	£	s.	d.	£	s.	d.
Stoke-by-Clare .	300	12	1	324	4	1¼
St. Neot's . .	206	12	6	241	11	4¼[2]
Cowick . . .	53	18	8	78	16	7¼

It is not possible to reach a satisfactory total for Goldcliff or Ogbourne since the estates had been broken up. But tenuous as the figures are, it seems that Wilsford alone had suffered permanent devastation and depopulation, possibly as much through the pestilence as through the confiscations. Elsewhere barns and byres might fall into ruin or woods be cut down, monastic buildings and the chancels of appropriated churches might crumble for lack of repairs,[3] but the damage could be made good by a prudent administrator in a few years. The land was probably saved by the leasehold movement; when the income of the prior was derived mainly from rents, failure to pay his full farm would be more likely to lead to an examination of his income and the pardon of his arrears than to distraint on the stock and corn which then belonged to his tenants. No doubt the royal exactions meant real hardship for the monks, who had to live on a diminutive income, and there can have been little, if any, spare capital to spend on improving the land; possibly, too, the desperate need for ready cash partly accounts for the multiplication of corrodies after the seizures began.[4] But

1 *Valor Ecclesiasticus*, iv. 262; iii. 471; ii. 382.

2 It is possible to compare the actual extents of the manor and town of St. Neot's and the nearby grange of Monk's Hardwick at three different dates. In 1324 (Exch. K.R., E. 106, 6/7) the estimated value was £72. 5*s*. 10*d*.; in 1370 (ibid. 10/1) it was £81. 3*s*. 2*d*.; in the *Valor Ecclesiasticus* (iv. 261–2) it was £91. 19*s*. 5*d*. after the deduction of various extraneous rents included under the same heading. The rise was probably in part due to trading prosperity, for the profits of the market rose from £3 to £6. 13*s*. 4*d*., and then to £9. 6*s*. 8*d*.; meanwhile rents soared from £10. 5*s*. 6*d*. to £20. 3*s*. 4*d*., and then to £56. 8*s*. 6*d*.; and since there was no appreciable decrease in the size of the demesne between 1324 and 1370, and afterwards it decreased only by about 50 per cent., it seems probable that town rents were rising.

3 The abbot of Tavistock drew a gloomy picture of the state of Cowick priory in the reign of Edward IV: 'The service of God was withdrawn, the church defouled with rude beasts, the place fallen in ruin and desolation, and the foundation broken, to the huge displeasure of God' (Cowick Priory Documents, D 82/32).

4 For example, at Goldcliff Richard de Careswell, king's serjeant, received a

on the estates of Bec at least most of the damage was made good during the fifteenth century.

The formal act suppressing the non-conventual alien priories in 1414[1] had no immediate effect on the dependencies of Bec. John, duke of Bedford, continued to farm the property in the bailiwick of Ogbourne for a few years. By 1421 his conscience was troubling him, and so 'considering that divers spiritual goods were annexed to the priory, the care of which was known to pertain to ecclesiastical persons, and that those things which are of the church of God are ordered to be rendered to God and ecclesiastical persons', he gave the spiritualities to the warden and canons of St. George's chapel, Windsor, on 3 December. Royal consent was obtained shortly afterwards.[2] As a Knight of the Garter the duke of Bedford had a special interest in the chapel; and his gift, which included the rich prebends of Ogbourne and Cleeve, four other rectories, and innumerable tithes and pensions, was a valuable and welcome windfall for the dean and canons. After his death in 1436 the religious of Bec petitioned for the restoration of their property without success.[3] The manors were farmed for a few years to various laymen, including Humphrey, duke of Gloucester:[4] but after 1440 a commission appointed to deal with the property of alien priories[5] began the process of distributing

corrody in 1375 (*C.Cl.R. 1374–7*, p. 247); John de Banham in 1385 (*C.Cl.R. 1385–9*, p. 109); Agnes Henyver, king's servant, in 1403 (*C.Cl.R. 1402–5*, p. 178); Thomas Ryngwode, yeoman of the king's robes, and Joan his wife in 1407 (*C.Cl.R. 1405–9*, p. 358); at Steventon William de la Garderobe, keeper of the king's lions, was granted a corrody in 1354 (*C.Cl.R. 1349–54*, p. 623); at St. Neot's Peter Sheford received a corrody in 1377 (*C.Cl.R. 1374–7*, p. 524); Henry Mancestre, the king's esquire, in 1387 (*C.Cl.R. 1385–9*, pp. 434–5); John Bilney in 1392 (*C.Cl.R. 1392–6*, p. 89); John de Oterhunte received a corrody in Stoke-by-Clare in 1315 (*C.Cl.R. 1313–18*, p. 226); and John Roos in Ogbourne in 1382 (*C.Cl.R. 1381–5*, p. 201). Some of these corrodians were probably appointed in accordance with the ordinary rights of patronage, but others may have been forced upon the priors in return for remission of debts. Priors in embarrassed financial circumstances were often obliged to sell life corrodies for a lump sum (cf. A. Hamilton-Thompson, 'A Corrody from Leicester Abbey, A.D. 1393–4' in *Transactions of the Leicestershire Archaeological Society*, 1925).

[1] *Rot. Parl.* iv. 22.

[2] *C.P.R. 1416–22*, pp. 441–2; *C.Cl.R. 1435–41*, pp. 24–5; Windsor, White Book, f. 90.

[3] MS. Lat. 13905, ff. 11–11*v*; Porée, ii. 217–18.

[4] *C.P.R. 1436–41*, pp. 92, 126, 189, 195, 259, 296, 303.

[5] Rymer, *Foedera*, x. 802–3.

them to St. Nicholas,—later King's—College, Cambridge, St. Mary's College, Eton, and other ecclesiastical foundations. Edward IV's omission of St. Nicholas, and Eton from the list of institutions exempted from his Act of Resumption,[1] and later his attempt to suppress Eton altogether in favour of St. George's, Windsor,[2] led to grave confusion in the descent of the estates; but they were finally divided as follows:

St. Nicholas, College, Cambridge: Atherstone,[3] Dunton Waylett,[4] Brixton-Deverill,[5] Combe,[6] Lessingham,[7] Monxton,[8] Ogbourne St. George and St. Andrew,[9] Ruislip.[10]

Eton College: Blakenham,[11] Povington and Milburne,[12] Bledlow,[13] Cottisford,[14] Weedon,[15] East Wretham.[16]

St. George's Windsor: All the spiritualities, including the rectory manors of Wantage and Hungerford, which followed the advowsons of the churches.[17]

Hospital of St. Katherine's by the Tower: Quarley,[18] Chisenbury.[19]

St. Mary's Guild in the chapel of St. Mary within the cemetery of Barking Church: Tooting Beck.[20]

Vicar of Ashford, for the endowment of the college founded by Sir John Fogg. Hooe,[21] Preston.[22]

Swyncombe became detached from the other manors before 1440; no clear grant of it is recorded, but in 1433 Thomas Chaucer died seised of it conjointly with others, possibly in virtue of his position as steward of the honour of

1 *Rot. Parl.* v. 463–75; Heywood and Wright, *The Ancient Laws of the Fifteenth Century for King's College Cambridge and for Eton College* (London, 1850), pp. 382–5.
2 H. Maxwell-Lyte, *A History of Eton College* (London, 1911), pp. 63 seq.
3 *C.P.R. 1441–6*, p. 269.
4 *C.P.R. 1446–52*, p. 428.
5 *C.P.R. 1441–6*, p. 181; *C.P.R. 1461–7*, p. 74.
6 *C.P.R. 1436–41*, p. 557; *C.P.R. 1461–7*, p. 74.
7 Ibid.
8 Ibid.; *C.P.R. 1436–41*, p. 557.
9 Ibid., pp. 521–2.
10 Ibid.
11 *C.P.R. 1467–77*, p. 63; *V.C.H. Suffolk*, ii. 153.
12 *C.P.R. 1446–52*, p. 417; *V.C.H. Dorset*, ii. 119.
13 *C.P.R. 1461–7*, p. 73.
14 Ibid.
15 *C.P.R. 1441–6*, p. 205.
16 Ibid.
17 *Supra*, p. 131.
18 *C.P.R. 1436–41*, p. 529; *V.C.H. Hants*, iv. 385.
19 *C.P.R. 1436–41*, p. 529; *C.P.R. 1461–7*, p. 140.
20 *Court Rolls of Tooting Beck*, p. vi.
21 *V.C.H. Sussex*, ix. 244–5.
22 *C.P.R. 1467–77*, pp. 42–3.

Wallingford, to which it had once belonged. Certainly it was added to the estates of the house of Suffolk when his daughter Alice married William de la Pole, and it remained continuously in lay hands.[1]

Goldcliff and Cowick had been given renewed life by the arrival of fresh monks from Bec during the reign of Henry IV.[2] Since they were conventual they ought not to have been affected by the act of suppression. However, their helplessness and isolation combined with the covetousness of neighbouring English abbeys to bring about their ruin. The last years of Goldcliff were stormy. The prior, Laurence de Bonneville, had been summoned to Bec in 1439 or 1440 to answer a charge of misappropriating the revenues of the priory, and since he did not go, he was deposed by the abbot. Possibly because they believed the priory to be vacant, the commissioners of alien priories presented to it as prior John Twining, monk of St. Peter's Gloucester, and he was instituted by the bishop of Llandaff. In 1441 Henry VI gave his assent to the appropriation of the priory by the abbot and convent of Tewkesbury after the death or resignation of John Twining, on condition that they should maintain a prior and two religious there; and Pope Eugenius IV confirmed the grant.[3] Laurence de Bonneville, who had been engaged in bitter strife with John Twining and had refused to resign, obtained a papal mandate restoring him to the priory in 1445.[4] In spite of this the monks of Tewkesbury contrived to retain possession until 1450, when Henry VI granted the priory to Eton College;[5] Edward IV restored it to Tewkesbury,[6] but in 1467 finally bestowed it on Eton.[7] Eton retained the manors of Goldcliff and Coudray in Monmouthshire, with all their appurtenances; but the Somersetshire and Devonshire property—the manors of Membury, Preston, and Monksilver and the

[1] H. A. Napier, *Historical Notices of the Parishes of Swyncombe and Ewelme*, (Oxford, 1858), pp. 19, 26–7, 29 seq.

[2] R. Graham, 'Four alien priories . . .' in *J.B.A.A.* xxxv (1929), 116; Rymer, *Foedera*, viii. 721.

[3] *C.P.L.* viii. 241–4.

[4] The full account of Laurence de Bonneville's resistance and the armed attacks upon the priory by John Twining and the monks of Tewkesbury is given by R. Graham, op. cit., pp. 118–19, and Porée, ii. 224–31.

[5] *C.P.R. 1446–52*, p. 457.

[6] *C.P.R. 1461–7*, p. 93.

[7] *C.P.R. 1467–77*, pp. 48, 62.

advowsons of the churches of Puriton and Woolavington—was given to St. George's, Windsor, in 1474.[1] In this way, rather by private intrigue than public policy, a conventual priory was crushed out of existence and its property given to non-monastic establishments, regardless of the fact that it had been served by eight monks of Bec in 1441.

Cowick priory remained independent for a little while longer. It had been among the alien priories granted by Henry IV to Queen Joan,[2] and was in the hands of another lay farmer in 1439.[3] Nevertheless it continued to be served by monks; the abbot of Bec sent Peter de Menneval to be prior in January 1420,[4] and William Donnebant, monk of Bec, succeeded him after his death in September of the same year.[5] Whilst he was prior he appealed to Henry VI to be discharged from further payment of his yearly farm of 24 marks, and obtained a remission of the farm in 1440, after proving that his priory was conventual. He drew a gloomy picture of its ruinous condition, showing that many of its possessions had been inundated by the great floods of the river Exe, and would be destroyed unless costly works of embankment were undertaken; that the church, cloister, and many of the priory buildings were so decayed that only speedy and expensive repairs could save them from collapse; and that the possessions were insufficient to allow for repairs and the maintenance of divine service unless the farm were remitted.[6] There was still a convent in existence in 1447, when Robert of Rouen or Becdenne, the last prior, was appointed,[7] but in 1451 Cowick was granted to Eton College.[8] Edward IV, after giving it first to Tavistock Abbey,[9] later restored it to Eton.[10] However, the abbot of Tavistock was not prepared to relinquish his claim and had cogent reasons drawn from canon law to support it. They are set out in an undated draft of the 'considerations of the

[1] *C.P.R. 1467–77*, p. 461.
[2] *C.P.R. 1408–13*, pp. 85–6; *C.P.R. 1413–16*, p. 165.
[3] *C.P.R. 1436–41*, p. 300.
[4] Cowick Priory Documents, D 82, no. 14.
[5] Ibid., nos. 15–17; *Reg. Lacy*, i. 4–5.
[6] *C.P.R. 1436–41*, p. 381.
[7] Cowick Priory Documents, D 82, no. 20; *Reg. Lacy*, i. 316.
[8] *C.P.R. 1446–52*, pp. 429, 563.
[9] *C.P.R. 1461–7*, pp. 222, 273.
[10] *C.P.R. 1467–77*, p. 63.

abbot of Tavistock, moving King Edward IV to make the grant of the priory of Cowick to the abbot'. Amongst others, we find that 'the said priory was perpetuell and conventuell accordyng to the exception of the acte anno 2 H. V, and no pryor nor monkes within, and that yt myght not stonde with Goddes lawe nor mannys lawe ne by gode reason the said pryory to be commyted to secular use, butte only to be occupied and servid with religiouse men yf eny coude be founde'.[1] In 1478 the abbot and convent of Tavistock obtained licence to sue before the pope, and secured confirmation of Edward IV's letters patent granting them the alien priory of Cowick.[2] In this way the last dependencies of Bec passed out of the control of the mother house in Normandy, though the name still lingered for some centuries. John Stow referred in his survey of London to the 'house called Ogbourne' in Castle Lane;[3] and in the seventeenth century the villagers of Henton and Clapcot were still paying to the dean and chapter of Windsor 'Beccherlewin's tithes'.[4]

[1] Cowick Priory Documents, D 82, no. 32. It must have been drawn up either before the first grant of the priory in 1462 or else after the restitution of it to Eton. The canons cited in support of the abbot's claims were *Decretum*, XIX. iii; *Lib. Sext. Decr.* III, tit. XXXVI, caps. ii, v; lib. III, tit. L, cap. vii; lib. III, tit. XXXV, cap. viii.

[2] *C.P.R. 1476–85*, p. 90.

[3] *A Survey of London*, ed. C. L. Kingsford, ii. 13–14.

[4] Windsor, XV 41/85; XV 41/159.

CONCLUSION

FOR over two centuries after the Norman Conquest a series of energetic and enterprising abbots had striven to maintain discipline in their English priories and run their English estates profitably, on the whole with notable success. The monks were united not only by the authority of the abbot and general chapter, but also by common liturgical observances, the white habit peculiar to the order,[1] and the personal bonds which naturally appeared when almost all monks made their profession at Bec[2] and were moved from priory to priory by the abbot; and the estates were directed for the welfare of the abbey. Local influence might leave its mark, and centrifugal tendencies might appear in the priories, but in the end it was war and political division, not peaceful growth, that wrenched them away from the abbey. During the period when they were being lost one by one the abbey itself fell upon evil days: occupied in turn by French and English soldiers, converted into a fortress at its own expense, and then partly demolished, it was heavily burdened with debts; and orderly religious life became practically impossible. Nevertheless it began to recover in the middle of the fifteenth century; the French priories were still united to it, general chapters met and legislated for changing needs, and the worst debts were paid. The English priories, however, were never to be recovered.

They are perhaps most remarkable as examples of stunted growth which, though they were never to become vital centres of monasticism, were just capable of being covered by the wide mantle of St. Benedict. One, the largest, was able to stand as an independent monastery after its denization. On their internal history the records are silent, and only their place in the growing order of Bec and their relationships with other authorities can be studied. The granges are in a different position. Priories only in name, existing solely to minister to the material needs of the monks of Bec, their primary importance is in the social and economic development of England. The manors in the

[1] Porée, i. 504–7.

[2] Ibid. ii. 272–3.

bailiwick of Ogbourne were widely scattered and included almost every type of rural economy: they were carefully organized for a special purpose, and it would be no exaggeration to say that the abbots of Bec had left their mark upon their Wiltshire manors long after the last monk of Bec had returned to France. Even the outlying cash manors illustrate, in their development, some of the fundamental economic changes that were taking place in fourteenth-century England. Lastly, the dependence of these manors on a French abbey had one consequence important for their future history. Whereas the estates of many English monasteries passed into lay hands at the Dissolution, the manors and churches of Bec were converted before that time into the endowments of colleges and chapels sufficiently in harmony with the new age to survive the sixteenth-century upheaval; and so, instead of being scattered amongst lay owners, they have continued until the present day to support religious and learned institutions of a different kind.

APPENDIX

PROPERTY IN THE BAILIWICK OF OGBOURNE

THE abbey of Bec received the greater part of its English estates from a small group of Norman families in the late eleventh and early twelfth centuries. The Clares were the most notable benefactors, with their kinsmen the Giffards. Miles Crispin and his wife, Maud of Wallingford, who later married Brian Fitz Count, also ranked high; Ernulf de Hesding and his wife and Hugh de Grantmesnil and his two daughters all bestowed manors on the monks. Gifts of tithes were particularly abundant; the two most extensive were Miles Crispin's gift of two-thirds of his demesne tithe in the honour of Wallingford, and Richard of Clare's gift of similar tithes in some of his Suffolk, Essex, and Surrey manors. The scattered tithes were so assiduously collected that the dean and chapter of Windsor, who came into the spiritualities in 1421, inherited tithes in forty-eight different parishes.

In the following list the property is grouped according to dioceses—prebends, churches, manors, and their appurtenances being grouped first, and separate tithes last. I have noted wherever a manor was clearly not conterminous with a vill; elsewhere the presumption is that it was.

Diocese of Salisbury

Ogbourne St. George and St. Andrew. The manors of Ogbourne St. George and Ogbourne St. Andrew were given to Bec before 1133 by Maud of Wallingford with the assent of Brian Fitz Count, her husband. The gift, which was made for the wardrobe of the monks, was confirmed by Henry I, and *c.* 1147–9 it was confirmed and augmented, with the approval of the young Henry Plantagenet and his mother.[1] The appropriation of the churches was granted by Hubert Walter, bishop of Salisbury, 1189–93, and confirmed by him as archbishop of Canterbury.[2] The abbot of Bec did not hold the whole of the two vills, since one carucate remained in lay hands and was held directly of the honour of Wallingford.[3]

The Prebend of Ogbourne. In 1208 Herbert Poore, bishop of Salisbury, erected the churches of both Ogbournes, with the churches of Wantage and Hungerford and the chapel of Shalbourne, into a prebend, and constituted the abbots of Bec canons of Salisbury. The

[1] Porée, i. 460–1; Windsor, XI G 11, nos. 19, 38; XI G 1; MS. Lat. 9211, no. 2; Dugdale, vi. 1016.

[2] Windsor, XI G 11, nos. 3, 7, 8.

[3] *R.H.* ii. 269.

abbots were obliged to maintain a stall vicar in the cathedral church and vicars in each of the appropriated prebendal churches.[1] Like the other Salisbury prebends Ogbourne was exempt from episcopal control, and the priors and monks who were later sent there were consequently exempt from episcopal visitation.[2] Canons of Salisbury normally enjoyed archidiaconal jurisdiction in their prebends,[3] and after a long struggle the abbots of Bec obtained formal recognition of their rights from Robert Bingham, bishop of Salisbury, and the archdeacons of Berkshire and Wiltshire.[4] Very few records of their peculiar jurisdiction have survived, but during the fourteenth century at least they appointed an 'Official of the prebendal jurisdiction of Ogbourne', whose duties certainly included receiving chaplains presented to the chantry of Holy Trinity in Hungerford church.[5] The chapel in the hospital of St. John Baptist, Hungerford, also came under the abbot's jurisdiction.[6] In 1422–3, just after the dean and canons of Windsor acquired the spiritualities of Ogbourne, the profits of the peculiar amounted to £1. 14*s.* 10*d.*[7]

Brixton-Deverill (Wilts.). The manor of Brixton-Deverill, which lay between the two Glastonbury manors of Monkton and Longbridge Deverill, was given to Bec by Queen Maud before 1086, and the monks held it at the time of the Domesday survey.[8] They gave up the church when the prebend of Ogbourne was erected,[9] and their rights were limited to a few of the small tithes.[10]

Charlton (Berks.). In 1316 the prior of Ogbourne held a quarter of a knight's fee in Charlton, but there is no record of the mode of acquisition.[11]

Chisenbury (Wilts.). Robert de Meulan gave the manor of Chisenbury to the kitchen of the monks in 1112, and his gift was confirmed by Henry I.[12] Another manor in the same vill pertained to the cathedral church of Salisbury.[13]

[1] *Vetus Registrum Sarisberiense*, i. 189 seq.

[2] *H.M.C.*, *Various Collections*, vii. 30–1.

[3] *Statutes and Customs of the Cathedral Church of the Blessed Virgin Mary of Salisbury*, ed. C. Wordsworth and D. Macleane, pp. 28, 194.

[4] Windsor, White Book, ff. 103–9*v*.

[5] Windsor, XV 31/56. For the history of the chantry see *V.C.H. Berks.* iv. 198; *C.P.R. 1324–7*, p. 191; *1330–4*, p. 178; *1334–8*, p. 300.

[6] Windsor, White Book, ff. 110–110*v*.

[7] Windsor, XV 48/7 (Roll of John Coryngham, Steward), 'Recepcio forinseca. Et de xxxiiij *s.* x *d.* receptis de perquisitis provenientibus de peculiari iurisdictione prebende de Okebourne, factis per Iohannem Colkyrke officialem ibidem.'

[8] *D.B.* i. 68; *L.F.* ii. 739; Porée, ii. 574.

[9] *Vetus Reg. Sar.* i. 189, n. 1.

[10] Windsor, XI G 20; XV 31/7.

[11] *F.A.* i. 51. Cf. ibid. 61.

[12] Windsor, XI G 11, no. 15; MS. Lat. 13905, f. 21*v*; Porée, i. 467; MS. Cinq Cents Colbert 190, p. 53. Cf. *R.H.* ii. 258.

[13] Ibid.

Compton (Wilts.). The chapel of Compton was given to Bec by Geoffrey de Brionne and confirmed by the count of Meulan.[1] It seems later to have been appropriated to St. Swithun's, Winchester, but a pension of one mark was still owed to Bec, and was payable annually at Chisenbury by the parson of Enford.[2]

Durrington (Wilts.). Land in Durrington was given by Ralph, son of Robert, son of Anquetil, in 1120, and confirmed by the earl of Leicester, Henry I, and Henry II.[3] There is no evidence that Bec held anything in Durrington after the beginning of the thirteenth century. Either the gift never took effect or the land was alienated; a deed in the Salisbury register states that the church was resigned into Bishop Herbert's hand when he created the prebend of Ogbourne.[4]

Eddington, with the hamlet of *Hidden* (Berks.). The manor of Eddington had been part of the endowment of Bec's priory at Beaumont-le-Roger. In 1147, by a decision of Pope Eugenius III, it was granted to the prior and canons of St. Frideswide, Oxford, who in return renounced their rights in the church of Beaumont-le-Roger. One-third of the tithe of villein land was, however, reserved to Bec.[5] In 1234 William de Guineville, proctor of Bec, leased tithes of Eddington and Hidden to St. Frideswide's at perpetual fee-farm for 40*s.* annually, payable at Hungerford.[6]

East Hendred (Berks.). In *c.* 1140 King Stephen gave to Bec a rent of 100*s.* which had formerly been paid to him by the abbot and convent of Reading for land in East Hendred.[7] In addition the tithes of the demesne land in the same manor were leased to the abbot and convent of Reading for 20*s.* by the abbot of Bec.[8]

Hungerford (Berks.). The church of Hungerford, with all its appurtenances, was given to Bec by the earl of Leicester and was held until 1421 with the rectory manor.[9] The church was appropriated to Bec, and together with its dependent chapel of Shalbourne it formed part of the prebend of Ogbourne.

[1] Windsor, XI G 11, no. 21; Porée, ii. 578.

[2] MS. Add. 24316, f. 24 (under Chisenbury): 'Persona de Eneford debet annuatim unam marcam ad festum S. Nicolai pro capella de Cumtona'; Windsor, White Book, f. 148: 'Pensio de persona de Enforde in comitatu Wiltes pro capella de Compton que modo appropriatur prioratui Sancti Swythini Wynchester, xiij *s.* iiij *d.*'

[3] Windsor, XI G 11, no. 17; Porée, i. 574.

[4] *Vet. Reg. Sar.* i. 189, n. 1.

[5] Windsor, XI G 11, no. 23; Porée, i. 419–20.

[6] Windsor, XI G 75. Cf. MS. Add. 24316, f. 37 [38] (under Hungerford): 'Prior Sancte Frideswithe Oxon' debet annuatim xl solidos pro decimis de Huddene ad terminos Sancti Iohannis et Sancti Martini.'

[7] Windsor, XI G 11, no. 30; MS. Lat. 13905, f. 25*v*; Porée, i. 470.

[8] Windsor, XI G 11, no. 33. Cf. MS. Add. 24316, f. 16 (under Wantage): 'De abbate de Rading pro Henrede, vj libre.'

[9] Porée, ii. 578; *V.C.H. Berks.* iv. 197–8.

Milburne (Dorset). A small manor in Milburne was given to Bec by R. count of Meulan.[1] In 1399 the prior of Ogbourne's tenement there was described as one knight's fee.[2]

Povington (Dorset). Robert, son of Gerold, gave Bec the manor of Povington which he had held at the time of the Domesday survey.[3] Lutton and Blackmanstone were both members of the manor, which was conterminous with the vill of Povington. The gift did not include the church, but the prior and convent of Bermondsey leased to Bec the tithes of Povington, Lutton, and Blackmanstone for 8*s*. annually.[4]

Shalbourne (Berks.). The chapel of Shalbourne was dependent on the church of Hungerford, and was probably given with it since no separate gift is recorded. It formed part of the Salisbury prebend. In 1234 the abbot and convent of Bec granted licence to William Estorny to found a chantry chapel on his demesne in Shalbourne.[5] The abbot also had some tenants at Bagshot in Shalbourne.[6]

Wallingford (Berks.). The abbot of Bec held some tenements which he had acquired either by purchase or from the parents of oblates.[7]

Wantage (Berks.). The church was given to Bec by Henry II, with one librate of land which formed the rectory manor.[8] The appropriation of the church was licensed by Pope Clement III and Hubert Walter,[9] and later it formed part of the prebend of Ogbourne.

Wareham (Dorset). A mill was held by the monks of Bec.[10]

Tithes

Miles Crispin's gift of his demesne tithes included tithes in *Clapcot*[11] (Berks.) and *Wootton Basset*[12] (Wilts.). His man Richard, son of Reinfrid, gave tithes in *Appleton* (Berks.).[13]

1 Porée, ii. 578.
2 *C.Cl.R. 1396–9*, p. 456.
3 *D.B.* i. 80; Porée, ii. 574.
4 Windsor, XI G 17.
5 Windsor, White Book, ff. 98–98*v*. See also *V.C.H. Berks.* iv. 233.
6 *L.F.* i. 295.
7 Details in ibid. 109.
8 Porée, ii. 573. Cf. *V.C.H. Berks.* iv. 324, 329.
9 Windsor, XI G 11, nos. 4, 6; Windsor, Denton Black Book, f. 27.
10 *Rot. Lit. Claus.* ii. 52, 67; *T.P.N.*, p. 184 *a*.
11 H. E. Salter, 'Two Deeds about the Abbey of Bec', in *E.H.R.* xl (1925), pp. 73–8; Windsor, XI G 47; White Book, ff. 113–113*v*, 148; XV 31/7. Clapcot lay within the parish of All Hallows, Wallingford, and the church paid a yearly portion of 40*s*. as composition for the tithes (*T.P.N.*, p. 188*a*; *V.C.H. Berks.* iii. 543).
12 Salter, loc. cit.
13 Ibid.; *T.P.N.*, p. 187 *a*; MS. Add. 24316, f. 16: 'De persona de Appelton, xxij solid'.'

Bec held the demesne tithes of *Langford* (Wilts.) and *Up Wimborne* (Dorset) of the gift of Walter Moubert.[1]

The following portions and pensions were also due to the abbey in the thirteenth century:

Barbury (Wilts.). 20*s.* annually from the prior of Avebury for tithe in Barbury, payable at Ogbourne.[2]

Boscombe (Wilts.). Pension of 13*s.* 4*d.* payable at Quarley by the parson of Boscombe.[3]

Denchworth (Berks.). Portion of 18*s.*[4]

Steeple (Dorset). Portion of 3*s.* 4*d.*[5]

Sparsholt (Berks.). Portion of 4*s.* 2*d.* payable at Wantage.[6]

Turnworth (Dorset). Pension of 20*s.* payable at Milburne by the abbot of Ford.[7]

Diocese of Bath and Wells

The Prebend of Cleeve (Somerset). The church of Cleeve was given to Bec with all its appurtenances by Robert, son of Gerold, in the early twelfth century.[8] His heir, William de Roumare, insufficiently informed about the gift, presented clerks to the church, and it was apparently claimed as a prebend of Wells by the dean and chapter of Wells. The production of the abbey's charters convinced William de Roumare of his error; he persuaded Reginald de Ver and M. Peter de Mesnilo, whom he had presented to the church, to resign it into the hands of Savaric, bishop of Bath and Wells. Savaric confirmed the gift and granted licence to appropriate in 1192–7; finally in 1198–9, to settle the claims of the chapter of Wells, he erected it into a prebend. The abbot and convent of Bec were to become canons of Wells and enjoy full fraternity with the church of Wells; since residence was impossible, they were to appoint a stall vicar and pay him 4 marks a year.[9] Almost immediately the abbot and convent of Bec leased the church of Cleeve at perpetual fee-farm to the abbot and convent of Cleeve for 44 marks annually, of which 4 marks were to be paid to the stall vicar.[10]

Robert's original gift included land in *Harwood in Cutcombe*

[1] Windsor, XI G 10; XV 31/7; XI G 68. Cf. *T.P.N.*, p. 178 *b*.

[2] MS. Add. 24316, f. 31 [32].

[3] Windsor, White Book, f. 148; MS. Add. 24316, f. 35 *v* [36*v*].

[4] *T.P.N.*, p. 187 *a*; Windsor, White Book, f. 101; XV 31/7.

[5] *T.P.N.*, p. 179 *b*; Windsor, White Book, f. 101.

[6] *T.P.N.*, p. 186 *b*; Windsor, White Book, f. 101; MS. Add. 24316, f. 16.

[7] *T.P.N.*, p. 178 *b*; Windsor, White Book, f. 101; MS. Add. 24316, f. 28.

[8] Windsor, XI G 11, no. 10.

[9] Ibid., nos. 9, 11, 24, 28, 37; Archives de l'Eure, H 11. Cf. *H.M.C. Wells*, i. 489; Porée, i. 486–7.

[10] Windsor, XI G 11, no. 39; *H.M.C. Wells*, ii. 549.

(Somerset) and *Lega*, which is probably to be identified with either *Leigh in Winsham* (Somerset) or *Leigh in Wimborne* (Dorset).

Diocese of Canterbury

Glynde (Sussex; exempt deanery of South Malling). Philip, canon of South Malling, granted to Bec with his brother William's consent the reversion of the church of Glynde and all its appurtenances after his death. The gift was confirmed (1139–50) by Theobald, archbishop of Canterbury, and the church was appropriated to the monks.[1] Their normal practice was to lease it, and this practice was approved by Walter Reynolds in 1327.[2]

Saltwood (Kent). Before 1122 Robert de Montford gave the church of Saltwood with all its appurtenances to Bec and St. Philbert, with the intention that it should be appropriated to them,[3] and the gift was confirmed by Ralph, archbishop of Canterbury, 1114–22,[4] and by Archbishop Theobald,[5] though it was never appropriated. A dispute about possession arose in the thirteenth century; and Stephen Langton ordained that the prior of St. Philbert was to receive a pension of 15 marks annually from the rector of Saltwood, whilst the patronage was to belong to the archbishop of Canterbury. The agreement was confirmed by the prior and convent of Christ Church,[6] and thenceforward the rights of the abbot of Bec were limited to the collection of the pension.[7]

Tithe

No gift of tithe is recorded, but 22*s.* was owed by the parson of Westcliffe-by-Dover for tithes of the demesne of Warin of Munchensy.[8]

Diocese of Chichester

Hooe (Sussex). A manor in Hooe was given to Bec and its dependent priory of St. Martin-au-Bosc by Henry, Count of Eu, in 1106.[9]

West Preston (Sussex). William, count of Mortain, gave the manor of Preston in Beddingham in 1153–9.[10] The abbey of Bec never held the churches of either Hooe or Preston.

1 Windsor, XI G 11, nos. 1, 2, 12; XI G 3.

2 Windsor, XI G 3, 54.

3 Windsor, XI G 29, no. 1. The charter contains the words 'in usus suos integre et plenarie in perpetuum possidendam'. Cf. Porée, i. 469–70.

4 Windsor, XI G 29, no. 2.

5 Ibid., no. 3.

6 Ibid., nos. 4, 5. Cf. *Reg. Epist. Joh. Peckham*, iii. 1014.

7 Windsor, XI G 43, 45.

8 MS. Add. 24316, f. 5*v*; Windsor, White Book, f. 148.

9 Dugdale, vi. 1016–17; Archives de la Seine Inférieure, D 20; *C.D.F.*, nos. 399–401; Porée, ii. 578.

10 Ibid. 574. Cf. *D.B.* i. 24; *R.H.* ii. 206.

Diocese of Coventry and Lichfield

Atherstone (Warwick). The manor was given by Hugh, earl of Chester, before 1101.[1] It was granted a yearly fair in 1246[2] and was successfully defended against Ralph de Cuylly in 1275.[3]

Diocese of Exeter

Christow (Devon). The manor was given temp. William I by Emma, wife of Baldwin, a cousin of the Clares.[4] From 1244 it was let at perpetual fee-farm to the prior of Cowick.[5] The church probably accompanied the manor, since the prior of Cowick had the advowson from the time that the episcopal registers begin.[6]

Diocese of Lincoln

Bledlow (Bucks.). A manor in Bledlow was acquired from Hugh de Gurnay in 1198 in exchange for tithes and other dues in Bray, Normandy.[7] Bec never had the advowson of the church.

Broughton (Bucks.). Hugh de Grantmesnil entered into an agreement with Peter, second abbot of Missenden, conveying land in Broughton to the abbot and convent of Missenden in return for 6 marks annually.[8] Some time before 1242 this rent was transferred to the abbey of Bec, and was collected annually at Ruislip.[9]

Cottisford (Oxon.). Two separate manors in Cottisford were given to Bec by the daughters of Hugh de Grantmesnil; one by Adeline and Ralph d'Ivri her husband, the other by Rohais and her husband Robert de Curcy, *c.* 1125.[10] The abbey also received from St. Évroult all that it possessed in Cottisford, including the patronage of the church.[11] During the thirteenth century the abbot of Bec held the whole vill.[12]

Hykeham (Lincs.). Four carucates in Hykeham were given by William de Rullos before 1123.[13] From the mid-thirteenth century it was farmed to the prior of Wilsford.[14]

1 Porée, ii. 574; Dugdale, *Warwickshire*, pp. 766–7; cf. *R.H.* ii. 227.

2 *C.Ch.R.* i. 307.

3 *Select Cases in the Court of King's Bench*, i. 16–19.

4 Salter, loc. cit. Cf. *R.H.* i. 84.

5 Oliver, *Monasticon*, pp. 156–7.

6 *Regs. Bronescombe and Quivil*, pp. 123, 127, and *passim*; *C.P.R. 1381–5*, p. 24 and *passim*.

7 MS. Cinq Cents Colbert 190, p. 163; *V.C.H. Bucks.* ii. 247; *F.A.* i. 97.

8 Windsor, XI G 11, nos. 13, 29.

9 MS. Add. 24316, f. 5*v*.

10 Ordericus Vitalis, *Historia Ecclesiastica*, ed. Le Prévost, iii. 25, n. 1; MS. Lat. 13905, f. 22*v*; Porée, i. 468.

11 Ibid., n. 1; Windsor, XI G 11, no. 32; *T.P.N.*, p. 31 *b*.

12 *R.H.* ii. 837; *L.F.* ii. 831.

13 Windsor, XI G 11, no. 18; MS. Cinq Cents Colbert 190, p. 53; *R.H.* i. 389.

14 *Supra*, p. 23.

Swyncombe (Oxon.). The manor was given by Miles Crispin before 1086, together with the tithes of his demesne in the honour of Wallingford.[1] The monks held the advowson of the church with the manor.[2]

Members of Swyncombe were at *Ewelme*, where the abbot held two virgates;[3] and at *Goring*. In Goring two mills and some land were given by Hugh de Druevalle;[4] and Thomas de Druevalle's gift of a mill and hide of land, together with the tithe of his demesne, was confirmed by Alexander III.[5]

Weedon (Northants.). William de Thibouville gave half the manor of Weedon to Bec and St. Lambert de Malassis in 1126, and his son William gave the other half with the church of Weedon.[6] A certain clerk, however, continued to hold the church, and it was given again to Bec by Robert, earl of Leicester.[7] The manor contained both the 3½ hides held by Hugh de Grantmesnil at the time of Domesday, and the ½ hide of the count of Mortain;[8] and the church was appropriated to Bec.[9] Although the Hundred Rolls state that the abbot of Eynesham with the abbot of Bec withheld suit of hundred court in Weedon, I can find no evidence that the abbot of Eynesham ever held any land here.

Tithes

Many of the manors in the honour of Wallingford lay in Oxfordshire and Buckinghamshire. Miles Crispin's gift included tithe in: *Aston Rowant*,[10] *Chalgrove*,[11] *Gatehampton*, *Great Haseley*,[12] *Kingston Blount*, *Mapledurham*,[13] *Newnham Murren*,[14] *Rotherfield Peppard*,[15] *North Stoke* with the chapel of *Ipsden*,[16] *Whitchurch* with *Hardwick*

[1] *D.B.* i. 159.
[2] *Rot. R. Grosseteste*, p. 457; *C.P.R. 1370–4*, p. 423; *T.P.N.*, p. 30 *b*.
[3] *R.H.* ii. 761.
[4] Windsor, XI G 11, no. 25.
[5] MS. Cinq Cents Colbert 190, p. 63; Windsor, Denton Black Book, ff. 26*v*–7; White Book, ff. 113–113*v*; *T.P.N.*, p. 30 *a*.
[6] MS. Cartulaire de St. Lambert, Collection Mancel de Caen, no. 200, pp. 2–4, 9, 12; Porée, ii. 574. Cf. *R.H.* ii. 10; *L.F.* ii. 1288.
[7] Windsor, XI G 11, no. 20; MS. Cart. de St. Lambert, pp. 2–4, 9.
[8] *D.B.* i. 223, 224; *V.C.H. Northants.* i. 370.
[9] *T.P.N.*, p. 38 *b*.
[10] All these places are enumerated in the deeds printed by H. E. Salter, loc. cit.
[11] MSS. of Magdalen College, Oxford, Chalgrove, first series, nos. 140, 157.
[12] *T.P.N.*, p. 31 *a*.
[13] Ibid., p. 30 *a*.
[14] *R.H.* ii. 777. Bec also received in Newnham the ninth sheaf from the land of Walter of Huntercumbe (Windsor, XI G 33).
[15] *T.P.N.*, p. 30 *b*; Windsor, XI G 31, 49.
[16] *T.P.N.*, p. 30 *a*.

(Oxon.);[1] *Eythorpe*, *Iver*, *Quainton*,[2] *Shabbington*,[3] *Waddesdon*,[4] and *Wycombe*[5] (Bucks.).

Bec received the following demesne tithes from the men of Miles Crispin: *Alkerton* (Oxon.) and *Ickford* (Bucks.) from Richard son of Reinfrid.[6] *Adwell*,[6] *Chesterton*,[7] and *Henton in Chinnor* (Oxon.) from Hugh son of Miles.[8]

The tithes of Aston Rowant, Eythorpe, Henton in Chinnor, Quainton, and Wycombe were, during the thirteenth century, collected at Bledlow.[9]

Bec also claimed, in 1327, tithe in *Bensington*, *Crowmarsh*, and *South Merton*,[10] and in 1377 in *Ewelme*,[11] though the validity of the first claim is doubtful. A pension of 7*s.* annually was received from the parson of *Barford* (Oxon.), probably for tithe.[12]

Diocese of London

Dunton Waylett (Essex). Nigel of Albiny, the founder of the house of Mowbray, had given land in *Smitham* (Warwicks.) *ad coquinam monachorum* between 1099 and 1114.[13] Between 1114 and 1124 he exchanged it for 20 librates of land in Dunton.[14] Both places had rich water-meadows, and possibly he hoped by his gift to supplement the cheese supply of the monastery. He gave also the church of Dunton after the death of Wido, his chaplain. It was never appropriated, but the monks of Bec held the advowson and received a pension of 4 marks,[15] and their title was confirmed by Richard Fitz-Neal, bishop of London.[16]

Langham (Essex). The manor of Langham was conferred on Bec by Hugh Tirel in 1138,[17] but the gift never took effect, for soon afterwards Hugh mortgaged the manor to Gervase, justiciar of London, and it passed into his family.[18]

[1] Salter, op. cit., p. 77; *T.P.N.*, p. 30 *a*.

[2] Windsor, XI G 56; Salter, loc. cit.

[3] *T.P.N.*, p. 34 *a*. In 1167–83 these tithes were let at perpetual fee-farm for 20*s.* to the prior and convent of Wallingford (Windsor, XI G 32).

[4] *T.P.N.*, p. 34 *a*.

[5] Ibid., p. 33 *a*; *V.C.H. Bucks.* iii. 133. From 1254 they were leased to Godstow nunnery.

[6] Salter, loc. cit.

[7] Ibid. Cf. MS. Add. 24316, f. 44 [46] (under Cottisford): 'Et sciendum quod debet quolibet anno serviens manerii recipere de persona de Cestr' . . . xv solidos.'

[8] Salter, loc. cit.; *T.P.N.*, p. 30 *b*.

[9] MS. Add. 24316, f. 67.

[10] Windsor, White Book, ff. 113–113*v*.

[11] Windsor, XV 31/7.

[12] MS. Add. 24316, f. 44 [46] (under Cottisford): 'Et sciendum quod debet quolibet anno serviens manerii recipere de persona de Bereford vij solidos.'

[13] Windsor, XI G 11, no. 36.

[14] Ibid., no. 26.

[15] Windsor, XI G 51; XI G 73; White Book, f. 101; *T.P.N.*, p. 22 *a*; Newcourt, *Repertorium*, ii. 230.

[16] Windsor, XI G 5; White Book, f. 115 *v*.

[17] Porée, i. 392; MS. Lat. 13905, f. 43*v*.

[18] Round, *Feudal England*, pp. 470–1.

London. The abbot of Bec possessed a number of tenements in London. The chief of these was the prior of Ogbourne's town-house in Baynardcastle Ward, which stood in Castle Lane between the river Thames and the Black Friars. It was, John Stow reports, 'the Prior's lodging when he repayred to London';[1] and was owned by him until, in 1352, financial difficulties compelled him to sell it.[2] London property in this district had been bought in the late twelfth century by Richard de Coleville, prior of Ruislip, from the abbot and convent of Westminster[3] and the dean and chapter of St. Paul's.[4] Some property was given by Hugh de Gurnay,[5] and possibly more was bought; the tenements still held in the early fifteenth century are enumerated in the patent rolls.[6]

Ruislip (Middlesex). The manor was given by Ernulf de Hesding *c.* 1090,[7] and probably the church accompanied it. About a hundred years later the church was appropriated to Bec by Richard Fitz-Neal, bishop of London,[8] and the appropriation was regularly confirmed by later bishops and archbishops.[9]

Tithes

Bec received in the diocese of London:

From Richard of Clare temp. William I two-thirds of the demesne tithe in *Little Sampford* (Essex)[10] and *Standon* (Herts.),[11] and from Garnerus his man similar tithes in *Chawreth* (Essex).[12]

From Hugh de Gurnay temp. William I two-thirds of the demesne tithe and one villein in *Liston*, *Fordham*, and *Ardleigh* (Essex).[13]

From Henry de Ferrers, temp. William I two-thirds of the demesne tithe and one villein in *Woodham Ferrers*, *Steeple*, and *Stebbing* (Essex).[14]

[1] *A Survey of London*, ed. C. L. Kingsford, ii. 13–14.

[2] *Supra*, p. 124.

[3] Porée, i. 469, n. 5; Windsor, XI G 11, no. 14.

[4] Porée, i. 469, n. 5; *Early Charters of the Cathedral Church of St. Paul*, ed. M. Gibbs, Camden Third Series, lviii (1939), no. 165.

[5] MS. Lat. 13905, f. 20: 'Dedit Hugo de Gornaco . . . quod habebat in Londonia de rege Willelmo patre Henrici regis.'

[6] *C.P.R. 1436–41*, pp. 565–6; *1446–52*, p. 429.

[7] Porée, ii. 574.

[8] Windsor, XI G 6.

[9] Windsor, XI G 51, 52, 64; White Book, ff. 112–13.

[10] Ibid., ff. 112–112*v*; *D.B.* ii. 41. Cf. Lunt, *The Valuation of Norwich*, p. 351.

[11] Salter, op. cit., p. 76; Windsor, XI G 4.

[12] Windsor, White Book, ff. 112–112*v*, 127; Salter, loc. cit.; *D.B.* ii. 103; cf. Lunt, op. cit., p. 361. In the mid-thirteenth century the tithes of Chawreth were leased to the prior of the hospital at Clerkenwell for 20 marks (MS. Add. 24316, f. 5*v*).

[13] MS. Lat. 13905, f. 45*v*; Salter, loc. cit.; *D.B.* ii. 89; Newcourt, *Repertorium*, ii. 269.

[14] Salter, loc. cit.; Windsor, White Book, ff. 112–112*v*; *D.B.* ii. 56–7.

From Simon, son of Arnold, similar tithes in *Finchingfield* and *Lashley* (Essex).[1]

From Maurice the sheriff similar tithes in *Tiltey* (Essex) and *Bicknacre* in Woodham Ferrers (Essex).[2]

From an unknown donor tithes in *Southall by Hayes* (Middlesex).[3]

Diocese of Norwich

Blakenham (Suffolk). The manor was given *c.* 1075 by Walter Giffard,[4] and the church probably accompanied it, for later presentations were made in the name of the prior of Ogbourne.[5]

Lessingham (Norfolk). Lessingham had been a royal manor at the time of the Domesday survey,[6] but was given to Bec *c.* 1090 by Gerard de Gurnay.[7] The advowson of the church went with it, and the abbot was a pensionary.[8]

East Wretham (Norfolk). Ralph de Toeni gave East Wretham in 1085–6.[9] There were members of the manor at Hocham[10] and Shropham.[11] As at Lessingham the abbot of Bec held the advowson of the church and received a pension.[12]

Tithes

Bec received gifts of tithes from four of the men of Richard of Clare, temp. William I:

In *Dalham* (Suffolk) from William Peccatum.[13]

In *Wimundestuna* (Suffolk, unidentified) from Giraldus.[14]

In *Witherfield* (Suffolk) from Wilardus.[15]

In *Great Wratting* (Suffolk) from Joffridus.[16]

During the thirteenth century these tithes were leased, at first for 28*s.* and then for one mark.[17]

[1] Windsor, White Book, ff. 112–112*v*; *D.B.* ii. 39, 101.

[2] Windsor, White Book, ff. 112–112*v*.

[3] Ibid., ff. 111–14; MS. Add. 24316, f. 6*v*; *T.P.N.*, p. 18 *a*.

[4] Porée, i. 451–2; MS. Lat. 12884, f. 95; Dugdale, vi. 1002.

[5] *C.P.R. 1381–5*, p. 62 and *passim*.

[6] *D.B.* ii. 133–4.

[7] Porée, ii. 574; MS. Lat. 13905, f. 20; Blomefield, ix. 328–9. Cf. *R.H.* i. 528.

[8] Blomefield, loc. cit.; Windsor, XI G 41; Porée, i. 466–7.

[9] King's College, M 102/15; MS. Lat. 13905, ff. 23, 88. Cf. *D.B.* ii. 236; *R.H.* i. 471, 473, 528; *L.F.* i. 128.

[10] Blomefield, i. 464–5; *T.P.N.*, p. 108 *a*; MS. Add. 24316, f. 59 [60]; Porée, i. 466–7.

[11] MS. Add. 24316, f. 59*v* [60*v*].

[12] Blomefield, i. 467; Windsor, XI G 41.

[13] Salter, loc. cit.; Windsor; White Book, f. 127; *D.B.* ii. 390.

[14] Salter, loc. cit.; Windsor, White Book, f. 127; *D.B.* ii. 391.

[15] Salter, loc. cit.; Windsor, White Book, f. 127.

[16] Ibid.; *D.B.* ii. 390.

[17] Windsor, XI G 30, 57, 60, 61, 63, 66.

Diocese of Rochester

Richard I of Clare gave one house in *Tunbridge* (Kent).[1]

Diocese of Winchester

Blissmore Hall (Weyhill, Hants). In 1346 the prior of Ogbourne was holding with Richard Crul a quarter of a knight's fee in Blissmore, but how he acquired it is not known.[2]

Combe (Hants). The manor was given before 1100 by Emmelina, wife of Ernulf de Hesding.[3]

The church was appropriated to Bec, and was valued at 20 marks in 1291.[4]

Hersham in Walton-on-Thames (Surrey). Three virgates of land were given by Richard I of Clare.[5]

Monxton (Hants). The manor was the gift of Hugh de Grandmesnil, *c.* temp. William II.[6] The advowson of the church followed the manor.

Quarley (Hants). Queen Maud gave the manor to Bec, though *c.* 1086 the gift had not yet become effective. The advowson of the church followed the manor.[7] A member of the manor lay in Amport. In 1226 Richard and Edith, son and widow of Henry Stratfield, granted the reversion of a carucate of land called Goldhord in Amport to Bec, and the abbey received other small gifts later to augment it.[8]

Tooting and Streatham (Surrey). Before 1086 Richard of Clare gave to Bec the manor of Tooting, and also Streatham, by which probably was meant the church of Streatham.[9] The church was not appropriated, but in 1322 the abbey claimed the following spiritualities in Tooting, where they had a chapel, and Streatham: All tithes great and small from their demesne lands in Tooting; two-thirds of the tithes from their tenants' land; 20*s.* pension from the church of Streatham and the right to compel all their tenants to come to their chapel at Tooting at the feast of the Purification and offer candles.[10]

Tithes

Richard I of Clare's gift included two-thirds of the demesne tithe

1 Windsor, White Book, f. 127.

2 *V.C.H. Hants*, iv. 396.

3 Windsor, XI G 11, no. 16; Porée, ii. 574; *V.C.H. Hants*, iv. 310–11.

4 *T.P.N.*, p. 212 *b*; Windsor, XV 31/7.

5 Salter, loc. cit.; Windsor, White Book, f. 127.

6 Porée, ii. 573–4; *V.C.H. Hants*, iv. 380.

7 Ibid. 385; Porée, ii. 574.

8 *V.C.H. Hants*, iv. 342–3; Windsor, XI G 38.

9 Windsor, White Book, ff. 127, 142*v*–143; *T.P.N.*, p. 207 *b* (portion valued at £4).

10 Windsor, XI G 78.

in *Betchworth*,[1] *Bletchingley and Chivington*,[2] *Chipstead*,[3] *Thorncroft in Leatherhead*,[4] *Talworth*,[5] *Walton Leigh*,[6] and *Woodmansterne*[7] (Surrey).

The abbey also held the tithes of the hide of land which Faranus de Colona gave to Bec in *Balham* by Clapham (Surrey).[8] The land itself does not appear to have been retained.

Tithes in *Sopley* (Hants) which were owed to the abbey of Bec were let at fee-farm to the prior of Christ Church for one mark.[9]

Diocese of Worcester

The possessions of Bec in the diocese of Worcester were limited to tithes.

Miles Crispin's gift included two-thirds of the demesne tithe of *Alderley* (Glos.);[10] which were farmed out by successive general proctors of Bec.[11]

The abbey also held two-thirds of the demesne tithe of *Hillsley* (Glos.).[12] Roger Hottot granted the tithe of his land called *Linda* by Worcester, which is possibly to be identified with *Lindridge*; but there is no indication that the monks retained this gift later.[13]

It has been impossible to identify the following places mentioned in charters and deeds:

Calumaye. Land given by Stephen, count of Boulogne.[14]

Cambaio. Alms given by William, earl of Essex.[15]

Cerlenton. One silver mark given by R. de Magneville, and confirmed by the count of Meulan.[16] It may possibly be Charlton (Dorset).

Pachem. £10 annual rent in the church given by William de Braose and confirmed by the earl of Leicester.[17]

[1] *D.B.* i. 35; Windsor, White Book, ff. 127–127*v*, 144.

[2] Salter, loc. cit.; Windsor, White Book, ff. 117–18, 127–127*v*; *T.P.N.*, p. 208 *a*.

[3] Salter, loc. cit.; Windsor, White Book, ff. 127–127*v*.

[4] Windsor, White Book, ff. 127–127*v*; *D.B.* i. 35; Windsor, White Book, f. 144.

[5] Windsor, White Book, ff. 127–127*v*.

[6] Windsor, White Book, ff. 127–127*v*; Salter, loc. cit.; Windsor, White Book, f. 144.

[7] Ibid.

[8] Dugdale, vi. 1003, 1068, 1017; *V.C.H. Surrey*, i. 324; Windsor, White Book, ff. 118*v*–119.

[9] Windsor, XI G 18; XV 31/7. Cf. MS. Add. 24316, f. 24: 'Prior Christi Ecclesie debet solvere apud Chisingebur' ad festum Sancti Michaelis pro decimis provenientibus de dominio Rogeri Mober in parochia de Sopeleya annuatim unam marcam.'

[10] Salter, loc. cit.

[11] MS. Add. 24316, f. 31 [32]; Windsor, XI G 59; White Book, ff. 120–120*v*.

[12] Windsor, XI G 59; White Book, f. 120*v*.

[13] Windsor, XI G 11, no. 34.

[14] MS. Cinq Cents Colbert 190, p. 61, 'Donation faite par Estienne comte de Boulogne à l'abbaye du Bec d'une terre appellée Calumaye.'

[15] Windsor, XI G 11, no. 35.

[16] Ibid., nos. 22, 31.

[17] Ibid., no. 27.

BIBLIOGRAPHY

MANUSCRIPT SOURCES

British Museum

MS. Cotton Domitian A XI.

MS. Additional 24316.

Public Record Office

Exchequer K.R., E. 106 (Alien Priories Bundles), 1–12.

Ministers' Accounts, S.C. 6, 917/26, 917/27, 937/19, 949/13, 949/14, 1015/6.

Ancient Correspondence, S.C. 1, 15/45–53, 32/70, 33/24–30, 37/185–6, 49/118.

Ancient Petitions, S.C. 8, 164/8157, 239/11950, 3133, E. 959, E. 1394.

Plea Rolls, K.B., 26/37, 27/129, 27/131, 27/137, 27/169, 27/207, 27/288.

Feet of Fines, Wilts., Case 250, nos. 6/171, 8/46 (124), 70/195, 8/50 (136); Norfolk, Case 156, no. 67/842; Suffolk, Case 214, no. 24/13, Case 215, no. 34/19.

King's College Cambridge

C 1–15. Composite Court rolls.

C 16–24. Court rolls of Ogbourne, Combe, Monxton, Quarley, Chisenbury and Brixton-Deverill.

Q 44–9. Court rolls of Ruislip.

Q 1–7. Charters of Ruislip.

Dd 1–32. Miscellaneous documents relating to Ogbourne.

Dd 33. Roll of manorial customs.

M 7–9. Court rolls of Dunton.

M 18, 19. Rentals of Dunton.

P 1–4. Court rolls of Lessingham.

H 1–3. Charters of Atherstone.

L 65–7. Charters of Combe.

M 1–3. Charters of Dunton.

T 1–3. Charters relating to the London property.

MSS. of Eton College

(These documents are still uncalendared, and only drawer references can be given.)

In drawer A 20: Account rolls of East Wretham.

In drawer B 11: Account rolls, charters and rentals of Weedon Beck.

In drawer C 5: Charters of Bledlow.

In drawer C 14: Charters and account rolls of Cottisford, and pipe roll of 1288–9.

In drawer D 5: Charters, account rolls and court rolls of Blakenham.

Windsor, Dean and Chapter Muniments

In box XI G and box XV 31: Miscellaneous documents relating to the spiritualities of Bec.

Arundel White Book (fifteenth-century register).

Denton Black Book (sixteenth-century register).

Westminster, Dean and Chapter Muniments

No. 7301. Copy of a plea roll.

Nos. 7396–7402, 7579. Deeds conveying Steventon to Westminster abbey.

Bibliothèque Nationale

MS. lat. 9211. Collection of 143 original charters of Bec.

MS. lat. 12884. D. Thibault: *Chronicon Beccense auctum et illustratum* (seventeenth century).

MS. lat. 13905. D. Jouvelin: Collection of transcripts (eighteenth century).

MS. Cinq Cents Colbert 190: *Inventaire général des titres de l'abbaïe du Bec faict en 1670.*

Archives de l'Eure

Charters, H 9–11, H 1345.

Archives de la Seine-Inférieure

Charters, H 5, D 17.

Bibliothèque de Caen

Collection Mancel, no. 200 *Cartulaire de Saint-Lambert*, written in 1457.

SELECT BIBLIOGRAPHY OF PRINTED SOURCES

AULT, W. O., *Court Rolls of the Abbey of Ramsey and of the Honor of Clare* (Yale, 1928).

BALLARD, A., and TAIT, J., *British Borough Charters, 1216–1307* (Cambridge, 1923).

——, *British Borough Charters, 1042–1216* (Cambridge, 1913).

BERLIÈRE, DOM U., 'Innocent III et la Réorganisation des Monastères Bénédictines', in *Révue Bénédictine*, xxxii (1920).

BIRDSALL, JEAN, 'The English Manors of La Trinité at Caen', in *Haskins Anniversary Essays* (Boston, Mass., 1929).

BLOMEFIELD, F., *An Essay towards a Topographical History of the County of Norfolk*, 11 vols. (London, 1816–40).

BOURGET, D., *The History of the Royal Abbey of Bec* (London, 1779).

Cartularium Monasterii de Rameseia, ed. W. de G. Birch, 3 vols. (Rolls Series, 1884–93).

Chapters of the English Black Monks, 1215–1540, ed. W. A. Pantin, 3 vols. (Camden Third Series, 1931–7).

Chronique du Bec et Chronique de François Carré, ed. A. A. Porée (Rouen, 1883).

Court Rolls of Tooting Beck Manor, ed. G. L. Gomme, vol. i (London County Council, 1909).

Custumals of Battle Abbey, ed. S. R. Scargill Bird (Camden Society, New Series, xli, 1887).

DAVENPORT, F. G., *The Economic Development of a Norfolk Manor* (Cambridge, 1906).

DELISLE, L., *Études sur la Condition de la Classe Agricole en Normandie au XIIe siècle* (Évreux, 1851).

DENHOLM-YOUNG, N., *Seignorial Administration in England* (Oxford, 1937).

DOUGLAS, D. C., *The Social Structure of Medieval East Anglia* (Oxford Studies in Social and Legal History, ix, 1927).

DUGDALE, W., *The Antiquities of Warwickshire* (Coventry, 1765).

Feet of Fines for Oxfordshire, transcribed and calendared by H. E. Salter (Oxfordshire Record Society, 1930).

GORHAM, G. C., *The History and Antiquities of Eynesbury and St. Neot's* (London, 1820).

——, *A Supplement to the History and Antiquities of Eynesbury and St. Neot's* (London, 1824).

GRAHAM, ROSE, 'Four Alien Priories in Monmouthshire', in *J.B.A.A.* xxxv (1929).

——, *English Ecclesiastical Studies* (London, 1929).

GRAS, N. S. B. and E. C., *The Economic and Social History of an English Village, Crawley, Hampshire* (Harvard Economic Studies, Cambridge, Mass., 1930).
HEARNSHAW, F. J. C., *Leet Jurisdiction in England* (Southampton, 1908).
Histoire de l'Abbaye de S. Pierre de Jumièges par un religieux bénédictin de la Congrégation de S. Maur, ed. J. Loth (Rouen, 1884).
HOLDSWORTH, W. S., *A History of English Law*, 3 vols. (London, 1903–9).
HUDSON, W., 'Status of "Villani" and Other Tenants in Danish East Anglia in pre-Conquest Times', in *T.R.H.S.*, 4th Series, iv (1921).
—— 'Three Manorial Extents of the Thirteenth Century', in *Norfolk Archaeology*, xiv (1901).
——, 'Traces of Primitive Agricultural Organisation as suggested by a Survey of the Manor of Martham, Norfolk', in *T.R.H.S.*, 4th Series, i (1918).
KNOWLES, DOM M. D., *The Monastic Order in England, 943–1216* (Cambridge, 1940).
——, *The Religious Houses of Medieval England* (London, 1940).
KOSMINSKY, E. A., 'Services and Money Rents in the Thirteenth Century', in *Economic History Review*, v (1935).
LEVETT, A. E., *Studies in Manorial History*, ed. H. M. Cam, M. Coate, and L. S. Sutherland (Oxford, 1938).
MARTÈNE, E., *De Antiquis Monachorum Ritibus*, 2 vols. (Lyons, 1690).
MOLITOR, RAPHAËL, *Aus der Rechtsgeschichte Benediktinischer Verbände*, vol. i (Münster, 1928).
NEILSON, N., *Customary Rents* (Oxford Studies in Social and Legal History, ii, 1910).
——, *Economic Conditions on the Manors of Ramsey Abbey* (Philadelphia, 1899).
NEW, C. W., *History of the Alien Priories in England to the Confiscation of Henry V* (privately printed, University of Chicago, 1916).
NEWCOURT, R., *Repertorium Ecclesiasticum Parochiale Londinense*, 2 vols. (London, 1708–10).
PAGE, F. M., *The Estates of Crowland Abbey* (Cambridge, 1934).
PERROY, E., *L'Angleterre et le Grand Schisme d'Occident* (Paris, 1933).
POLLOCK, F., and MAITLAND, F. W., *History of English Law*, 2 vols. (London, 1923).
PORÉE, A. A., *Histoire de l'Abbaye du Bec*, 2 vols. (Évreux, 1901).

POSTAN, M. M., 'The Chronology of Labour Services', in *T.R.H.S.*, 4th Series, x (1937).

POWER, EILEEN, *The Wool Trade in English Medieval History* (Oxford, 1941).

Records of the Templars in England in the Twelfth Century, ed. B. A. Lees (British Academy, 1935).

Regestrum Visitationum Archiepiscopi Rothomagensis, Journal des visites pastorales d'Eude Rigaud, archévêque de Rouen (1248–1269), ed. T. Bonnin (Rouen, 1852).

Rentalia et Custumaria Michelis de Ambresbury et Rogeri de Ford, Abbatum Monasterii Beate Marie Glastonie, ed. C. J. Elton (Somerset Record Society, 1891).

ROGERS, J. E. THOROLD, *A History of Agriculture and Prices*, vols. i, ii (1866).

SAUVAGE, R. N., *L'Abbaye de St. Martin de Troarn* (Mémoires de la Société des Antiquaires de Normandie, Caen, 1911).

Select Pleas in Manorial and Other Seignorial Courts, ed. F. W. Maitland (Selden Society, vol. ii, 1889).

STOW, JOHN, *A Survey of London*, ed. C. L. Kingsford, 2 vols. (Oxford, 1908).

'Two Deeds about the Abbey of Bec', ed. H. E. Salter, *English Historical Review*, xl (1925).

VINOGRADOFF, P., *Villainage in England* (Oxford, 1892).

Warwickshire Feet of Fines, abstracted . . . by E. Stokes, ed. F. C. Wellstood and F. T. S. Houghton (Dugdale Society, ix, 1932).

WRETTS-SMITH, M., 'Organisation of Farming at Crowland Abbey', in *Journal of Economic and Business History*, iv (1932).

WYLIE, J. H., and WAUGH, W. T., *The Reign of Henry the Fifth*, 3 vols. (Cambridge, 1914–29).

——, *History of England under Henry the Fourth*, 4 vols. (London, 1884–98).

INDEX

PRINTED IN GREAT BRITAIN AT THE UNIVERSITY PRESS, OXFORD
BY JOHN JOHNSON, PRINTER TO THE UNIVERSITY